The Christological Case for Compatibilism

Analyzing Theology Series

The Christological Case for Compatibilism

Randall K. Johnson

CASCADE *Books* • Eugene, Oregon

THE CHRISTOLOGICAL CASE FOR COMPATIBILISM

Cascade Books
An Imprint of Wipf and Stock Publishers
199 W. 8th Ave., Suite 3
Eugene, OR 97401

www.wipfandstock.com

PAPERBACK ISBN: 979-8-3852-2771-6
HARDCOVER ISBN: 979-8-3852-2772-3
EBOOK ISBN: 979-8-3852-2773-0

Cataloguing-in-Publication data:

Names: Johnson, Randall K. [author].

Title: The christological case for compatibilism / Randall K. Johnson.

Description: Eugene, OR: Cascade Books, 2026 | Series: Analyzing Theology | Includes bibliographical references and index.

Identifiers: ISBN 979-8-3852-2771-6 (paperback) | ISBN 979-8-3852-2772-3 (hardcover) | ISBN 979-8-3852-2773-0 (ebook)

Subjects: LCSH: Free will and determinism—Religious aspects—Christianity. | Free will and determinism. | Jesus Christ—Person and offices. | Philosophical theology.

Classification: BT40 J646 2026 (paperback) | BT40 (ebook)

03/03/26

To Heather

"And he went on, and there was a yellow light, and fire within; and the evening meal was ready, and he was expected. And Rose drew him in, and set him in his chair, and put little Elanor upon his lap."

—J. R. R. TOLKIEN, *THE RETURN OF THE KING*

Contents

Analyzing Theology

The 1980s witnessed a sea change in the academic, philosophical study of Christian doctrines on the heels of a renewal in philosophy of religion initiated by such prominent figures as Alvin Plantinga, Marilyn McCord Adams, William P. Alston, Eleonore Stump, and Nicholas Wolterstorff. At the turn of the second millennium, interest in the analysis of Christian doctrine only grew more profound as analytic philosophers and systematic theologians began to interact in more substantive ways. These interactions eventuated in the rise of analytic theology, an explicitly constructive theological program equipped with the tools and methods of analytic philosophy.

Despite its significant promise for driving theology forward in both the academy and the church, much of analytic theology remains outside the grasp of nonspecialists. One of the fundamental goals of this series is to broaden analytic theology's audience and influence.

Analyzing Theology is a series of books in Christian theology that showcases cutting-edge work in analytic and systematic theology. Monographs in the series are aimed at: (i) introducing cutting-edge analytic and systematic theology, (ii) providing a platform for original contributions in analytic and systematic theology, and (iii) connecting questions of theoretical significance to theology with the practices of actual theological communities.

Analytic theology is an emerging methodology that draws from the tools and methods of contemporary analytic philosophy to serve the ends of constructive systematic theology. Those methods make use of contemporary logical and conceptual analysis, emphasize the virtues of clarity and concision (as employed within the analytic philosophical tradition), and typically include a commitment to the objectivity of truth, goodness, justice, and rationality.

The monographs in the series span a range of Christian traditions and encompass a range of subject matter. This includes discussions of the method of analytic theology, exploring its engagements with other theological disciplines (such as biblical studies), as well as exemplifying this method by addressing underexplored theological topics from an analytic perspective.

Foreword

Timothy J. Pawl

I'm a fan of Randy Johnson. Happily, I'm also a fan of his work, otherwise his asking me to write a foreword for this book would have been an uncomfortable experience.

Johnson's goal in this work is to argue that *classical Christology*—by which term he means the Christology expressed in the creedal statements of the first seven ecumenical councils, plus the affirmation the Christ is and always has been impeccable—*entails the truth of compatibilism*—by which he means the thesis that human free will is compatible with every action or event (including acts of human freedom) being "necessitated by a set of prior and sufficient conditions." If classical Christology is true, says Johnson, then so is compatibilism. His is an important project for multiple reasons.

First, Johnson's dialectic charts a new path forward for the free will debate, which, in the metaphysical discussions, has been caught in a loop of never-ending epicycles for decades now. Here we have a novel approach to arguing for compatibilism, one to which standard moves in the philosophical debate don't apply neatly. The book breaches the impasse.

Second, the project has, somewhat paradoxically, a narrow-yet-broad application. Narrow, because the only people who would be inclined to use Modus Ponens on the entailment thesis, and so to derive compatibilism from Johnson's reasoning, are those who accept certain forms of Christianity. As such, he is moving the dialectic forward only in a specific community. But, that said, he has chosen the broadest swath of that community as his interlocutor in employing classical Christology as his backdrop. This is because classical Christology, as he defines it, is common to the majority of past and present Christians, including Catholics, the Orthodox, and many confessional Protestants. So, the project is valuable to a not inconsiderable segment of the contemporary debates.

Third, Johnson does an exemplary job of combining philosophical analysis with systematic and historical sophistication. He draws deeply from scripture, the councils, the early fathers, the medievals, and reformers like Calvin, Turretin, and Edwards. But at the same time, he is thoroughly seeped in the contemporary analytic discussions of freedom, determinism, moral responsibility, and innumerable other salient topics. The result is a book that clearly avoids the common stereotypical objections that analytic theology is historically unmoored and biblically sophomoric, or that historical and systematic theology are deficient in perspicuous reasoning. It is because of books like this one that such uninformed stereotypes are becoming rarer.

For these three reasons, I think that this book will be of great value to the contemporary debates on freewill and Christology. With this book, Johnson has given a gift to analytic and systematic theology. Join me in thanking him for it.

Acknowledgments

This book began as a PhD dissertation, so I would like to thank my advisor, Steve Wellum, for his guidance and encouragement throughout the research and writing process. Indeed, his course on the person of Christ has had the greatest effect on my understanding of Scripture and theology. His influence is plain to see in this book. I would also like to thank Guillaume Bignon, Paul Helm, and Bruce Ware who served as readers and committee members for my dissertation defense, and whose feedback was invaluable. I am grateful to Tim Pawl who has been a constant encouragement and advocate. The structure of this book is indebted to conversations with him. I thank Jordan Wessling for constructive feedback on my manuscript. I would also like to thank several former professors: Paul Helseth, who introduced me to Reformed theology, and Alicia Finch and Doug Blount, whose courses on metaphysics and free will prepared me well for writing this book. I am especially grateful for nights discussing life and theology with Alex Tibbott, Torey Teer, Henry Lyan, Daniel Scheiderer, Drew Sparks, and David King. Finally, I am grateful to my lovely wife, Heather, for her love and support.

Soli Deo Gloria

Abbreviations

BDAG	Arndt, William, Frederick W. Danker, Walter Bauer, and F. Wilbur Gingrich. *A Greek-English Lexicon of the New Testament and Other Early Christian Literature.* 3rd ed. Chicago: University of Chicago Press, 2000
JAT	*Journal of Analytic Theology*
JETS	*Journal of the Evangelical Theological Society*
JRT	*Journal of Reformed Theology*
ST	*Summa Theologiae.* Translated by Laurence Shapcote. 8 vols. Green Bay, WI: Aquinas Institute, 2012
WTJ	*Westminster Theological Journal*

Introduction

1. Introduction

In this book, I argue that classical Christology entails compatibilism. This thesis contains three key terms. First is "classical Christology." Classical Christology is the teaching about Jesus Christ found in Scripture and affirmed in historical Christian orthodoxy. Central to classical Christology is the belief that the historical man Jesus Christ is the eternal Son of God. This Son is fully divine and fully human: one person subsisting in two natures. Classical Christology affirms such notions as the eternal pre-existence of the Son, his consubstantiality with the Father and Holy Spirit, the hypostatic union, the *communicatio idiomata*, the *extra calvinisticum*, dyothelitism, impeccability, and non-contrariety of wills. It affirms the virgin birth, and also the life, death, resurrection, and imminent bodily return of Jesus. It denies adoptionism, Arianism, docetism, monophysitism, monothelitism, and Nestorianism.[1] Rest assured, these key features of classical Christology will be explained in chapter 2 and rehearsed throughout the book.

1. The pre-existence of the Son is the notion that God the Son eternally exists, and his eternal existence precedes his becoming man. To say that the Son is consubstantial with the Father and the Holy Spirit is to say that Father, Son, and Holy Spirit share the numerically same essence and being. The hypostatic union is the personal union of Christ's divine and human natures; Christ is one person in two natures. The *communicatio idiomata* is the communication of properties (attributes, idioms); the properties of each of Christ's natures are properly applied to his person. The *extra calvinisticum* is the doctrine that the Son was not limited or contained by his humanity during his earthly ministry. Rather, the world was upheld and contained by the omnipotent, omniscient, and omnipresent Son. Dyothelitism is the doctrine that Christ has two wills, one according to each nature. To say that Christ is impeccable is to say that he cannot sin. And to affirm non-contrariety of wills is to deny that Christ's human and divine wills can be at odds with one another. Adoptionism is the view that Jesus became God by adoption. Arianism is the view that the Son is not consubstantial with but subordinate to the

The second key term is "entails." Entailment is a logical relation between propositions. A proposition (or set of propositions) is said to *entail* another proposition when the latter is a necessary consequence of the former. In this case, classical Christology is a set of propositions (beliefs about Jesus Christ) that entails compatibilism. Compatibilism is a necessary consequence of classical Christology.

"Compatibilism" is the third key term. Compatibilism concerns the debate over the relationship between determinism and freedom and moral responsibility. An action or event is determined if it is necessitated by a set of prior and sufficient conditions. It is impossible for those prior conditions to obtain without the event happening; if those prior conditions obtain, there is exactly one possible future. Thus, determinism is the thesis that every event is determined by prior and sufficient conditions. Compatibilism, then, is the thesis that freedom and moral responsibility are compatible with determinism.

Therefore, my sparse thesis can be expanded to the following parsed thesis: That freedom and moral responsibility are compatible with determinism is a necessary consequence of the teaching about Jesus Christ found in Scripture and affirmed in historical Christian orthodoxy.

Compatibilism is not the only view about the relationship between determinism and freedom and moral responsibility. Incompatibilism, as the name suggests, is the thesis that freedom and moral responsibility are incompatible with determinism. Incompatibilism is a family of views. The species of incompatibilism that affirms determinism but denies freedom and moral responsibility is called "hard determinism." The variety of incompatibilism that affirms freedom and moral responsibility is called "libertarianism." Libertarianism itself is divided into two groups: that which affirms and prioritizes the principle of alternative possibilities (PAP), called "PAP libertarianism" and that which prioritizes the source of the action (and may accept or reject PAP), called "sourcehood libertarianism."[2] Therefore, the main camps in the freedom and moral responsibility debate are hard determinism, PAP libertarianism, sourcehood libertarianism, and compatibilism.

In this book, I will argue that Jesus Christ's perfect obedience and conformity to the divine will can be maintained only by a compatibilist

Father. Docetism is the view that Jesus only appeared to take on flesh but did not really become true man. Monophysitism is the view that Christ has one nature, a confusion or mixture of his divinity and humanity. Monothelitism is the view that Christ has only one will. And Nestorianism is the view that Christ is two persons.

2. What I call "PAP libertarianism" is sometimes called "leeway theory" or "leeway libertarianism." Sourcehood libertarianism is also known as "source theory" or "sourcehood incompatibilism." These terms will be discussed at length in chapter 1.

paradigm, contra hard determinism, PAP libertarianism, and sourcehood libertarianism. Jesus' actions were significantly free and morally appraisable yet determined by a set of prior and sufficient conditions. Therefore, Jesus' actions prove the compatibility of freedom, moral responsibility, and determinism. If compatibilism must be true in the case of Jesus, then compatibilism must be true *simpliciter*—freedom and moral responsibility are, indeed, compatible with determinism.

2. Significance

A christological case for compatibilism is a significant contribution to the contemporary discussions about free will, moral responsibility, and the incarnation. Classical Christology is shared by Roman Catholic, Orthodox, and Protestant churches. To show Christology's implications on freedom and responsibility, then, has the potential to influence every major branch of Christianity. My broadest goal (perhaps "wish" would be a better term), then, is to persuade all Christians to become compatibilists.

A narrower goal—and one more likely to be achieved—is to bolster the credibility and necessity of compatibilism in Protestant circles. And this goal, from a Reformed compatibilist perspective, is directed both outward and inward. I hope to influence Arminians, Molinists, and Reformed libertarians; if they hold to classical Christology, then they ought to be compatibilists. I also hope to encourage my fellow Reformed compatibilists in the assurance that our theological system is internally consistent. A consistent Reformed understanding of total depravity, regeneration, biblical inspiration, and final states depend on the truth of compatibilism. Moreover, compatibilism makes the most sense of the doctrines of election, divine foreknowledge and providence, sanctification, and others. Therefore, by demonstrating that Christology entails compatibilism, I will have strengthened multiple doctrines and the Reformed system as a whole.

A christological case for compatibilism is also a unique contribution to the contemporary discussions about freedom and the incarnation. Rather than asking how we should think about Christ in light of our understanding of freedom, I consider how we should understand freedom in light of Christ.[3] Most contemporary defenses of compatibilism either arise from

3. This book could be considered a work of christological anthropology. See Cortez, *ReSourcing Theological Anthropology*. Whereas Cortez argues for a *comprehensively* christological anthropology in which "(a) Christology warrants ultimate claims about true humanity such that (b) the scope of those claims applies to all anthropological data," for present purposes, I need only to affirm a *minimally* christological anthropology in which "(a) Christology warrants important claims about what it means to be

philosophical speculation or are derived from the doctrines of predestination, providence, anthropology, sin, or salvation. But, in this book, I follow the tradition of my theological forbears in looking to the person and work of Christ for an answer to the question of free will. I adopt the christological case for compatibilism and update it for contemporary discussion.

This book poses a danger, unfortunately. For those absolutely committed to libertarianism, my argument may have the effect of leading them to deny classical Christology—which, I believe, would be worse than denying compatibilism. For that reason, I provide biblical and historical motivations for affirming classical Christology in the coming chapters.

3. Method

This book concerns the intersection of a locus of theology and a branch of philosophical inquiry: Christology and human moral agency. Because these fields of study are so significant and have been debated for millennia, it is impossible to cover everything in one book. For that reason, the scope is limited to contemporary views of free agency and models of the incarnation that are *prima facie* consistent with classical Christology.

Regarding human freedom, I focus on the contemporary philosophical and philosophico-theological literature, especially in the analytic tradition. Because I argue that classical Christology entails compatibilism, the conclusion is a philosophical and philosophico-theological one.[4] As such, the best interlocutors are philosophers and philosophical theologians. Because compatibilism has contemporary proponents and opponents, it is appropriate to engage primarily with the most recent literature on the issue. And because the analytic tradition has produced the clearest, most rigorous, and most voluminous literature on human freedom, I shall converse predominantly with the analytic tradition.

---

human and (b) the scope of those claims goes beyond issues like the image of God and ethics." Cortez, *ReSourcing Theological Anthropology*, 21.

4. Because I interact significantly with analytic philosophical theology (i.e., analytic theology), this book may be considered a work of analytic theology. I understand analytic theology to be a species of systematic theology that utilizes the analytic philosophical method. The method of analytic philosophy includes certain tools (e.g., deductive arguments, thought experiments, symbolic logic, and possible worlds semantics) and values (e.g., precision, clarity, rigor, and certitude). So, analytic theology applies that method to the theological task. Analytic theology, as a species of systematic theology, still requires proper exegesis, hermeneutics, biblical theology, and historical theology. See Crisp and Rea, *Analytic Theology*; McCall, *Invitation to Analytic Christian Theology*; cf. Crisp, *Analyzing Doctrine*.

Although the book's conclusion is a philosophical one (with theological implications), the arguments are premised on theological commitments—a commitment to Scripture and to classical Christology, especially as expressed in the creeds of Chalcedon and Constantinople III.[5] The most poignant elements of classical Christology for this project are dyothelitism, non-contrariety of wills, and impeccability. For these elements, I pay close attention to Maximus the Confessor and Thomas Aquinas. Maximus was a key figure in defending dyothelitism in the seventh century, which led to the anathematizing of monothelitism in Constantinople III. And Thomas discussed the two wills of Christ with his characteristic precision and comprehensiveness. Further confirmation of classical Christology is found throughout church history.

Several key theologians in the history of the Reformed tradition have made christological arguments for compatibilism. I review the arguments from John Calvin, Francis Turretin, and Jonathan Edwards. My christological case for compatibilism is indebted to these theologians.

4. Overview of Chapters

This book is divided into three parts. Part 1 (chapters 1–3) covers preliminary issues. In chapter 1, I review the contemporary literature on free will and moral responsibility. I present a taxonomy of views of freedom and moral responsibility and divide the debate into four main camps: PAP libertarianism, sourcehood libertarianism, hard determinism, and compatibilism. I also present the variations within the main camps. Chapter 2 clarifies what I mean by "classical Christology." I distinguish "classical Christology" from similar terms such as "conciliar Christology." I also expound on three essential features of classical Christology: dyothelitism, volitional non-contrariety, and impeccability. Chapter 3 serves as a bridge between the descriptive and the argumentative parts of the book. I survey the christological arguments for compatibilism from three prominent Reformed theologians: Calvin, Turretin, and Edwards. Then, I present my own argument as a conditional of which the antecedent is classical Christology and the consequent is a disjunction between hard determinism, PAP libertarianism, sourcehood libertarianism, and compatibilism. The rest of the book demonstrates that PAP libertarianism, sourcehood libertarianism, and hard

5. For that reason, this project may also be considered a work of theological philosophy. I understand theological philosophy to be the discipline that answers philosophical questions by way of a theological method. In other words, theological philosophy asks what the whole Bible teaches and entails about a particular philosophical question.

determinism are inconsistent with classical Christology. Therefore, if classical Christology is true, then compatibilism must be true.

Part 2 (chapters 4–7) is an argument against incompatibilism. Chapter 4 demonstrates that PAP cannot be true if classical Christology is true. Jesus' prayer in Gethsemane is an instance of a voluntary and morally significant action (Jesus' submission to God's will), and yet, Jesus could not have done otherwise than that action. Because PAP is false, PAP libertarianism is false. Chapter 5 shows that sourcehood libertarianism is inconsistent with classical Christology. I argue that Jesus is a moral agent who deserves moral praise; yet the ultimate source of Jesus' actions is not found in his humanity but in his divinity; thus, he fails to meet the sourcehood condition. Therefore, sourcehood libertarianism is false. Chapters 6 and 7 consider the matters of divine and human action more closely. In chapter 6, I examine the nature of the harmony between Christ's human and divine will. I argue that Christ's human will is ultimately caused by the divine will. In chapter 7, I argue that this divine causation is tantamount to theological determinism. Because Christ is still a moral agent despite his actions being divinely necessitated, hard determinism is false.

Part 3 (chapters 8–10) is a positive argument for compatibilism. Because part 2 shows that classical Christology is incompatible with PAP libertarianism, sourcehood libertarianism, and hard determinism, compatibilism is the only viable option. Part 3 shows the consistency of classical Christology with compatibilism. In chapter 8, I show that Jesus' teaching about himself and humanity supports compatibilism. Chapter 9 argues that the biblical-historical unfolding of God's plan necessitates the advent and obedience of Christ. In chapter 10, I review the systematic theological features of classical Christology to show how they produce a positive argument for compatibilism.

The conclusion summarizes the christological case for compatibilism and reflects on its significance. I connect my research to five broader subjects. First is classical Christian theology, which is the confluence of classical theism, classical trinitarianism, and classical Christology. Second is christological anthropology, which considers how our doctrine of Christ informs our doctrine of humanity. Third is scholarship in Reformed views of freedom. Fourth is theological compatibilism—the genus in which christological arguments for compatibilism are a species. And fifth is the debate over models of divine providence, which is intimately related to the debate over free will.

Part I:

Philosophical, Theological, and Historical Context for Compatibilism

1

Freedom and Moral Responsibility

1. Introduction

The history of the free will debate is long and complex. The nature of the debate has taken various forms throughout history and across cultures and contexts. Different motivations, commitments, fears, languages, and worldviews have contributed to the diversity of the debate. The focus of this book is on contemporary views of human freedom. The immediate history of contemporary views of human freedom stems from debates in Reformation, Counter-Reformation, and post-Reformation theology, philosophical debate in the modern period, and the rise of analytic philosophy at the beginning of the twentieth century.

In this chapter, I provide an overview of the contemporary freewill debate. First, I discuss the various perceived threats to human freedom and moral responsibility. Second, I narrow the discussion to determinism. Third, I present incompatibilism and its various permutations. Fourth, I present compatibilism and its various permutations.

2. Threats to Human Freedom

The perceived threats to human freedom may be categorized into three main genera: (1) fatalism, (2) determinism, and (3) internal necessity.[1] Each of these genera has two dominant species—one that is of particular concern to scientists, philosophers, or psychologists, and one that is of particular concern to theologians or philosophers of religion.

1. This way of organizing and labeling threats to human freedom is just one way to do it; there are many ways one could organize and label these threats. For an overview of the perceived threats to human freedom, see Kane, *Significance of Free Will*, 3–12.

Fatalism is concerned with the certainty of future events.[2] Fatalism comes in two main varieties: logical and theological. *Logical fatalism* rests on the premise that all propositions are either true or false (i.e., bivalence and the law of the excluded middle), including propositions about the future.[3] If it is true that I will eat an apple on January 1, 2045, then the proposition, "Randy eats an apple on January 1, 2045," is true.[4] But if that proposition is true, then it is always (or eternally) true, and there is nothing I or anyone else can do to make that proposition false. I will certainly eat an apple on January 1, 2045. *Theological fatalism*, similarly, is concerned with the certainty of future events. Theological fatalism presupposes that God is omniscient, or, at least, that God knows the future actions of human agents. If God knows that I will eat an apple on January 1, 2045, then I will certainly eat an apple on January 1, 2045; and there is nothing I or anyone else can do to change it. Theological fatalism is sometimes known as "the problem of divine foreknowledge."[5]

Determinism is the notion that every event is necessitated by a set of prior and sufficient conditions.[6] Indeterminism is the denial of determinism. Determinism comes in two main varieties. *Physical determinism*[7] is the thesis that the state of the world a long time ago (at or near the beginning of our universe) plus the laws of nature causally determine or logically entail every event that ever happens, including human actions.[8] Every event is caused by a prior event; and these events form a causal chain that reaches

2. The notion of fate is an ancient one. Here, I consider only contemporary forms of fatalism—even if the contemporary forms have ancient roots. I am not using the term "fatalism" to mean that the world is ruled by blind fate or chance, that future events are uncaused, or that the certainty of future events is unrelated to our choices.

3. Aristotle is famous for denying bivalence because of the threat of fatalism, in chapter 9 of *De Interpretatione*. Kane writes, "Most philosophers, beginning with Aristotle, believed there were ways to avoid its conclusion, but there is no general agreement about the best way to avoid it," in *Significance of Free Will*, 8. For more on logical fatalism, see Finch, "Logical Fatalism," 191–202.

4. I first wrote this paragraph in December of 2020.

5. See Fischer and Todd, *Freedom, Fatalism, and Foreknowledge*; Fischer, *Our Fate*.

6. Philosophers use the term "determinism" in various ways (see below). Here, I am using "determinism" to refer to forms of *causal* determinism.

7. Physical determinism may also be called "causal determinism," "natural determinism," or "nomological determinism."

8. How to understand natural laws is not a settled matter. If the laws of nature are governing, then it seems that the state of the world a long time ago plus the laws of nature *determine* every event that follows. If the laws of nature, however, are non-governing (i.e., the Humean view of the laws of nature), then it seems that the state of the world a long time ago plus the laws of nature merely *entail* every event that follows. For the debate between natural laws as governing or non-governing, see Beebee, "Non-Governing Conception of Laws of Nature," 571–94.

from the present all the way back to state of the world a long time ago—perhaps since the beginning of time—and they extend into the future with no seeming end in sight. *Theological determinism* is the thesis that every event is caused directly by God. God's activity is the prior and sufficient condition for every event in creation.[9] Whether any real causation exists between events within creation is a matter of debate.[10] Robert Kane writes:

> More than a few Western theologians, including Luther, Calvin, Jonathan Edwards, and perhaps even Augustine, believed that God's power, omniscience, and providence would be unacceptably compromised if one attributed to humans an ultimate control over their choices and actions such as the notion of free will required. And yet theologians on the other side, including Arminians, argued with equal force that if humans did not have such ultimate control, it was hard to see how they could be responsible for their actions in a manner that would justify divine rewards and punishments.[11]

Internal necessity is concerned with factors internal to the agent that necessitate certain choices or actions. One species of internal necessity is *psychological determinism*, which is the thesis that every human action (or choice) is necessitated by the human agent's mental states at, or just prior to, the moment of action (or choice).[12] Kane describes psychological determinism as "the idea that choices and actions are determined by prior motives and character, which in turn are the ultimate products of birth and upbringing. A special version of psychological determinism debated by the ancients was related to the Socratic doctrine that we can never freely act against what we believe to be our good."[13] He continues, "The more general version of psychological determinism is the view . . . that we are always determined to act by the strongest motives or desires, which are in turn the inevitable products of birth and upbringing."[14] Another species of internal necessity is the Augustinian/Reformed view of the *bondage of the will* either to sin

9. Note that theological determinism is not fully synonymous with meticulous providence, omnicausality, or divine sovereignty. See below for a detailed discussion of theological determinism's relation to these theological concepts.

10. Occasionalism is the thesis that God causes everything, and there are no other causes. A commitment to theological determinism is not necessarily a commitment to occasionalism.

11. Kane, *Significance of Free Will*, 7.

12. Psychological determinism is tantamount to freedom of inclination. See below.

13. Kane, *Significance of Free Will*, 6.

14. Kane, *Significance of Free Will*, 6.

or to Christ.[15] Because of original sin and corruption, we cannot do that which pleases God apart from God's grace. Rather, we are born into a state of *non posse non peccare* (not able not to sin). Similarly, the work of the Holy Spirit in regeneration and sanctification renders us incapable of rejecting God's grace—we *must* have faith and repentance. This moral necessity is even clearer in our final states. In the eschaton, the elect can never sin, and the reprobate can never repent.

3. Determinism

Questions and answers regarding free will and moral responsibility must be relative to one or more of the threats mentioned above. One may be free with respect to one threat but not with respect to another threat. Kane puts all the threats mentioned above under the label "determinism." He writes:

> Any event (including a choice or action) is determined . . . just in case there are conditions (such as the decrees of fate, antecedent physical causes plus laws of nature, or foreordaining acts of God) whose joint occurrence is (logically) sufficient for the occurrence of the event. In other words, it must be the case that, if these determining conditions obtain (e.g., physical causes and laws of nature), then the determined event occurs.[16]

W. Matthews Grant explains in greater detail: "Determinism, thus, requires that there be a certain sort of relationship between any determined event, or *determinatum*, and its *determinans*, or thing determining it; namely, the *determinans* must be *prior* to the *determinatum* and must be a *sufficient condition* for the *determinatum*."[17] Grant clarifies that "sufficient" refers to "logically sufficient": "*a* is logically sufficient for *b* just in case it is not possible for *a* to exist (or occur, or obtain) without *b*'s existing (or occurring, or obtaining)."[18] And "'Prior' can mean 'temporally prior,' but 'prior' is also frequently used to characterize one thing *a*'s relation to another *b*, when *b* asymmetrically depends on *a*, whether or not a temporally precedes b."[19]

I prefer not to label *all* the threats above as "determinism." For example, on one proposed solution to theological fatalism, God's (fore)knowledge of

15. See Augustine, *On Free Choice of the Will* and *On Grace and Free Choice;* Luther, *Bondage of the Will*; Calvin, *Bondage and Liberation of the Will.*

16. Kane, *Significance of Free Will*, 8.

17. Grant, *Free Will and God's Universal Causality*, 6.

18. Grant, *Free Will and God's Universal Causality*, 6.

19. Grant, *Free Will and God's Universal Causality*, 6.

free creaturely actions is not prior to the creatures' actions; thus it does not fit the description of determinism.[20] In that case, it seems that one could be free with respect to some form of fatalism but not with respect to some form of determinism. Furthermore, there seems to be an important difference between fatalism and determinism. Whereas fatalism merely entails *that* an event certainly happens, determinism provides the reason *why* an event certainly happens, e.g., God or the laws of nature determined it. It should also be noted that, unlike psychological determinism, the bondage of the will does not seem to determine an agent to a particular token action but rather to a type action. In other words, a slave to sin may freely sin in one particular way rather than another—even if he is unable not to sin. Thus, the bondage of the will is not so much a form of determinism as a form of moral necessity or inability.

Most of the debate surrounding free will in philosophical circles concerns causal (i.e., physical, nomological) determinism. In these circles, the term "determinism" is often coterminous with causal determinism. Most of the debate surrounding free will in theological circles, however, concerns either theological determinism or bondage of the will. Here, it is important to distinguish theological determinism from meticulous providence, omnicausality, and divine sovereignty. Calvinists,[21] Thomists,[22] and Molinists[23] all believe that God's will is meticulous. Calvinists typically believe that God is the primary cause of all events. Molinists, however, argue that, in the case of free human actions, God weakly actualizes his will (i.e., "brings about") rather than strongly actualizing his will (i.e., "causes');[24] and some Thomists deny that God's primary causation is prior and sufficient.[25] Many who deny meticulous providence still affirm divine sovereignty. For God to be sovereign, then, is for him to be in ultimate control, like a good king—even if he does not direct every event meticulously.[26] Thus, theological determinism should not be confused with these other concepts.

20. See, for example, Book V of Boethius, *Consolation of Philosophy*.

21. See Bavinck, *Reformed Dogmatics*; Helseth, "God Causes All Things."

22. See Garrigou-Lagrange, *God, His Existence and His Nature*.

23. See Molina, *On Divine Foreknowledge*; cf. Flint, *Divine Providence*.

24. On "weak" versus "strong" actualization, see A. Plantinga, *Nature of Necessity*, 172–73.

25. See the recent work by Grant: "Divine Universal Causality Without Occasionalism (and with Agent-Causation)," 175–200; and "Divine Universal Causality and Libertarian Freedom," 214–33.

26. For example, see Cottrell, *What the Bible Says About God the Ruler*; cf. Olson, *Arminian Theology*.

In what follows, I shall use the term "determinism" to refer simply to the thesis that every event is determined by a set of prior and sufficient conditions. Physical determinism, theological determinism, and psychological determinism fit this description. Even so, the conclusions of this project are relevant to the debates about human freedom with respect to the other perceived threats. With respect to freedom and determinism, one is either an incompatibilist or a compatibilist.[27]

4. Incompatibilism

Incompatibilism is the thesis that freedom and moral responsibility are incompatible with determinism. Incompatibilists are either hard determinists or libertarians.[28] Hard determinism is the belief that (1) determinism is true, and (2) humans are never free.[29] Libertarianism is the belief that (1) determinism is false, and (2) humans are free at least sometimes.[30] In this section, I discuss one of the strongest arguments for incompatibilism. Then I consider the main varieties of incompatibilism.

4a. The Consequence Argument

Peter van Inwagen proposed one of the most influential arguments for incompatibilism.[31] The consequence argument (CA) claims that if (nomological) determinism is true, then our actions are the consequence of the state of the world from the distant past plus the laws of nature. Neither the state of the world from the distant past nor the laws of nature are up to us. Therefore, our actions are not up to us; thus, we are not free. Here, I present the modal version of CA.

27. I include semicompatibilism as a form of compatibilism. See below.

28. For an overview of libertarianism, see Ginet, "Libertarianism," 587–612.

29. Soft determinism is the belief that (1) determinism is true, and (2) humans are free at least sometimes. Therefore, soft determinists are compatibilists.

30. Neither compatibilists nor libertarians claim that all human actions are free. Compatibilists deny that *involuntary* actions are free, e.g., being tripped by a dog or having a muscle spasm. Many libertarians will deny that even certain *voluntary* actions are free, e.g., a drug addiction hinders a person's freedom to refrain from drugs even though the addict takes the drugs voluntarily. See van Inwagen, "When Is the Will Free?," 399–422.

31. Van Inwagen, *Essay on Free Will*, 55–105. Manipulation arguments are, likewise, strongly influential arguments for incompatibilism. See Mickelson, "Manipulation Argument," 166–78.

CA reasonably presupposes that the laws of nature and the distant past are fixed. Beyond these presuppositions, CA posits two novel rules of inference. A rule of inference is a valid argument form that allows us to derive conclusions from premises. The new rules of inference are Rule α and Rule β:

- Rule α: "For any sentence *p*, the result of prefixing *p* with 'N' may be regarded as an abbreviation for the result of flanking 'and no one has, or ever had, any choice about whether' with occurrences of *p*."[32] In other words, if *p* is necessarily true, then no one has any choice about whether *p* is true.
- Rule β: The conjunction of N*p* and N(if *p* then *q*) entails N*q*. In other words, if no one has any choice about whether *p* is true, and no one has any choice about whether *if p then q* is true, then no one has any choice about whether *q* is true.

With these presuppositions and rules of inference clarified, let P_0 be a description of the state of the world in the distant past; let L be a description of the laws of nature; and let *p* be any true proposition. In the following argument, the left side represents the steps of the argument, and the right side represents the justification for each step.

1. Necessarily: if (P_0 and L) then *p*.	Consequence of determinism
2. Necessarily: if P_0 then (if L then *p*).	Derived from 1
3. No one has any choice about: if P_0 then (if L then *p*).	Derived from 2 and Rule α
4. No one has any choice about: P_0.	Premise
5. No one has any choice about: if L then *p*.	Derived from 3, 4, and Rule β
6. No one has any choice about: L.	Premise
7. No one has any choice about: *p*.	Derived from 5, 6, and Rule β[33]

This argument shows that if nomological determinism is true, then no one has any choice about whether *p* is true. Remember, *p* designates any true proposition, including propositions about our actions. So, if determinism is true, then it is not up to us what we do, and so, we have no free will.[34]

32. Van Inwagen, *Essay on Free Will*, 93.

33. Van Inwagen, *Essay on Free Will*, 94–95. I translated the logical symbols for the sake of accessibility.

34. Almost every major work on free will since 1983 has interacted with CA.

A similar argument may be made in the case of theological determinism. Rather than the conjunction of the state of the world in the distant past and the laws of nature, we might posit the will of God as the *determinans*. Let W be the will of God and let *p* be any true proposition.

1. Necessarily: if W then *p*.	Consequence of (theological) determinism
2. No one has any choice about: if W then *p*.	Derived from 1 and Rule α
3. No one has any choice about: W.	Premise
4. No one has any choice about: *p*.	Derived from 3 and Rule β

This argument shows that if theological determinism is true, then, again, no one has any choice about whether *p* is true; therefore, no one has free will. Because these arguments are valid, incompatibilists must reject the truth of either free will (as hard determinists do) or determinism (as libertarians do).

4b. Libertarianism

Libertarians may be divided into those who claim alternative possibilities are necessary for free choice and those who deny it. The former I shall call "PAP libertarians"; the latter I shall call "sourcehood libertarians." Kevin Timpe writes, "Both Leeway Incompatibilism and Source Incompatibilism agree that the truth of causal determinism would be sufficient for the lack of moral responsibility, but they differ in terms of what is most fundamentally required for moral responsibility."[35]

4c. PAP Libertarianism

Most libertarians believe that free will and moral responsibility require that an agent have alternative possibilities. The agent must have the ability or power to do otherwise. Harry G. Frankfurt calls this principle the Principle

Perhaps the most famous response to CA comes from Lewis, "Are We Free to Break the Laws?," 113–21. See also McKay and Johnson, "Reconsideration of an Argument against Compatibilism," 113–22; Finch and Warfield, "Mind Argument and Libertarianism," 515–28.

35. Timpe, *Free Will*, 146. For Timpe, "Leeway Incompatibilism" is tantamount to PAP libertarianism, assuming people have free will at least sometimes.

of Alternative Possibilities (PAP).[36] Van Inwagen explains a common and intuitive notion of free will:

> When I say of a man that he "has free will" I mean that very often, if not always, when he has to choose between two or more mutually incompatible courses of action—that is, courses of action that it is impossible for him to carry out more than one of—each of these courses of action is such that he can, or is able to, or has it within his power to carry it out. A man has free will if he is often in positions like these: he must now speak or now be silent, and he *can* now speak and *can* now remain silent; he must attempt to rescue a drowning child or else go for help, and he is *able* to attempt to rescue the child and *able* to go for help; he must now resign his chairmanship or else lie to the members, and he has it within his power to resign and he has it within his power to lie.[37]

How one understands this power to do otherwise is crucial but contested.[38] To say that an agent can do otherwise is to say that it is *possible* for an agent to do otherwise. Because possibility is a modal notion, one must ask, "In *what way* is it possible?"

The broadest type of possibility is logical possibility. Something is logically possible if it does not violate the laws of logic. Physical (a.k.a. nomological) possibility is narrower than logical possibility. Something is physically possible only if it does not violate the laws of nature. But libertarians are concerned with an even narrower possibility. I shall call this kind of possibility to do otherwise "categorical possibility"; agents have the categorical ability to do otherwise if it is categorically possible for them to do otherwise.[39] The categorical ability to do otherwise claims that an agent S with respect to some action A at time *t* could have done A or not-A. Nothing before or at *t* determines whether S does A or not-A. If S chose A at *t*, and we rewound time to a moment just before *t*, without adjusting any of the variables about the laws of nature or the state of the world or S's mental state or God's will, S would be able to choose not-A at *t*. For PAP libertarians, S is

36. Frankfurt, "Alternative Possibilities and Moral Responsibility," 1.

37. Van Inwagen, *Essay on Free Will*, 8. Kane writes, "The agent has *alternative possibilities* (or can do otherwise) with respect to A at t in the sense that, at t, the agent *can* (has the *power* or *ability to*) do A and *can* (has the *power* or *ability to*) do otherwise." Kane, *Significance of Free Will*, 33.

38. Most compatibilists agree that free actions require that the agent be able to do otherwise in *some* sense.

39. This categorical possibility is sometimes called "narrow metaphysical possibility."

directly free and morally responsible with respect to A at *t* only if S has the categorical ability to do otherwise than A.[40]

4d. Sourcehood Libertarianism

Sourcehood libertarians believe that free will and moral responsibility require that an agent be the ultimate source of the agent's actions—that the agent be ultimately *responsible* for the agent's actions. Determinism is incompatible with an agent's being the source of the agent's actions because, if determinism is true, then the ultimate source of an agent's action is found outside the agent rather than inside the agent. Timpe points out that there are two subcategories of sourcehood libertarianism: "narrow" and "wide" types of sourcehood libertarianism. Timpe explains, "The reason for this is that some Source Incompatibilists do think there is an alternative-possibilities condition for free will; what makes them Source Incompatibilists, however, is that the source condition is more 'fundamental' or 'important' in some sense for free will (and thus also for moral responsibility)."[41] These libertarians are wide sourcehood libertarians. Narrow sourcehood libertarians, however, "think that an agent could be the required source of her action even if she has no alternative possibilities whatsoever."[42] He continues, "For these Source Incompatibilists, it is not the case that the sourcehood condition is simply more fundamental than the alternative-possibilities condition; according to them, there is no required alternative-possibilities condition for free will and moral responsibility at all."[43]

Kane is an example of a wide sourcehood libertarian. He argues that the issue of determinism and free will "requires attention to *two* conditions in the historical literature on free will that seem to imply incompatibility. The second condition, which I will call the condition of Ultimate Responsibility, or UR, is less familiar than Alternative Possibilities or AP, and far less frequently discussed. Yet it is, to my mind, of even greater importance."[44] For us to be ultimately responsible for our actions "demand[s] that the

40. PAP libertarians may affirm that S is *indirectly* free and morally responsible with respect to A at *t* even if S does not have the categorical ability to do otherwise than A only if S was *directly* free with respect to some prior action that resulted in S's inability to do otherwise at *t*. For example, S may have (directly) freely chosen to drink to the point of intoxication at *t*-1, and S's drunkenness hindered S's ability to do otherwise with respect to A at *t*.

41. Timpe, *Free Will*, 146.

42. Timpe, *Free Will*, 147.

43. Timpe, *Free Will*, 147.

44. Kane, *Significance of Free Will*, 33.

ultimate source of our wills lies in us and not in something outside us."[45] Derk Pereboom belongs to Timpe's category of wide sourcehood *incompatibilism* but not the category of wide sourcehood *libertarianism*. Pereboom agrees with Kane that ultimate sourcehood is more fundamental to freedom—even though Pereboom denies we have this kind of freedom. He writes, "the incompatibilist intuition about actual causal histories . . . is more fundamental than any incompatibilist intuition about alternative possibilities."[46]

Three prominent narrow sourcehood libertarians are Linda Zagzebski, David Hunt, and Eleonore Stump.[47] For narrow sourcehood libertarians, PAP is unnecessary for free will and moral responsibility, as Zagzebski writes, "The presence of alternate possibilities may be a reliable sign of the presence of the agency needed for responsibility, but it is not necessary for it."[48] Yet, causal determinism is still incompatible with freedom. Hunt writes, "The threat posed by causal determinism . . . does not appear to vanish in the fact of Frankfurt's argument against PAP."[49] Eleonore Stump explains that an "agent is the ultimate source of her action," when

> the ultimate cause of her action is found in her intellect and will; she does what she does only because of her own beliefs and desires, and there is no cause of what she does. She is therefore ultimately responsible for what she does. Nonetheless, it isn't necessary for her to have ultimate responsibility that she have alternative possibilities available to her. Her intellect and will might be such that all options but one are unthinkable for her.[50]

Free actions must ultimately be within the agent's control and not the result of causal determinism.

4e. *Sourcehood Accounts*

One way to divide libertarians is by their view of the necessary and sufficient conditions for free will and moral responsibility. This division results in both PAP libertarians and sourcehood libertarians, as explained

45. Kane, *Significance of Free Will*, 71.

46. Pereboom, *Living Without Free Will*, 33. See below for more on Pereboom's hard incompatibilism.

47. See Timpe's discussion and critique of narrow sourcehood incompatibilism in *Free Will*, 141–61.

48. Zagzebski, "Does Libertarian Freedom Require Alternate Possibilities?," 245.

49. Hunt, "Moral Responsibility and Unavoidable Action," 223.

50. Stump, "Alternative Possibilities and Moral Responsibility," 324.

above. Another way of dividing libertarians is by their account of sourcehood (i.e., self-determination): event-causal libertarianism,[51] agent-causal libertarianism,[52] and non-causal libertarianism.[53]

Event-causal libertarianism claims that "self-determining an action requires, at minimum, that the agent cause the action and that an agent's causing his action is *wholly reducible* to mental states and other events involving the agent nondeviantly causing his action."[54] For example:

> Consider an agent's raising his hand. According to the event-causal model at its most basic level, an agent's raising his hand consists in the agent's causing his hand to rise and his causing his hand to rise consists in *apt* mental states and events involving the agent—such as the agent's desire to ask a question and his belief that he can ask a question by raising his hand—*nondeviantly* causing his hand to rise.[55]

Moreover, "self-determination requires nondeterministic causation, in a nondeviant way, by an agent's reasons."[56]

Agent-causal libertarianism claims that "self-determination requires that *the agent herself* play a causal role over and above the causal role played by her reasons."[57] "Agent causation is *irreducible substance causation*. The agent, the person, is a metaphysical substance whose causal activity grounds autonomous agency (and responsibility)."[58] Self-determined actions are, therefore, not reducible to "nondeterministic causation by apt mental states: agent-causation does not reduce to event-causation."[59] Agent causal libertarianism maintains that the causal role played in free will is identical with the agent's own self—not merely the agent's mental states.

Non-causal libertarianism claims that "exercises of the power of self-determination need not (or perhaps even cannot) be caused or causally structured. According to this view, we control our volition or choice simply in virtue of its being ours—its occurring in us. We do not exert a

51. For a defense of event-causal libertarianism, see Kane, *Significance of Free Will*. See also Ekstrom, "Event-Causal Libertarianism," 62–71.

52. For a defense of agent-causal libertarianism, see O'Connor, *Persons & Causes*.

53. For a defense of non-causal libertarianism, see McCann, *Creation and the Sovereignty of God*, 92–112.

54. O'Connor and Franklin, "Free Will."

55. O'Connor and Franklin, "Free Will."

56. O'Connor and Franklin, "Free Will."

57. O'Connor and Franklin, "Free Will."

58. Griffith, "Agent Causation," 73.

59. O'Connor and Franklin, "Free Will."

special kind of causality in bringing it about; instead, it is an intrinsically active event, intrinsically something we do."[60] Hugh J. McCann writes, "free agency . . . is simply not a causal relationship, and certainly does not consist in our creating our own actions."[61] McCann argues that free agency consists of three features. First, "the operations of free will cannot be the product of independent event-causal conditions."[62] That is, free agency cannot be the result of deterministic or even indeterministic causes. Second is the phenomenal experience of being "active in making the decision."[63] Third is that the act is intentional. "When we engage in acts of the will, we mean to be doing exactly what we are doing, exactly when and as we are doing it. We are committed, not just to the goal we set up or pursue, but to the decision and pursuit themselves."[64]

4f. Hard Determinism, Freewill Skepticism, and Hard Incompatibilism

Hard determinism is the thesis that freedom and moral responsibility are incompatible with determinism, and determinism is true. Determinists believe that everything is determined—whether by God or by the laws of nature and antecedent conditions; free will is incompatible with determinism; therefore, no one has free will. Baruch Spinoza is perhaps the father of modern hard determinism: "In the mind there is no absolute, or free, will. The mind is determined to this or that volition by a cause, which is likewise determined by another cause, and this again by another, and so ad infinitum."[65] Hard determinism is less popular today than libertarianism, perhaps because the deterministic bend of Newtonian physics appears to be undermined by quantum physics. Many believe that the universe has an element of chance or indeterminism, at least at the smallest level of reality.

Hard determinism is not only a species of incompatibilism but also a species of freewill skepticism—the family of views that maintains a critical stance toward the reality of free will and/or moral responsibility.[66] Another species of freewill skepticism is hard incompatibilism, which is the thesis

60. O'Connor and Franklin, "Free Will."

61. McCann, *Creation and the Sovereignty of God*, 101.

62. McCann, *Creation and the Sovereignty of God*, 101.

63. McCann, *Creation and the Sovereignty of God*, 102.

64. McCann, *Creation and the Sovereignty of God*, 102.

65. Spinoza, *Ethics*, IIP48, 95.

66. See Pereboom, "Skeptical Views About Free Will," 121–35.

that free will is incompatible with determinism *and* indeterminism. Greg Caruso explains:

> Against the view that free will is compatible with causal determination of our actions by natural factors beyond our control (i.e., compatibilism), most hard incompatibilists maintain that there is no relevant difference between this prospect and our actions being causally determined by manipulators (e.g. Pereboom 2001, 2014a).... Against *event-causal libertarianism*, hard incompatibilists generally advance the "luck" or "disappearing agent" objection, according to which agents are left unable to *settle* whether a decision/action occurs and hence cannot have the control in action required for moral responsibility (Pereboom 2001, 2014a; 2017c; Waller 1990, 2011, N. Levy 2008, 2011 ...). The same problem, they contend, arises for *non-causal libertarian accounts* since these too fail to provide agents with the control in action needed for basic desert (Pereboom 2014a). While *agent-causal* libertarianism could, in theory, supply this sort of control, hard incompatibilists argue that it cannot be reconciled with our best physical theories (Pereboom 2001, 2014a; Waller 2011; Harris 2012; cf. N. Levy 2011) and faces additional problems accounting for mental causation. Since this exhausts the options for views on which we have the sort of free will needed for basic desert moral responsibility, hard incompatibilists conclude that moral responsibility skepticism is the only remaining position.[67]

To summarize, incompatibilists believe that free will and moral responsibility are incompatible with determinism. Libertarians think that humans are free at least sometimes, so determinism must be false. PAP libertarians believe that alternative possibilities are necessary for free will and moral responsibility, but sourcehood libertarians aver that free will and moral responsibility require only that the agent be the ultimate source of the action. Hard determinists think that determinism is true, so humans are never free; and hard incompatibilists argue that free will and moral responsibility are impossible because they are incompatible with both determinism and indeterminism.

67. Caruso, "Skepticism About Moral Responsibility." Caruso cites the following sources in this block quote: Pereboom, *Living Without Free Will*; Pereboom, *Free Will, Agency, and Meaning in Life*; Pereboom, "Responsibility, Regress, and Protest," 21–140; Waller, *Freedom Without Responsibility*; Waller, *Against Moral Responsibility*; Levy, "Bad Luck Once Again," 749–54; Levy, *Hard Luck*; Harris, *Free Will*.

5. Compatibilism

Compatibilists believe that human freedom and moral responsibility are compatible with determinism. Because it is so rare for someone to affirm compatibilism yet deny that humans are free at least sometimes, compatibilism may just as well be the thesis that human freedom and moral responsibility are compatible with determinism *and humans are free*. Semicompatibilists, however, argue that moral responsibility is compatible with determinism regardless of whether freedom is compatible with determinism. Thus, whereas most positions in the debate hold that freedom and moral responsibility are inseparable (i.e., one cannot be morally responsible if one is not free), semicompatibilists believe that moral responsibility does not depend on freedom. In this section, I discuss one of the most influential arguments for compatibilism. Then I sketch classical compatibilism, contemporary species of compatibilism, and semicompatibilism.

5a. Arbitrariness Objection

The arbitrariness objection is really a closely related family of arguments for compatibilism (or freewill skepticism) concerning the element of luck, randomness, or indeterminacy on libertarian models of free will.[68] These arguments show that indeterminism makes human choices irrational, incompatible with free will and moral responsibility, or both. A basic outline of the objection is as follows: If an agent is undetermined with respect to an action, then the agent performs that action seemingly arbitrarily (i.e., by luck or chance). Although an agent might have a reason for choosing A and a reason for choosing not-A (for example, choosing to exercise because it is healthy and choosing not to exercise because it is difficult), according to libertarianism, there can be no *sufficient* reason why the agent might choose A rather than not-A. In other words, libertarianism cannot explain why the agent might choose A rather than not-A; the agent might as well have chosen not-A instead of A. Therefore, the choice seems arbitrary. Furthermore, if an agent acts arbitrarily, the act is not a free or morally responsible act. If indeterminism is true, then an agent does not have the kind of control necessary for free and morally responsible action. "According to these

68. The arbitrariness objection is sometimes called the "Mind Argument" because of its frequent appearances in the journal *Mind*; e.g., Nowell-Smith, "Freewill and Moral Responsibility," 45–61. See van Inwagen's discussion in *Essay on Free Will*, 126–52. See also Franklin, "Luck and *Mind* Arguments," 203–12. Justin J. Daeley argues that theistic compatibilists ought not to use the arbitrariness objection because it would imply that God himself acts arbitrarily in "Divine Freedom and Contingency," 563–82.

arguments [i.e., arbitrariness objections], undetermined action cannot be something over which agents exercise sufficient control either for the action to be free or the agent to be morally responsible for it."[69] Therefore, free will and moral responsibility *require* determinism.

5b. *Classical Compatibilism*

Compatibilists may be divided according to their understanding of the sufficient conditions for freedom and responsibility and their philosophy of action. Classical compatibilists maintain that an agent is free only if he is able to do what he wants unimpeded and without compulsion.[70] This view of freedom is also called (or is closely related to) "freedom of inclination" or "freedom of action."

Classical compatibilists may affirm or deny that alternative possibilities are necessary for freedom and moral responsibility, but none will affirm that alternatives are categorically possible. Rather, when classical compatibilists do affirm the necessity of alternative possibilities, they are working with a different sense of "possible" than libertarians are. They affirm a conditional possibility: *if things had been different*, the agent could have done otherwise. For example, an agent S could have done otherwise than A at *t* if S had wanted to do other than A at *t* (or, "if the laws of nature had been different right before *t*," or "if God had so willed," etc.). In this way, compatibilists agree that humans often have the ability to do otherwise—if they wanted to do otherwise.

Classical compatibilists often had a view of the soul centered on faculties and powers, most importantly, the intellect and the will. For these classical compatibilists, the will inevitably follows the final dictate of the intellect. Therefore, the agent always chooses what the agent understands to be the best choice—all things considered.

5c. *Contemporary Compatibilisms*

New forms of compatibilisms emerged in analytic philosophy in the twentieth century. Contemporary compatibilists fall into five main groups: identification models, dispositional models, reasons-responsive models, reactive-attitudes models, and epistemic-standpoint models. These models

69. Franklin, "Luck and *Mind* Arguments," 211.

70. Notable classical compatibilists include Thomas Hobbes, David Hume, John Locke, and Jonathan Edwards. See Edwards, *Freedom of the Will*.

grew especially out of discussions surrounding CA and Frankfurt-style counterexamples (FSCs) to PAP. First, I explain FSCs. Second, I offer a brief overview of each group of models.

5c.i. Frankfurt-Style Counterexamples

Harry G. Frankfurt argues that moral responsibility does not require that the agent have alternative possibilities.[71] In other words, Frankfurt argues that PAP is false. Frankfurt proposed several thought experiments involving two men, Jones and Black, that purported to undermine PAP. In each case, Jones is presented with a choice between two actions (say, A or B). Black resolves that he would intervene (by threat, force, or even hypnosis) in order to prevent Jones from choosing A if Jones were ever about to choose A. In this way, it would be impossible for Jones to choose A. But in each case, Jones chooses B because he wants to choose B, not because Black prevents him from choosing A. Thus, Jones' inability to choose A does not explain why he chooses B. Jones chooses B because that is the action he wants to choose—even though he could not have chosen otherwise. These thought experiments provide counterexamples to PAP, as Frankfurt explains:

> The fact that he could not have done otherwise clearly provides no basis for supposing that he *might* have done otherwise if he had been able to do so. When a fact is in this way irrelevant to the problem of accounting for a person's action it seems quite gratuitous to assign it any weight in the assessment of his moral responsibility.[72]

Jones is responsible for his choice because that choice is the one he chose—not because he could have chosen otherwise. Counterexamples to PAP have since been dubbed "Frankfurt-style counterexamples" (FSCs).

5c.ii. Identification Models

Identification models (a.k.a. "mesh theories" or "hierarchical models") "trace the capacity for freedom of the will to the differentiation in the agent's psychology such that the agent can fully identify with some of his desires, or more broadly, motivating attitudes, to make them deeply his own and internal."[73]

71. Frankfurt, "Alternative Possibilities and Moral Responsibility," 1–10.
72. Frankfurt, "Alternative Possibilities and Moral Responsibility," 8.
73. Jaworska, "Identificationist Views," 15.

The most famous identification model comes from Frankfurt who argues that a person is a being with a certain volitional structure.[74] This structure begins with first-order desires "which are simply desires to do or not to do one thing or another."[75] For example, a person may desire to eat French fries. Next are second-order desires, which are desires concerning first-order desires: what one wants to desire. For example, a person may want to desire to eat broccoli. Human persons may have a more but not less complex hierarchy of desires (e.g., third-order or fourth-order desires). According to Frankfurt, a person's will is the effective first-order desire, i.e., "one that moves (or will or would move) a person all the way to action."[76] A second-order volition is a second-order desire that a first order desire be one's will. For example, a person may want to will to eat broccoli. Frankfurt continues, "Now it is having second-order volitions, and not having second-order desires generally, that I regard as essential to being a person."[77] Only persons, as such, are able to have freedom of the will. Frankfurt argues that "it is in securing the conformity of his will to his second-order volitions, then, that a person exercises freedom of the will."[78] Thus, a person has freedom of the will when the person "is free to will what he wants to will, or to have the will he wants."[79]

5c.iii. Dispositional Models

Dispositional compatibilism is a broad group of views—some of which overlap with identification and reasons-responsive models.[80] "The dispositional compatibilist says that our commonsense beliefs about free will can be understood in a way that is consistent with our other beliefs about the natural world and our place in it, and which is neutral with respect to the truth or falsity of determinism."[81] Dispositional compatibilists view alternative possibilities as necessary to free will and moral responsibility.[82] Agents

74. See Frankfurt, *Importance of What We Care About.*

75. Frankfurt, "Freedom of the Will and the Concept of a Person," 12.

76. Frankfurt, "Freedom of the Will and the Concept of a Person," 14.

77. Frankfurt, "Freedom of the Will and the Concept of a Person," 16.

78. Frankfurt, "Freedom of the Will and the Concept of a Person," 20–21.

79. Frankfurt, "Freedom of the Will and the Concept of a Person," 20.

80. For example, see Vihvelin, "Free Will Demystified," 427–50; Haji, "Obligation, Reason, and Frankfurt Examples," 288–308.

81. Vihvelin, "Dispositional Compatibilism," 55–56.

82. Michael Patrick Preciado calls these compatibilist models "leeway theories," in *Reformed View of* Freedom, 153–57.

have freedom of the will when they have the right dispositions or "bundles of abilities in virtue of which [they] think and deliberate and make decisions and choices and form intentions about what to do."[83] Agents have freedom of action when they have the bundles of abilities that allow them to act upon their will. Thus, agents have the ability to do otherwise when they have the dispositions to will and act freely. For example, suppose I chose to eat pistachio ice cream last night rather than strawberry ice cream. I was free to choose otherwise because I had the abilities required to choose otherwise—I had the ability to understand the options, deliberate between them, decide on one of them, and act on that decision. Determinism does not undermine an agent's having dispositions to think and act freely; therefore, free will is compatible with determinism.

5c.iv. Reasons-Responsive Models

Reasons-responsive models argue that freedom consists in responding in the appropriate way to internal reasons. E.g., I did *this* because I had reason to do *this*, but I would not have done *this* if I had reason not to do *this*.[84] Reasons-responsive models argue that being the source of one's actions is necessary for freedom and moral responsibility (i.e., the sourcehood condition). When an agent's actions are traceable to the agent's internal reasons for acting, the agent can be considered the proper source of the action. Michael McKenna explains:

> Reasons-responsive theorists develop a familiar compatibilist strategy of distinguishing between kinds of causes of actions, some of which are freedom-defeating and others that are not. In a wide range of conditions in which the causes of an agent's actions are freedom-defeating (compulsion, psychosis, phobia, coercion, delusion, and so on) the agent is not reasons-responsive.[85]

Determinism is not a freedom-defeater. An agent may act according to the agent's reasons even if the agent was causally determined to act so. Therefore, freedom and moral responsibility are compatible with determinism.

83. Vihvelin, "Dispositional Compatibilism," 58.

84. For examples of reasons-responsive models, see Wolf, *Freedom Within Reason*; Fischer and Ravizza, *Responsibility and Control*.

85. McKenna, "Reasons-Responsive Theories of Freedom," 29–30.

5c.v. Reactive-Attitudes Models

Reactive-attitudes models distinguish between reactive and objective attitudes to show that we have practical reasons for having moral responsibility even if determinism is true.[86] A reactive attitude (e.g., resentment or indignation) is one that holds someone morally responsible (e.g., for some wrongdoing). An objective attitude is a detached, non-emotive attitude that takes into consideration the causes of an action. Moral responsibility *just is* the moral reactive attitude we have when we wrong someone or someone wrongs us. For determinism to be proven true or false would have no bearing on whether we should continue reacting with moral attitudes. The question of determinism is a theoretical issue, but the question of responsibility is a practical one. "These attitudes, relations, and expectations are so much an expression of natural, basic features of our social lives—of their emotional textures—that it is practically inconceivable to imagine how they *could be* given up."[87]

5c.vi. Epistemic-Standpoint Models

Epistemic-standpoint models hold that freedom depends on an agent's not knowing what she might choose before she chooses. From the epistemic standpoint of an agent S, S's choice is open to S; S could choose A or not-A.[88] In other words, A is epistemically possible for S at *t* if S does not know that S will not perform A. For example, it is epistemically possible for me right now that I will take a walk outside today because I do not know that I will not take a walk outside today. Even if it turns out that the laws of nature or God's will determined that I not take a walk outside today, it is still epistemically possible for me to take a walk outside today because I do not know otherwise. Epistemic freedom is enough for moral responsibility. Tomis Kapitan argues, "Doxastic freedom of the empirical self is all the freedom X needs to be minimally responsible for P, while an additional efficacy of the will over responsibility-making attitudes is needed for higher degrees."[89] Whereas determinism undermines metaphysical freedom, it does not

86. For an example of a reactive-attitudes model, see Strawson, "Freedom and Resentment," 1–25.

87. McKenna and Coates, "Compatibilism."

88. For examples of an epistemic-standpoint model, see Kapitan, "Doxastic Freedom"; Velleman, "Epistemic Freedom."

89. Kapitan, "Doxastic Freedom," 37.

undermine epistemic freedom. Therefore, the kind of freedom necessary for moral responsibility is compatible with determinism.

5d. Semicompatibilism

Semicompatibilism is the view that moral responsibility is compatible with determinism (and fatalism) regardless of whether freedom is compatible with determinism (or fatalism). "A crucial element of the doctrine of semicompatibilism is that the compatibility of causal determinism and moral responsibility does not hinge on the compatibility of causal determinism and freedom to do otherwise."[90] Semicompatibilists tend to think that freedom does require that human beings be able to do otherwise in some sense. Free will and PAP are inseparable. Yet, semicompatibilists also tend to think that CA is sound. If determinism is true, then human beings really cannot do otherwise. But semicompatibilists also tend to think that FSCs demonstrate that moral responsibility is not dependent on the ability to do otherwise. Thus, semicompatibilists separate freedom from moral responsibility.

As has been shown above, some libertarians reject the necessity of PAP for freedom and moral responsibility. Rather, they appeal to sourcehood—the notion that freedom and moral responsibility require that one be the ultimate source of one's actions. "But," as John Martin Fischer notes, "there is a perfectly reasonable notion of "sourcehood," according to which the source's being internal to the agent is compatible with causal determination."[91] If an agent is the source of the agent's action, then the agent is morally responsible for that action, even if the agent was causally determined to that action and not free with respect to that action. For example, "The President of the United States might wonder who is the source of a leak of sensitive information to the press. Ascertaining who the source is does not require a presupposition of causal determinism!"[92] The reasons-responsive model of Fischer and Mark Ravizza, for example, is actually a type of semicompatibilism because it affirms that the ability to do otherwise is necessary for freedom but unnecessary for moral responsibility.

To summarize, compatibilists believe that free will and moral responsibility are compatible with determinism. Semicompatibilists believe that moral responsibility—but not free will—is compatible with determinism. Classical compatibilists are content to say that an agent is free when the agent is able to do what the agent wants to do. Classical compatibilists may

90. Fischer, "Semicompatibilism," 5.

91. Fischer, "Semicompatibilism," 9.

92. Fischer, "Semicompatibilism," 9.

appeal to a conditional analysis of alternative possibilities—"I could have done otherwise, *if I wanted to do otherwise*." Contemporary compatibilisms arose in response to more powerful and complex arguments for incompatibilism. Identification models argue that freedom is a matter of personally identifying with the right acts of will. Dispositional models posit freedom in the agent's dispositional powers to do otherwise. Reasons-responsive models contend that freedom is acting or choosing according to one's reasons for acting or choosing. Reactive-attitudes models argue that moral responsibility has to do with societal reactions toward certain behavior, and thus, it does not hinge on the truth or falsity of determinism. Epistemic-standpoint models maintain that humans are free when their choices seem genuinely open to them.

6. The Christological Case for Compatibilism

Thus far, I have presented the main positions in the contemporary free will debate. In the coming chapters, I argue that classical Christology entails compatibilism. *But which compatibilism?* Rather than argue for a particular model of compatibilism, I argue that every alternative to compatibilism is inconsistent with classical Christology; thus, *some* form of compatibilism must be true. To argue for a particular model of compatibilism may require that I present a fuller philosophy of action, moral psychology, or metaphysic than is warranted by classical Christology. Instead, I shall merely eliminate two types of models: the reactive-attitudes and the epistemic-standpoint models.

Reactive-attitudes models are skeptical about retributive and desert-based moral responsibility: human agents do not have the kind of power or control over their actions that could make them objectively morally responsible for their actions. This moral responsibility skepticism is contrary to the moral realism of Christianity. Christians believe that people are held morally responsible and accountable to God. There is a moral character to reality, and it does not depend on social construction. Jesus Christ himself was certainly a moral realist; and Scripture and tradition teach that he dealt with a real moral problem (humanity's sin). Classical Christology, then, is best interpreted within the framework of moral realism.

Epistemic-standpoint models are problematic for two reasons. First, they add an unnecessary component to freedom and moral responsibility, namely, ignorance. Moral responsibility ought to be grounded in something the agent has or does—not in something the agent lacks. Furthermore, it seems counterintuitive to affirm that the less an agent knows the *more* responsible the agent is. Second, epistemic-standpoint compatibilism is *prima facie* incompatible with classical Christology because it implies that Jesus was not free or morally responsible for any action for which he knew the outcome beforehand. But Jesus *did* know the outcome beforehand in many instances, and he was morally responsible for his actions in those instances.

Classical Christology may be consistent with various iterations of classical, identification, reasons-responsive, or dispositional compatibilisms. I am especially sympathetic, however, to the argument set out by Michael Patrick Preciado that the Reformed view of freedom is compatible with a reasons-responsive model. I show in chapter 3 that the Reformed tradition argued for compatibilism from classical Christology. As Preciado's argument is a further development of compatibilistic freedom in continuity with the Reformed tradition, so this book is a further development of a particular kind of argument for compatibilism in continuity with the Reformed tradition. I consider the reasons-responsive model to be a form of compatibilism (rather than semicompatibilism) because I reject that the categorical ability to do otherwise is necessary for free will. If the reader stipulates that free will *just is* the categorical ability to do otherwise, then the matter is merely semantic, in which case, the reader may understand my thesis to be "classical Christology entails semicompatibilism."

2

Classical Christology

1. Introduction

In this chapter, I discuss the key features of classical Christology. Classical Christology, because it is biblical, traditional, and classical, does not change in substance; rather, it is refined and clarified over time and often through controversy.[1] For this project, I affirm a minimalist account of classical Christology—only that which is needed to defend the central argument.[2] In what follows, first, I discuss the term "classical Christology" as distinct from other terms, especially "conciliary Christology." Second, I describe the key features of classical Christology: dyothelitism, volitional non-contrariety, and impeccability. Finally, I consider the matter of Christ's freedom.

2. Which Christology?

This book concerns *classical* Christology. The term "classical Christology" overlaps significantly with terms such as "biblical Christology," "traditional Christology," "Chalcedonian Christology," "orthodox Christology," "confessional Christology," and "conciliar Christology." These Christologies share

1. Begin with Wellum, *God the Son Incarnate*, for an in-depth overview of the biblical, theological, and historical development of the doctrine of Christ. Then see Duby, *Jesus and the God of Classical Theism*. For a short introduction to Christology from the perspective of philosophy of religion, see Pawl, *Incarnation*. See also Crisp, *Divinity and Humanity*, for philosophico-theological arguments for a classical view of Christ's divine and human natures.

2. That is, I do not take into consideration other issues in Christology such as theories of atonement or Christ's relation to the church and the sacraments (or ordinances). Of course, I care deeply about issues beyond a minimalist account, but those issues detract from the thesis and potentially minimize my audience.

the same basic features. These terms, however, are not perfect synonyms. In this section, I focus on the difference between *conciliar* and *classical* Christology.

Timothy Pawl, a Roman Catholic philosophical theologian, explains his use of the term "conciliar Christology":

> Conciliar Christology embraces all of the teachings about Christ found in the accepted texts of the first seven ecumenical councils. Such texts range from the definitions of faith, anathemas, creeds, and canons to letters accepted by the conciliar participants as conveying dogmatic exposition. Thus, Leo's Tome to Flavian was accepted at Chalcedon as part of the conciliar pronouncement. As such, anything included in that Tome concerning Christology is part of Conciliar Christology.[3]

Pawl notes that "Catholics believe the councils never to have erred in matters of faith and morals. . . . Orthodox Christians, too, see the seven ecumenical councils as authoritative and binding."[4] Protestants churches, however, have varied deference to the ecumenical councils. Protestants almost universally affirm the creeds of the first four councils: Nicaea in 325, Constantinople I in 381, Ephesus in 431, and Chalcedon in 451. For many contemporary Protestants, the Chalcedonian Creed (as a clarification of Scripture) is the final word on christological orthodoxy.[5] Historically, the majority of Protestant churches have affirmed the teachings of the final three ecumenical councils—Constantinople II in 553, Constantinople III in 680, and Nicaea II in 787—regarding the person of Christ but not regarding the use of icons. Protestants are less likely to affirm the ancillary documents associated with the councils to be as authoritative as the creedal definitions themselves. Despite these differences with regard to the authority of the councils and tradition, Gregg Allison is right when he writes, "When it comes to the person of Jesus Christ, the Roman Catholic Church, the Orthodox Church, and Protestant churches share a common belief. Although each might have slightly different emphases, a remarkable agreement exists about Jesus Christ."[6]

3. Pawl, *In Defense of Extended Conciliar Christology*, 16.

4. Pawl, *In Defense of Extended Conciliar Christology*, 13–14. For the history and theology leading up to and including the ecumenical creeds, see Kelly, *Early Christian Doctrines*; Davis, *First Seven Ecumenical Creeds (325–787)*; Grillmeier, *Christ in Christian Tradition*. For the creeds themselves, see Tanner, *Decrees of the Ecumenical Councils*.

5. Wellum laments, "In Protestant and Evangelical theology, the conclusions of the post-Chalcedonian Councils are either little known or ignored. This is especially true of the Third Council of Constantinople (681)." Wellum, *God the Son Incarnate*, 338.

6. Allison, *Historical Theology*, 365.

As a Protestant, I am not obligated to embrace all of the documents associated with the ecumenical councils, but I do affirm the councils' teachings on the person of Christ as expressed in the creeds. I shall present the key features of those creeds as they relate to my project below. But, in order to avoid confusion with Pawl's use of "conciliar Christology," I shall use the term "classical Christology."

In some ways, classical Christology has fewer boundaries than conciliar Christology (i.e., because it is committed to the teachings of fewer documents), but there is at least one way that classical Christology—as I use the term—is an addition over conciliar Christology. Whereas Christ's impeccability is nowhere explicitly and uncontestably affirmed in the ecumenical councils, I believe it is an essential feature of classical Christology.[7] Although impeccability may not be strictly conciliar, it is classical.

3. Key Features of Classical Christology

In this section, I discuss the key features of classical Christology as they pertain to this project: dyothelitism, volitional non-contrariety, and impeccability. These features are essential to the classical model of the incarnation, but they do not exhaust the model. Before moving to these key features, I shall lay the foundation.

Classical Christology is a two-natures model of the incarnation. Jesus Christ is one person with two natures. That Jesus is one person with both a divine nature and a human nature is the core of classical Christology. In full, the Chalcedonian Creed reads:

> In agreement, therefore, with the holy fathers, we all unanimously teach that we should confess that our Lord Jesus Christ is one and the same Son, the same perfect in Godhead and the same perfect in manhood, truly God and truly man, the same of a rational soul and body, consubstantial with the Father in Godhead, and the same consubstantial with us in manhood, like us in all things except sin; begotten from the Father before the ages as regards His Godhead, and in the last days, the same, because of us and because of our salvation begotten from the Virgin Mary, the *Theotokos*, as regards His manhood; one and the same Christ, Son, Lord, only-begotten, made known in two natures without confusion, without change, without division, without

7. Pawl, for example, discusses Christ's impeccability not as essential to conciliar Christology but as an extension of conciliar Christology. See Pawl, *In Defense of Extended Conciliar Christology*, 132–64.

> separation, the difference of the natures being by no means removed because of the union, but the property of each nature being preserved and coalescing in one *prosopon* and one *hupostasis*—not parted or divided into two *prosopa*, but one and the same Son, only-begotten, divine Word, the Lord Jesus Christ, as the prophets of old and Jesus Christ Himself have taught us about Him and the creed of our fathers has handed down.[8]

Pawl summarizes the two-natures model: "There was (and is) one person, Jesus Christ, the Second Person of the Holy Trinity, who, after the incarnation, has two complete and distinct natures."[9]

The nature-person distinction is key to understanding classical Christology.[10] "Person" refers to the subject—the *who*. "Nature" refers to that which makes a thing the thing that it is—the *what*. The Trinity is a unity of three persons—three subjects of a rational nature (i.e., the one divine nature). The Son is the subject of two rational natures (i.e., the one divine nature and a particular human nature). Herman Bavinck explains:

> But "nature" is the substratum, the presupposition, that by which a thing is what it is, the "principle by which"; and "person" is the subject not of a given nature in general but of a rational nature, the individual substance of a rational nature, the "principle which." "Person" is what exists in and for itself, the owner, possessor, and master of the nature, a completion of existence, sustaining and determining the existence of a nature, the subject that lives, thinks, wills, and acts through nature with all its abundant content, by which nature becomes self-existent and is not an accident of another entity.[11]

To be divine is to be absolute, simple, immutable, omnipotent, etc. To be human is to be created, to have a human body, to have a human soul, etc. The Son is the one person—the one subject, the *who*—of these two natures. Jesus is Christ is fully God and fully man.

Because Jesus is God and consubstantial with the Father, all of the divine perfections, operations, and prerogatives are properly predicated of

8. From Kelly, *Early Christian Doctrines*, 339–40.

9. Pawl, *In Defense of Extended Conciliar Christology*, 16. To say that Jesus Christ is two persons, however, is to affirm Nestorianism. Nestorianism is the ancient heresy that the man, Jesus, and the divine Logos are distinct persons who are united in a moral union. See Grillmeier, *Christ in Christian Tradition*, 443–87; cf. Kelly, *Early Christian Doctrines*, 310–17.

10. For more on the nature-person distinction, see Wellum, *God the Son Incarnate*, 260–65.

11. Bavinck, *Reformed Dogmatics*, 3:306.

him. The perfections of God are his communicable and incommunicable attributes. Jesus is omnipotent, omniscient, omnipresent, eternal, *a se*, and everything else that the Father and Spirit are by nature. The classical trinitarian principle *opera trinitatis ad extra indivisa sunt* affirms that all the external works of God are works of the whole Trinity. Because Father, Son, and Spirit share the same divine nature—the same principle of operation—each person is involved in every act of God. Jesus is as much involved in God's providence as he is in God's salvation of sinners. Furthermore, because he is God, Jesus shares the divine prerogatives with the Father and Spirit—he receives prayer, worship, and praise, and he judges, condemns, justifies, and forgives.

Jesus Christ has a complete human nature, including a body and soul.[12] Pawl writes, "The other nature is a human nature. This nature either (a) is composed of a body ensouled by a rational soul, or (b) entails that the bearer, at least during life, have a body ensouled by a rational soul. According to this nature, Christ is like us in all ways—including having a created will—except sin."[13]

3a. Dyothelitism

Dyothelitism is the teaching that Christ has two wills. Christ has two wills because he has two complete and distinct natures. Chalcedon affirms "our Lord Jesus Christ is one and the same Son, the same perfect in Godhead and the same perfect in manhood, truly God and truly man, the same of a rational soul and body."[14] Chalcedon denies a union of Logos and mere

12. I take Christ's human nature to be a concrete particular. For the distinction between abstract and concrete natures as it pertains to Christ, see A. Plantinga, "On Heresy, Mind, and Truth," 182–93; Pawl, *In Defense of Extended Conciliar Christology*, 22–28; Crisp, *Divinity and Humanity*, 34–71. Most concretist accounts are also relational accounts. Relational accounts of the incarnation maintain that the Logos entered into some type of relation with a concrete human nature. That relation is often understood as some form of composition (mereological or non-mereological). Compositional accounts of the incarnation maintain that the Son of God is composed of parts. Two-part compositional accounts contend that the incarnate Son is composed of the Logos and a human body. This view is usually interpreted as monothelitic. Three-part compositional accounts contend that the incarnate Son is composed of the Logos, a human body, and a human soul. This view is usually interpreted as dyothelitic. For more on three-part concretist accounts of the incarnation, see Crisp, *Divinity and Humanity*; Leftow, "Humanity of God," 20–44; See also Flint, "Should Concretists Part with Mereological Models of the Incarnation?," 67–87.

13. Pawl, *In Defense of Extended Conciliar Christology*, 17.

14. Kelly, *Early Christian Doctrines*, 339. For more on Chalcedonian Christology, see Grillmeier, *Christ in Christian Tradition*, 543–58.

flesh, i.e., a Word–flesh paradigm. The Logos does not replace the human will in Christ. Rather, the Logos took to himself a complete human nature—body *and* rational soul—i.e., a Word–human paradigm. The Logos assumes a complete human nature, including a human will. The Third Council of Constantinople makes this notion explicit:

> And we proclaim equally two natural volitions or wills in him and two natural principles of action which undergo no division, no change, no partition, no confusion, in accordance with the teaching of the holy fathers. And the two natural wills not in opposition, as the impious heretics said, far from it, but his human will following, and not resisting or struggling, rather in fact subject to his divine and all powerful will. For the will of the flesh had to be moved, and yet to be subjected to the divine will, according to the most wise Athanasius.[15]

Therefore, dyothelitism is conciliar orthodoxy. Christ has both a human and a divine will. Monothelitism (one will in Christ) was rejected.[16]

Constantinople III is indebted to the theology of Maximus the Confessor, the champion of dyothelitism.[17] Maximus makes a crucial distinction between a natural (faculty of) will and an object of the will, as Thomas Watts explains:

> Maximus distinguishes between two different Greek words for "will," θέλημα and θελητὸν. The term θέλημα refers to the "creative and essential will of God." The term θελητὸν refers to the "object of that will." . . . θέλημα/θέλησι and θελητὸν/θεληθέν relate to each other as the eye relates to what is being observed by it. The eye itself is distinct from what is seen; similarly, the faculty of the will is distinct from what is willed. Therefore when

15. Tanner, *Decrees of the Ecumenical Councils*, 128.

16. Calvin writes:

> Now this refutes the error of Apollinaris, as well as that of the so-called Monothelites. Apollinaris claimed that Christ had an eternal spirit instead of a soul, so that he was only half a man. As if he could atone for our sins in any other way than by obeying the Father! But where is inclination or will to obey except in the soul? We know that it was for this reason that his soul was troubled: to drive away fear and bring peace and repose to our souls. Against the Monothelites, we see that he did not will as man what he willed according to his divine nature. I pass over the fact that, with a contrary emotion, he overcame the fear of which we have spoken. (Calvin, *Institutes* 2.16.12)

17. See Maximus, *Disputation with Pyrrhus*. For more on Maximus and dyothelitism, see Bathrellos, *Byzantine Christ*; Watts, "Two Wills in Christ?," 455–87; Davidson, "'Not My Will but Yours Be Done,'" 178–204.

> a person's human will is one with God's divine will, it is not the faculty of will itself that is referred to, but the object of that will.[18]

Although Christ has *two distinct, natural wills* (i.e., one divine and one human), these wills could (or must) terminate on the *same object*. For example, Christ willed the salvation of humanity according to both his human and divine wills.

Wellum cites three reasons that the church has defended dyothelitism. First, dyothelitism maintains Christ's full humanity against Word–flesh Christologies such as monophysitism, Apollinarianism, and monothelitism which deny that Christ has a uniquely created human will. Second, "the church insisted that Jesus cannot be our Redeemer without a human will, since it is by the Son's obedience as a man, in his life and death, that he accomplishes our salvation and serves as 'the model for all Christians.'"[19] Hence, dyothelitism is important for soteriology and sanctification.[20] Third, trinitarian theology requires dyothelitism. Wellum explains:

> "Will" is best located in the nature of God, not the person, thus in pro-Nicene Trinitarianism, what is common to all three divine persons is their operation, power, nature, and deity, including a shared will. Yet the Father shares the one will in accordance with his mode of subsistence as the Father, and the same is true of the Son and Spirit. But since monothelitism places the "will" in the person, it seems to entail two serious implications. If there is only one will in God, which orthodoxy has affirmed, then this would require that there is only one person, hence modalism. The only alternative is to insist that there are three wills in God, but this runs the risk of surrendering the divine unity.[21]

For these reasons, dyothelitism is a key feature of classical Christology.[22]

18. Watts, "Two Wills in Christ?," 460–61. See also Bathrellos, *Byzantine Christ*, 99–174.

19. Wellum, *God the Son Incarnate*, 339–40. Wellum quotes Watts, "Two Wills In Christ?," 467.

20. For more on dyothelitism and its relation to soteriology, see Stamps, "Atonement in Gethsemane," 118–38.

21. Wellum, *God the Son Incarnate*, 340.

22. For more on Christ's human nature and dyothelitism, see Crisp, *Divinity and Humanity*, 34–71.

3b. Volitional Non-Contrariety

Volitional non-contrariety (VNC) is the teaching that Christ's human will was never contrary but always in conformity to the divine will according to its object. Christ's two wills acted in harmony. For example, Christ willed humanity's salvation through both his human and divine wills. VNC is codified in Constantinople III, as quoted above. Recall this line: "And the two natural wills not in opposition, . . . but his human will following, and not resisting or struggling, rather in fact subject to his divine and all powerful will. For the will of the flesh had to be moved, and yet to be subjected to the divine will . . . ."[23] VNC secures the unity of the person of Christ while also affirming the duality of Christ's natures, wills, and operations.

VNC is an especially crucial, yet complex, feature of classical Christology. It connects the doctrines of Christ's two natures and dyothelitism with his impeccability. VNC is especially complex because it brings together matters of human psychology, theology, and metaphysics.

3c. Impeccability

To say that Christ is impeccable is to say that Christ could not sin (*Christus non potest peccare*).[24] Christ's impeccability belongs to classical Christology as a key element because it is implied by Scripture, is entailed by other elements of classical Christology, and has a distinguished pedigree of adherents, including Augustine, Aquinas, and Calvin.[25] Although the Bible does not explicitly claim that Christ could not sin, it is implied. Bavinck explains:

> Scripture, however, prompts us to recognize in Christ, not just an empirical sinlessness, but a necessary sinlessness as well. He is the Son of God, the Logos, who was in the beginning with God and himself God. He is one with the Father and always carries out his Father's will and work. For those who confess this of Christ, the possibility of him sinning and falling is unthinkable. For that reason Christian theology maintained, against Arians,

23. Tanner, *Decrees of the Ecumenical Councils*, 128.

24. Berkhof writes, "This means not merely that Christ could avoid sinning (*potuit non peccare*), and did actually avoid it, but also that it was impossible for Him to sin (*non potuit peccare*) because of the essential bond between the human and the divine natures." Berkhof, *Systematic Theology*, 318.

25. See McKinley, *Tempted for Us*; Pawl, *In Defense of Extended Conciliar Christology*, 132–35. Those who deny Christ's impeccability are outliers in Reformed Christology. See, for example, Hodge, *Systematic Theology*, 2.457; Erickson, *Christian Theology*, 736.

> Pelagians, and nominalists such as Duns Scotus, Biel, Durandus, Molina, and others that Christ could not sin. For in that case either God himself would have to be able to sin—which is blasphemy—or the union between the divine and the human nature is considered breakable and in fact denied.[26]

As Bavinck suggested, denying Christ's impeccability would put us in a dilemma between two untenable horns. If Christ can sin, then we must say one of two things. On the one hand, we might infer that God can sin because (1) Christ can sin, and (2) Christ is God. Few are willing, however, to doubt God's impeccability (and rightly so).[27] On the other hand, we might say that Christ is not truly or fully God, so Christ can sin without it entailing that God sinned. But in that case, we would have to affirm something like adoptionism, Arianism, or Nestorianism—each of which has been deemed a condemnable heresy. Therefore, we ought to agree that Christ is impeccable.[28]

4. Challenges to Classical Christology

I take classical Christology to be the starting point—the presupposition—for this project. Classical Christology's fidelity to Scripture and tradition—as well as its internal and external coherence—is its own defense. But there have always been challenges to the classical view, and it would be appropriate to note these before proceeding. In this section, therefore, I present a summary of contemporary challenges to classical Christology. For the reader who is interested in these debates, I provide extensive footnotes.

26. Bavinck, *Reformed Dogmatics*, 3:314. Pawl cites part of this passage from Bavinck in *In Defense of Extended Conciliar Christology*, 133.

27. In addition to Scriptural support (e.g., Jas 1:3; 1 John 1:5), the matter of God's impeccability "is independently settled on the basis of perfect-being theology; and is almost universally conceded by compatibilists and incompatibilists alike without much of a dispute." Bignon, *Excusing Sinners and Blaming God*, 105. There are those, however, who deny divine impeccability by arguing that there is at least some sense in which God can sin, even if he certainly will not sin (e.g., Pike, "Omnipotence and God's Ability to Sin," 208–16). A slightly more vexed issue is whether God is morally praiseworthy despite his inability to sin or do moral wrong. Scripture unambiguously portrays God as praiseworthy for who he is and what he has done (e.g., Ps 148; Rev 4), but some (e.g., Morris, *Anselmian Explorations*) view divine praiseworthiness as axiological rather than moral. Because God has no moral duties, he cannot be held morally responsible. Rather, God acts analogically *in accordance with* but not *from* moral duties. Whether God is morally praiseworthy or merely axiologically praiseworthy does not undermine Christ's moral responsibility. The man, Jesus Christ, was obligated to obey God's commands.

28. Affirming Christ's impeccability does not entail denying the validity of his temptations. For various models of impeccability and temptation, see McKinley, *Tempted for Us*. I address the issue of Jesus' temptations in chapters 4 and 10.

First, classical Christology has significant ties to classical theism, and classical theism is out of vogue in many Christian circles. Classical theism views God as the most perfect being—as that than which nothing greater can be conceived.[29] God is simple, absolute, *a se*, immutable, impassible, timelessly eternal, infinite, omnipotent, omniscient, omnipresent, omnibenevolent, most just, most wise, most good, etc.[30] God's simplicity, immutability, impassibility, and timelessness are especially criticized.[31] Classical theism is often associated with the Creator–creature distinction and the doctrine of analogy, which teaches that human predication about God is neither univocal nor equivocal but analogical.[32] The major critics of classical theism are process theists, open theists, and theistic mutualists.[33]

Second, classical Christology is connected closely with classical trinitarianism, and classical trinitarianism has competitors.[34] Classical trinitarianism views the Father, Son, and Spirit as three subsistences distinguished only by their relations of opposition: the Father begets; the Son is begotten; and the Spirit proceeds from the Father and the Son.[35] God is one center of consciousness, knowledge, will, and power, according to classical trinitarianism.[36] The two biggest competitors of classical trinitarianism are social trinitarianism—which views the Trinity as three centers of consciousness—and relative trinitarianism—which draws from the notion of relative identity and material constitution to solve the threeness–oneness problem.[37]

29. See Anselm, *Proslogion*.

30. For a contemporary overview of classical theism and God's attributes, see Rogers, *Perfect Being Theology*; Barrett, *None Greater*.

31. For a defense of divine simplicity, see the works of Dolezal: *All That Is in God* and *God Without Parts*. See also Duby, *Divine Simplicity*. For divine timelessness, see Helm, *Eternal God*. For a defense of divine immutability and impassibility, consider the works of Weinandy, *Does God Change?* and *Does God Suffer?*

32. For the relationship between God, Scripture, metaphysics, and language, see Duby, *God in Himself*; Horton, "Hellenistic or Hebrew?," 317–41; Caneday, "Veiled Glory," 149–99.

33. For process theism, see the works of process philosopher Alfred North Whitehead, then the works of theologians John B. Cobb Jr. and Charles Hartshorne. See also Cobb and Pinnock, *Searching for an Adequate God*. For open theism, see Pinnock et al., *Openness of God*; Pinnock, *Most Moved Mover*; Sanders, *God Who Risks*. For theistic mutualism, see Frame, *Doctrine of God*; Ware, *God's Greater Glory*.

34. Classical trinitarianism is sometimes called "Latin trinitarianism" or "Western trinitarianism."

35. See Augustine, *De Trinitate*. See also Sanders, *Triune God*.

36. See Leftow, "Latin Trinity," 76–106.

37. For social trinitarianism, see C. Plantinga, "Social Trinity and Tritheism," 21–47; Morris, *Our Idea of* God, 174–84; Horrell, "Toward a Biblical Model of the Social Trinity," 399–421; Moreland and Craig, "Trinity," 21–43. For relative trinitarianism, see

Both classical theism and classical trinitarianism allow for a degree of variance on the finer details.[38] And although I, myself, hold to both classical theism and classical trinitarianism, the central argument of this book does not require everything included in classical theism or classical trinitarianism. I deal only with those aspects of God and the Trinity as is necessary to uphold classical Christology and to prove my thesis. I am confident that most classical theists and many theistic mutualists will readily affirm the minimalist account of theism and trinitarianism undergirding this project.

Third, many theologians and philosophers reject dyothelitism in favor of monothelitism.[39] Monothelites are almost always kenoticists (and social trinitarians). Kenoticism is the view that, in the incarnation, God the Son emptied himself of (or abstained from using) certain (e.g., omnipotence, omniscience, and omnipresence) or all his divine attributes.[40] Likewise, most (but not all) Spirit Christologies are kenotic and monothelitic.[41] Dyothelitism has been championed, however, by some outside classical Christology, theism, and trinitarianism.[42] Dyothelitism is central to every constructive chapter of this book, so the christological case for compatibilism that *I* make requires it. But I believe a similar christological case for compatibilism could be made on a monothelitic model, but I think it would have to draw more from the divine decree and/or providence than my case does. In this way, it would not be a strictly christological case for compatibilism but a theological case for compatibilism with christological elements.

Cain, "Doctrine of the Trinity and the Logic of Relative Identity," 141–52; Rea, "Relative Identity and the Doctrine of the Trinity," 431–45; Brower and Rea, "Material Constitution and the Trinity," 57–76; Van Inwagen, "Three Persons in One Being," 126–42. See also McCall, *Which Trinity? Whose Monotheism?*

38. See Crisp's discussion of classical theism and trinitarianism in *Analyzing Doctrine*, 33–100. See also Stump, *God of the Bible and the God of the Philosophers.*

39. For example, see DeWeese, "One Person, Two Natures," 114–53.

40. For contemporary defenses of kenotic models of the incarnation, see Evans, *Exploring Kenotic Christology*; Forrest, "Incarnation," 127–40; Senor, "Drawing on Many Traditions," 88–114.

41. Spirit Christologies come in a wide variety. A contemporary adoptionistic model can be found in Dunn, *Jesus and Spirit*. An example of a kenotic model can be found in Hawthorne, *Presence & the Power*; cf. Ware, *Man Christ Jesus*. There are two kinds of dyothelitic Spirit Christologies in the literature: Sturchian and Owenite. For the former, see Sturch, *Word and the Christ*. For the latter, see Owen, *ΠΝΕΥΜΑΤΟΛΟΓΙΑ*; Claunch, "Son and the Spirit." The Owenite model is consistent with classical Christology. For a critique of the Owenite model by another classical Christologian, see Crisp, "John Owen on Spirit Christology," 5–25.

42. See Morris, *Logic of God Incarnate*; Swinburne, *Christian God*; Bayne, "Inclusion Model of the Incarnation," 125–41.

Fourth, the majority of Christians throughout history have affirmed Christ's impeccability and temptation, but there are nuances to the discussion.[43] Theologians continue to debate the nature of Christ's temptation and whether Christ is peccable in any sense.[44] I take impeccability to be the categorical inability to sin and an entailment of the hypostatic union and VNC. I address the matter of Christ's temptations in chapters 4 and 10.

4. The Freedom of Christ

This book is concerned with the freedom of Christ. I argue that compatibilism is true because Christ's actions were determined yet free and morally significant. I demonstrate in the following chapters that classical Christology entails compatibilism. But it is important to note that many christologians believe that Christ must have had libertarian freedom, at least sometimes, during his earthly ministry. These christologians may even deem Christ's libertarian freedom as essential to classical Christology. I, however, have not included compatibilistic freedom as essential to classical Christology because his freedom is precisely what is under consideration. I argue that the key features listed above preclude Christ's having libertarian freedom. If Christ's libertarian freedom were essential to classical Christology, then classical Christology would be an inconsistent set of beliefs. In chapter 6, I evaluate several attempts at reconciling a libertarian view of freedom with classical Christology. But here, I echo Pawl's thoughts when he writes:

> If compatibilism were true, then one would be able to reconcile the freedom of Christ's human will with the divine determination of that will very easily. We could let the divine moving of the human will be as strong as determinism, and yet, given compatibilism, that would not imply that Christ is not free. . . .
>
> If God were to determine that CHN [Christ's human nature] never sins despite being free and tempted (or, put in a different way, that the Son never acts sinfully by means of his human nature), then we have the human freedom of Christ, the temptation of Christ, and the sinlessness of the Incarnate Christ, all without any heavy metaphysical lifting. In a similar way, if

43. For a discussion of Christ's impeccability and temptation throughout church history, see McKinley, *Tempted for Us*. For a denial of Christ's temptation, see Best, *Christ Could Not Be Tempted*. For a denial of Christ's impeccability, see Hodge, *Systematic Theology*, 2.457; Erickson, *Christian Theology*, 736.

44. Many today will say that Christ, the person, is impeccable, but his (unassumed) human nature is peccable; cf. Pawl, *In Defense of Extended Conciliar Christology*, 132–64.

> compatibilism were true, then the worrisome logical determination that might result from Christ's foreknowing in his human intellect all the future free actions of any agents would dissipate. For Christ's foreknowing, even if it determined the later actions of agents, wouldn't for that reason preclude their being free, given the truth of compatibilism.[45]

Of course, Pawl denies compatibilism—at least for the sake of his argument for Christ's incompatibilist freedom. I argue that these issues in classical Christology are what provide good reason to affirm compatibilism.

In the next chapter, I show that christological arguments for compatibilism were common in the Reformed tradition and epitomized by John Calvin, Francis Turretin, and Jonathan Edwards. The central argument of this book is consistent with and a continuation of that tradition.

45. Pawl, *In Defense of Extended Conciliar Christology*, 125.

3

Christological Arguments for Compatibilism in the Reformed Tradition

1. Introduction

This chapter bridges the descriptive and the argumentative parts of the book.[1] I begin by considering the christological arguments for compatibilism from three prominent theologians in the Reformed tradition: John Calvin, Francis Turretin, and Jonathan Edwards. Then, I draft a formal argument for compatibilism from classical Christology. I see my christological argument as aligned with the Reformed tradition and also an advancement of that tradition. In the subsequent chapters, I defend each premise of the formal argument.

2. Historical Christological Arguments for Compatibilism

Calvin, Turretin, and Edwards are representatives of the Reformed tradition's legacy of christological arguments for compatibilism. Their prominence as Reformed theologians, their writing and influence on freewill debates, and their commitment to classical Christology make them appropriate representatives. Paul Helm writes, "Both Turretin and Edwards were classical theists, and adherents to Chalcedonian Christology. They were therefore committed to God's infinite knowledge, power and wisdom, and the impeccability of the human nature of Jesus Christ. And both were explicitly committed to the freedom of God and of the Son of God incarnate, Jesus."[2] Calvin was

1. A version of this chapter appears in Johnson, "Christological Arguments for Compatibilism in Reformed Theology," 125–39.

2. Helm, *Reforming Free Will*, 151.

likewise committed to Chalcedonian Christology, Christ's impeccability, and the freedom of God and his Son.[3]

Christological arguments for compatibilism appear in three forms: (1) appeals to Christ's wills and impeccability, (2) appeals to the necessity of the incarnation and the atonement, and (3) appeals to Christ's teaching. First, Christ was unable to sin and unable to will contrary to the divine will, i.e., he was unable to act otherwise than he did. Yet, he acted freely and willingly. Therefore, compatibilism is true. Second, because of the fact of sin and God's nature, decree, and promise, the incarnation and atonement were made necessary. Jesus' life and death were ordered by necessity. Yet, he acted freely and willingly. Therefore, compatibilism is true. Third, Jesus' teaching about himself and about human nature implied compatibilism. Each of these argument forms may be found in Calvin, Turretin, and Edwards to some degree or other (whether explicitly or implicitly), but no theologian devotes equal attention to each. In what follows, I present these historical christological arguments, attending to each theologian's own emphases.

2a. John Calvin (1509–64)

John Calvin has had a tremendous influence on both Christology and the freewill debate.[4] Calvin's writing on the nature of free will is less developed and organized than that of Turretin or Edwards, so an explanation of his view requires a few more steps. Calvin is considered to be a theological determinist and compatibilist, but his discussions of free will are predominantly related to humanity's post-fall condition. In what follows, I present a sketch of Calvin's multilayer view of free will and then show how he uses the words of Jesus to support his view.

2a.i. Providence

Calvin taught that everything happens according to God's meticulous will and providence—"nothing at all in the world is undertaken without his determination."[5] He writes:

3. See Book II of Calvin, *Institutes*. For a summary of the Reformer's contribution to Christology, see Letham, "Person of Christ," 313–46.

4. For introductions to Calvin's Christology, see Blocher, "Atonement in John Calvin's Theology," 279–303; George, *Theology of the Reformers*, 220–31. For Calvin's view of freedom, see Helm, *John Calvin's Ideas*, 157–83; Helm, *Calvin at the Center*, 227–72.

5. Calvin, *Institutes* 1.16.6.

> But anyone who has been taught by Christ's lips that all the hairs of his head are numbered [Matt 10:30] will look farther afield for a cause, and will consider that all events are governed by God's secret plan. And concerning inanimate objects we ought to hold that, although each one has by nature been endowed with its own property, yet it does not exercise its own power except in so far as it is directed by God's ever-present hand. These are, thus, nothing but instruments to which God continually imparts as much effectiveness as he wills, and according to his own purpose bends and turns them to either one action or another.[6]

This deterministic providence extends not only to inanimate objects, but to *all* events, including the thoughts and actions of human beings.[7] Yet, Calvin believed that his view of divine providence was consistent with God holding people morally accountable for their actions.[8] Furthermore, God does not govern merely the morally appraisable actions of free creatures, he also governs the morally insignificant actions:

> Even though we have touched upon the matter above, we have not yet explained what freedom man may possess in actions that are of themselves neither righteous nor corrupt, and look toward the physical rather than the spiritual life. . . .
>
> The force of God's providence extends to this point: not only that things occur as he foresees to be expedient, but that men's wills also incline to the same end. Indeed, if we ponder the direction of external things, we shall not doubt that to this extent they are left to human judgment. But if we lend our ears to the many testimonies which proclaim that the Lord also rules men's minds in external things, these will compel us to subordinate decision itself to the special impulse of God.[9]

It is important to note that Calvin was not a necessitarian. Necessitarianism is the idea that everything that happens—including God's decisions and all events in creation—happen with absolute necessity. Calvin preserved God's freedom despite the necessity of the world conforming to God's will. He writes, "But what God has determined must necessarily so take place, even though it is neither unconditionally, nor of its own peculiar

6. Calvin, *Institutes* 1.16.2.
7. Calvin, *Institutes* 1.16.
8. Calvin, *Institutes* 1.17.5.
9. Calvin, *Institutes* 2.4.6.

nature, necessary."[10] Helm summarizes, "The particular outcomes that He wills are thus hypothetically or conditionally necessary, and those He does not choose may be conditionally impossible."[11]

2a.ii. The Soul

Calvin's deterministic view of divine providence is just one layer of his understanding of human freedom. The next layer concerns the faculties of the soul considered simply (apart from the fall, sin, and depravity).[12] Calvin posits two faculties of the soul: understanding (represented by the mind) and will (represented by the heart):

> Thus let us, therefore, hold . . . that the human soul consists of two faculties, understanding and will. Let the office, moreover, of understanding be to distinguish between objects, as each seems worthy of approval or disapproval; while that of the will, to choose and follow what the understanding pronounces good, but to reject and flee what it disapproves. . . . [L]et it be enough for us that the understanding is, as it were, the leader and governor of the soul; and that the will is always mindful of the bidding of the understanding, and in its own desires awaits the judgment of the understanding.[13]

The will is dependent and subsequent to the understanding. The will must choose what the understanding judges to be good. This view of the soul's faculties is characteristic of Reformed compatibilism.[14] The will cannot do otherwise than the understanding dictates.

2a.iii. The Bondage of Sin

The final layer to Calvin's compatibilism concerns the bondage of sin. He writes, "Because of the bondage of sin by which the will is held bound, it cannot move toward good, much less apply itself thereto."[15] This bondage of sin does not take away the will but the "soundness of will."[16] Because of the

10. Calvin, *Institutes* 1.16.9.
11. Helm, *Reforming Free Will*, 85.
12. For Calvin's view of the soul, see Helm, *John Calvin's Ideas*, 129–56.
13. Calvin, *Institutes* 1.15.7; cf. 2.2.2.
14. Helm, *Reforming Free Will*, 195–232.
15. Calvin, *Institutes* 2.3.5.
16. Calvin, *Institutes* 2.3.5.

fall and original sin, people sin necessarily, though not by compulsion. He explains the difference:

> But it offends those who know not how to distinguish between necessity and compulsion. Suppose someone asks them: Is not God of necessity good? Is not the devil of necessity evil? What will they reply? God's goodness is so connected with his divinity that it is no more necessary for him to be God than for him to be good. But the devil by his fall was so cut off from participation in good that he can do nothing but evil. But suppose some blasphemer sneers that God deserves little praise for His own goodness, constrained as He is to preserve it. Will this not be a ready answer to him: not from violent impulsion, but from His boundless goodness comes God's inability to do evil? Therefore, if the fact that he must do good does not hinder God's free will in doing good; if the devil, who can do only evil, yet sins with his will—who shall say that man therefore sins less willingly because he is subject to the necessity of sinning?[17]

The bondage of sin inclines the will toward evil and away from God. The will may be inclined toward God by God's grace alone, through regeneration by the Spirit. "Surely there is ready and sufficient reason to believe that good takes its origin from God alone. And only in the elect does one find a will inclined to good. Yet we must seek the cause of election outside men. It follows, thence, that man has a right will not from himself, but that it flows from the same good pleasure by which we were chosen before creation of the world [Eph 1:4]."[18]

As I have shown, Calvin's view of free will is complicated by three layers: providence, the faculties of the soul, and the bondage of sin. These three, interestingly, align with three of the "threats" to human freedom, namely, theological determinism, psychological determinism, and bondage of the will.[19]

2a.iv. Christological Support for the Bondage of the Will

Calvin supports his compatibilism from the very words of Jesus. On the bondage of the will toward evil, Calvin writes, "If the whole man is depicted by these words of Christ, 'What is born of flesh, is flesh' [John 3:6] (as is easy

17. Calvin, *Institutes* 2.3.5.

18. Calvin, *Institutes* 2.3.8.

19. See chapter 2. Because he also espoused divine omniscience and exhaustive foreknowledge, the "threat" of theological fatalism also appears in Calvin.

to prove), man is very clearly shown to be a miserable creature."[20] In Calvin's view, "flesh," here, refers not particularly to the body but to whatever is opposed to the Spirit. The flesh is "so perverse that it is wholly disposed to bear a grudge against God [and] cannot agree with the justice of divine law, can, in short, beget nothing but the occasion of death."[21] A person who is born of flesh cannot do good, and he must be born again, just as Jesus declares in John 3.

Jesus taught that regeneration by the Spirit is necessary in order to have a right understanding of God (mind) and a will inclined toward God (heart); "man's mind can become spiritually wise only in so far as God illumines it."[22] Calvin continues, "Christ also confirmed this most clearly in his own words when he said: 'No one can come to me unless it be granted by my Father' [John 6:44 p.]. . . . [N]othing is accomplished by preaching him if the Spirit, as our inner teacher, does not show our minds the way. Only those men, therefore, who have heard and have been taught by the Father come to him."[23] Apart from regeneration, people cannot but will evil: "Do you see that people can will only evil until by a wonderful transformation their will is changed from evil to good?"[24] Calvin shows that Jesus himself understood that God determines who will come to him: "Now can Christ's saying ('Every one who has heard . . . from the Father comes to me' [John 6:45, cf. Vg.]) be understood in any other way than the grace of God is efficacious of itself."[25] Yet, God's efficacious grace is not compulsion:

> True, indeed, as to the kind of *drawing*, it is not violent, so as to compel men by external force; but still it is a powerful impulse of the Holy Spirit, which makes men willing who formerly were unwilling and reluctant. It is a false and profane assertion, therefore, that none are *drawn* but those who are willing to be *drawn*, as if man made himself obedient to God by his own efforts; for the willingness with which men follow God is what they already have from himself; who has formed their hearts to obey him.[26]

20. Calvin, *Institutes* 2.3.1.

21. Calvin, *Institutes* 2.3.1; cf. Calvin, *Commentaries on the Gospel of John*, 75–76.

22. Calvin, *Institutes* 2.2.20.

23. Calvin, *Institutes* 2.2.20.

24. Calvin, *Bondage and Liberation of the Will* 3.308.

25. Calvin, *Institutes* 2.3.10. And God's efficacious grace places a necessity on the receiver: "Again, as Christ formerly affirmed that men are not fitted for believing, until they have been drawn, so he now declares that the grace of Christ, by which they are drawn, is efficacious, so that they necessarily believe." Calvin, *Commentaries on the Gospel of John*, 183.

26. Calvin, *Commentaries on the Gospel of John*, 182.

Jesus taught that all blessing comes from God alone, and apart from God's efficacious government of our wills, we cannot do good.

> Christ has given a testimony of his benefits clear enough so that they cannot be spitefully suppressed. "I am," he says, "the vine, you the branches [John 15:5]; my Father is the cultivator [ch. 15:1]. Just as branches cannot bear fruit of themselves unless they abide in the vine, so can you not unless you abide in me [ch. 15:4]. For apart from me you can do nothing" [ch. 15:5]. If we no more bear fruit of ourselves than a branch buds out when it is plucked from the earth and deprived of moisture, we ought not to seek any further the potentiality of our nature for good. Nor is this conclusion doubtful: "Apart from me you can do nothing" [John 15:5]. He does not say that we are too weak to be sufficient unto ourselves, but in reducing us to nothing he excludes all estimation of even the slightest ability. If grafted in Christ, we bear fruit like a vine—which derives the energy for its growth from the moisture of the earth, from the dew of heaven, and from the quickening warmth of the sun—I see no share in good works remaining to us if we keep unimpaired what is God's. In vain this silly subtlety is alleged: there is already sap enclosed in the branch, and the power of bearing fruit; and it does not take everything from the earth or from its primal root, because it furnishes something of its own. Now Christ simply means that we are dry and worthless wood when we are separated from him, for apart from him we have no ability to do good, as elsewhere he also says: "Every tree which my Father has not planted will be uprooted" [Matt. 15:13, cf. Vg].[27]

Apart from Christ, our wills cannot be inclined toward good.

2a.v. Christological Support for Moral Responsibility

Even though Christ taught that people are born into flesh and are unable to incline their wills toward God apart from regeneration, people are still moral agents responsible for their actions. Calvin shows that Jesus himself taught moral responsibility.

First, even though anyone who does good, does so by the grace of God, people are rewarded for their good works:

> While the Lord enriches his servants daily and heaps new gifts of his grace upon them—because he holds pleasing and acceptable

27. Calvin, *Institutes* 2.3.9.

> the work that he has begun in them, he finds in them something he may follow up by greater graces. This is the meaning of the statement, "To him who has shall be given" [Matt. 25:29; Luke 19:26]. Likewise: "Well done, good servant; you have been faithful in a few matters, I will set you over much" [Matt. 25:21, 23; Luke 19:17; all Vg., conflated]. But here we ought to guard against two things: (1) not to say that lawful use of the first grace is rewarded by later graces, as if man by his own effort rendered God's grace effective; or (2) so to think of the reward as to cease to consider it of God's free grace.[28]

Calvin explains, "[God] rewards, as if they were our own virtues, those graces which he bestows upon us, because he makes them ours."[29] The good works that God does through people are worthy of praise.

Second, despite the fact that no one can come to the Father unless he be drawn by the Father, Calvin shows that Christ still saw exhortation as important: "Christ does not neglect the teacher's office, but with his own voice unremittingly summons those who need to be taught within by the Holy Spirit in order to make progress."[30] That Christ saw exhortation as valid and necessary implies moral responsibility. If people are not morally responsible for their actions, they would not need to know how to live in a right relationship with God and their neighbor.

Third, Calvin addresses the objection that if people do not have the ability to do good on their own, then the reproofs in Scripture are pointless. Calvin points out that Jesus prays for his people: "Hence also Christ asks the Father to keep us from evil [John 17:15, cf. Vg.]."[31] That Christ prays for his people is evidence that the reproofs in Scripture are not pointless. And the fact that reproofs are important is evidence for moral responsibility.

Calvin sees a three-tiered determinism: God's efficacious providence, the understanding's determination of the will, and the bondage of sin. Calvin makes a christological argument for compatibilism by appealing to Jesus own teachings on the necessity of God's grace.

28. Calvin, *Institutes* 2.3.11.

29. Calvin, *Institutes* 2.5.3.

30. Calvin, *Institutes* 2.5.5.

31. Calvin, *Institutes* 2.5.11.

2b. Francis Turretin (1623–87)

Francis Turretin, like Calvin, was a theological determinist.[32] He argues that the divine decree necessitates all events in history. He explains, "All things were decreed of God by an eternal and unchangeable counsel; hence they cannot but take place in the appointed time; otherwise the counsel of God would be changed, which the Scriptures declare to be impossible (Is. 46:10; Eph. 1:9)."[33] Moreover, all things are preserved, concurred, and governed by God's will in providence.[34] But, he argues, "Predetermination does not destroy, but conserves the liberty of the will. By it, God does not compel rational creatures or make them act by a physical or brute necessity. Rather he only effects this—that they act both consistently with themselves and in accordance with their own nature, i.e., from preference (*ek proaireseōs*)

32. There is a significant debate as to whether Turretin was, in fact, a theological determinist. I am convinced that Turretin's view amounts to soft theological determinism. Some scholars, however, deny that Turretin fits into any modern category of free will: determinist, indeterminist, compatibilist, incompatibilist. Part of the debate concerns the distinction between diachronic contingency and synchronic contingency. Richard A. Muller explains, "The difference . . . between synchronic and diachronic contingency is that, according to synchronic contingency, if Socrates is sitting at a particular moment T1, it is also possible (albeit not simultaneously actualizable) at T1 that Socrates run—whereas in the diachronic contingency model, if Socrates is sitting at T1, it is not possible that Socrates run at T2." Muller, *Divine Will and Human Choice*, 52. Even more clearly, Helm explains synchronic contingency:

> So by synchronic contingency is meant a contingency of logically simultaneous willings. Suppose a world and an agent. The agent is free in the synchronically contingent sense if at the moment the agent chooses A (when the external world and the state of a free agent's "internal" world is in state S) it is possible that at that very moment (the world being in state S) the agent chooses not-A or B instead. (Helm, *Reforming Free Will*, 46)

Van Asselt, J. Martin Bac, and Roelf T. te Velde argue that Turretin espoused synchronic contingency; see van Asselt et al., *Reformed Thought on Freedom*, 171–200. Muller disagrees with the editors of *Reformed Thought on Freedom*. He argues that Turretin believed in a real contingency in the world, but neither the modern concept of compatibilism nor the novel concepts of synchronic or diachronic contingency accurately describe Turretin's view; see Muller, *Divine Will and Human Choice*. Helm and Michael Patrick Preciado, however, argue that Turretin's view amounts to compatibilism; see Preciado, *A Reformed View of Freedom*; Helm, *Reforming Free Will*. I take the view of Helm and Preciado. Turretin's arguments about the necessity of the incarnation and atonement and Christ's impeccability are, themselves, further reasons to believe that he was a compatibilist.

33. Turretin, *Institutes* 1:320.

34. Turretin, *Institutes* 1:501–5.

and spontaneously (to wit, they are so determined by God that they also determine themselves)."[35]

Turretin makes both an implicit and an explicit christological argument for compatibilism. His implicit christological argument comes from the conjunction of the necessity of Christ's mediatorial work and his free and willing obedience. Turretin's explicit christological argument for compatibilism is in a discussion about free will considered absolutely.[36]

2b.i. Christ's Work as Necessary and Willing

Turretin argues that Christ's person and work were absolutely necessary—not a *simple* absolute necessity but a *consequent* absolute necessity, i.e., following God's will to redeem humanity, the incarnation and atonement were absolutely necessary.[37] First, the incarnation was necessary on account of "sin and the decree of God concerning the redemption of men."[38] The incarnation was necessary "as God cannot deny his own justice, he could not free men without a satisfaction being made first. Satisfaction could not be made to infinite justice except by some infinite ransom (*lystron*); nor could that infinite ransom (*lystron*) be found anywhere except in the Son of God."[39] Moreover, God's work of redemption could be performed only by the God-man.

35. Turretin, *Institutes* 1:508.

36. "Free will can be viewed either in the genus of being and absolutely (as belonging to a rational being in every state); or in the genus of morals and in relation to various states (either of sin or of righteousness)" (Turretin, *Institutes* 1:665).

37. Turretin parts ways with Augustine, Aquinas, and many of the Reformers by rejecting a mere hypothetical necessity of the incarnation and atonement. For example, Augustine writes, "we must also show, not indeed that no other possible way was available to God, since all things are equally within his power." Augustine, *De Trinitate*, 13.10. Aquinas, likewise: "In the first way [i.e., the sense of necessity 'when the end cannot be without it'] it was not necessary that God should become incarnate for the restoration of human nature. For God with His omnipotent power could have restored human nature in many other ways." *ST* III, Q. 1, A 2. Cf. Calvin, who writes, "Now it was of the greatest importance for us that he who was to be our Mediator be both true God and true man. If someone asks why this is necessary, there has been no simple (to use the common expression) or absolute necessity. Rather, it has stemmed from a heavenly decree, on which men's salvation depended. Our most merciful Father decreed what was best for us." Calvin, *Institutes* 2.12.1. For Turretin, the incarnation and atonement were not necessary merely because of the divine decree to bring about an incarnation and atonement (i.e., on account of the divine will); rather, following Athanasius and Anselm, the incarnation and atonement were necessary because of the divine nature.

38. Turretin, *Institutes* 2:301.

39. Turretin, *Institutes* 2:302.

Second, Turretin sees a necessity in the nature of Christ's mediatorial work. It was necessary that Christ fulfills the threefold office of prophet, priest, and king: "The acts of a Mediator could not be performed otherwise. For two things were necessary: that he should act for us with God (*ta pros ton theon*) and for God with us (*ta pros hēmas*)."[40] His prophetic office is shown to be necessary "(1) From the necessity of a revelation because there can be no knowledge of God and divine things without a revelation . . . . (2) From the method of salvation because no means of salvation was given except faith . . . . (3) From the oracles of the Old Testament which promise that prophecy, which must necessarily be fulfilled."[41]

Third, Turretin affirms that Christ's satisfaction was necessary. Satisfaction was of "absolute necessity, so that God not only has not willed to remit our sins without a satisfaction, but could not do so on account of his justice."[42] Christ legitimately takes the place of sinners and satisfies God's wrath because he meets the following conditions:

> (1) A common nature that sin may be punished in the same nature which is guilty (Heb. 2:14). (2) The consent of the will that spontaneously and willingly (without compulsion) he should take that burden upon himself: "Lo, I come to do thy will" (Heb. 10:9). (3) Power and dominion over his own life so that he may rightfully determine respecting it: "No man taketh it from me, but I lay it down myself. I have power to lay it down, and I have power to take it again" (Jn. 10:18). (4) The power of bearing all the punishment due to us and of taking it away as much from himself as from us. Otherwise, if he could himself be held by death, he could free no one from it. That Christ, God-man (*theanthrōpōs*), possesses this power, no one can doubt. (5) Holiness and immaculate purity, that being polluted by no sin, he might not have to offer sacrifice for himself, but only for us (Heb. 7:25–27).[43]

Christ's death, then, was both voluntary and necessary. Christ "willingly took the punishment upon himself."[44]

Turretin derives the necessity of satisfaction from the justice of God, the nature of sin, the sanction of the law, the preaching of the gospel, the greatness of God's love, and the glory of the divine attributes (namely, his

40. Turretin, *Institutes* 2:394.
41. Turretin, *Institutes* 2:398.
42. Turretin, *Institutes* 2:418.
43. Turretin, *Institutes* 2:421.
44. Turretin, *Institutes* 2:422.

holiness, justice, wisdom, and love).[45] The Christ-event is not necessary merely for our salvation, i.e., if we are to be saved, then God must save us. Rather, it was necessary that God act in *this* way for God to be God, given the fact that God had decided to redeem humanity.

The fact that Christ's incarnation and mediatorial work were necessary is not a direct argument for or proof of compatibilism. But implicit to this necessity is that Jesus was incarnated at the right time, was perfectly obedient in his life and death, and was an appropriate satisfaction to God—*and that it could not have been otherwise.*

2b.ii. Indifference Not Required for Christ's Freedom

Turretin produces an explicit christological argument against the notion that freedom requires indifference. For Turretin, freedom consists in rational willingness, not in indifference. By "indifference" in this case, he means "in a compound sense . . . —whether the will (all requisites being posited; for example, the decree of God and his concourse; the judgment of the practical intellect, etc.) is always so indifferent and undetermined that it can act or not act."[46] He denies that freedom consists in such indifference: "First, such an indifference to opposites is found in no free agent, whether created or uncreated: neither in God, who is good most freely indeed, yet not indifferently (as if he could be evil), but necessarily and immutably; *nor in Christ, who obeyed God most freely and yet most necessarily because he could not sin.*"[47] Although, necessarily, Christ could not have sinned, he was still free.

Turretin poses the objection, "That Christ, although he never sinned, still was not absolutely unable to sin; and that it is not repugnant to his nature, will or office to be able to sin?"[48] In other words, the objection states that Christ was peccable; he could have sinned. But Turretin answers:

45. Turretin, *Institutes* 2:422–25.

46. Turretin, *Institutes* 1:666.

47. Turretin, *Institutes* 1:666 (emphasis mine).

48. Turretin, *Institutes* 1:666. Similarly, Wilhelmus à Brakel argues,

> The Lord Jesus Christ could not will to be either obedient or disobedient to His Father. He could not do anything but be willing to obey His Father. Was not His will absolutely free? . . . In all these things there is an absolute freedom of will, but there is no neutrality as far as being willing or not willing to do something, or to will a certain thing or its opposite. Thus, freedom of the will does not consist in neutrality, but is one of necessary consequence. (Brakel, *Christian's Reasonable Service*, 1:409)

> We answer that far be it from us either to think or say any such thing concerning the immaculate Son of God whom we know to have been holy (*akakon*), undefiled (*amianton*), separate from sinners; who not only had no intercourse with sin, but could not have both because he was the Son of God and because he was our Redeemer (who if he could have sinned, could not also have saved us). Nor if he could be miserable could he for the same reason be a sinner. Misery for a time is not opposed to his most holy nature and contributed to the execution of his office because he was bound to pay the punishment of our sin and so to bear it by suffering. But he could not deserve it.[49]

It is not the case that Christ merely did not sin; he *could* not sin. Turretin affirms Christ's impeccability according to both his person ("he was the Son of God") and his work ("he was our Redeemer").[50]

According to Turretin, freedom consists in "(1) the choice (*to proairetikon*) so that what is done is not done by a blind impulse and a certain brute instinct, but from choice (*ek proaireseōs*) and the previous light of reason and the judgment of the practical intellect; (2) the voluntariness (*to hekousion*) so that what is done may be done spontaneously and freely without compulsion."[51] Thus, being rational is coextensive with being free. "Hence it follows that it is an inseparable adjunct of the rational agent, attending him in every state so that he cannot be rational without on that very account being free; nor can he be deprived of liberty without being despoiled also of reason."[52] The obedience of Christ, then, consists not in his ability to obey or disobey (because he was "immutably determined to obey the Father") but that he obeys willingly.[53]

49. Turretin, *Institutes* 1:666.

50. Turretin, *Institutes* 1:666.

51. Turretin, *Institutes* 1:667.

52. Turretin, *Institutes* 1:667.

53. Turretin, *Institutes* 1:667. Compare with Calvin, who writes, "And truly, even in death itself his willing obedience is the important thing because a sacrifice not offered voluntarily would not have furthered righteousness. . . . And we must hold fast to this: that no proper sacrifice to God could have been offered unless Christ, disregarding his own feelings, subjected and yielded himself wholly to his Father's will." Calvin, *Institutes* 2.16.5.

2c. Jonathan Edwards (1703–58)

Jonathan Edwards is perhaps the most widely recognized defender of Reformed compatibilism.[54] In order to show that liberty of indifference was not necessary for moral responsibility, Jonathan Edwards argued that Jesus' actions were necessary, and yet, they were morally praiseworthy. In section 3 of part 2 in *Freedom of the Will*, he argues two points:

> And, first, I would show, that his holy behavior was necessary; or that it was impossible it should be otherwise, than that he should behave himself holily, and that he should be perfectly holy in each individual act of his life. And secondly, that his holy behavior was properly of the nature of virtue, and was worthy of praise; and that he was the subject of law, precepts or commands, promises and rewards; and that he was in a state of trial.[55]

In what follows, I trace Edwards' argument.

2c.i. Jesus' Acts Were Necessary

Edwards affirms the essential features of classical Christology, and in particular, dyothelitism, volitional non-contrariety, and impeccability. He writes, "It was impossible, that the acts of will of the human soul of Christ should, in any instance, degree or circumstance, be otherwise than holy, and agreeable to God's nature and will."[56] Edwards makes eleven points to support this position. Most of his points are appeals to God's promises and their necessary fulfillments in Christ, but he also references Christ's impeccability. Therefore, we might categorize Edwards' arguments into the second and third forms of argument: appeals to Christ's wills and impeccability, and appeals to the necessity of the incarnation and atonement.

First, "God promised so effectually to preserve and uphold him by his Spirit, under all his temptations, that he should not fail of reaching the end for which he came into the world; which he would have failed of, had he fallen into sin."[57] "Through God's help, he should be immovable, in a way of obedience, under the great trials of reproach and suffering he should meet

54. For an introduction to Jonathan Edwards, read Beeke and Pederson, "Jonathan Edwards," 193–233. For more on Edwards' compatibilism, see Preciado, *Reformed View of Freedom*, 183–216.

55. Edwards, *Freedom of the Will*, 281.

56. Edwards, *Freedom of the Will*, 281.

57. Edwards, *Freedom of the Will*, 281.

with."[58] Edwards cites Isaiah 42:1–8, 49:7–9, and 50:5–9 as proof of God's promise, and Matthew 12:18 as his promise fulfilled.

Second, likewise, God promised that the Messiah would be successful in his office of mediator (e.g., Ps 2:6–7; 110:4) which required perfect obedience. He writes, "God's absolute promise of any things makes the things promised *necessary*, and their failing to take place absolutely *impossible*: and in like manner it makes those things necessary, on which the thing promised depends, and without which it can't take effect."[59]

Third, again, God promised "that God would give them a righteous, sinless Savior" (e.g., Isa 9:6–7; Jer 23:5–6).[60] The New Testament confirms the fulfillment of these promises, e.g., "Luke 24:44: 'That all things must be fulfilled, which were written in the law of Moses, and in the prophets, and in the Psalms concerning me.'"[61]

Fourth, these promises are meant for our comfort because they "show it to be impossible that Christ should not have persevered in perfect holiness."[62] These promises were solemn and often made with an oath, e.g., Genesis 22:16–17, wherein God swears by his own Name to bless the nations through the seed of Abraham. Edwards considers the argument of Hebrews 6:17, which comments on Genesis 22: "Wherein God willing more abundantly to shew to the heirs of promise the immutability of his counsel, confirmed it by an oath; that by two *immutable* things, in which it was *impossible* for God to lie, we might have strong consolation."[63] Edwards explains that in Hebrews 6, "the *necessity* of the accomplishment, or (which is the same thing) the *impossibility* of the contrary, is fully declared."[64]

Fifth, "all these promises imply, that the Messiah should perfect the work of redemption; and this implies, that he should persevere in the work which the Father had appointed him, being in all things conformed to his will. . . . And therefore it was impossible, that the Messiah should fail, or commit sin."[65]

Sixth, God promised Mary and Joseph that Jesus would save people from their sins (Matt 1:21; Luke 1:32–33). It would be impossible for Jesus

58. Edwards, *Freedom of the Will*, 282–83.
59. Edwards, *Freedom of the Will*, 283.
60. Edwards, *Freedom of the Will*, 283.
61. Edwards, *Freedom of the Will*, 284.
62. Edwards, *Freedom of the Will*, 284.
63. Edwards, *Freedom of the Will*, 285.
64. Edwards, *Freedom of the Will*, 285.
65. Edwards, *Freedom of the Will*, 286.

to "fail of persevering in integrity and holiness" because that would be inconsistent with God's promises to Mary and Joseph.[66]

Seventh, because God eternally decreed that Jesus would provide salvation, it would be impossible that Jesus would fail in his mission. "God could not decree before the foundation of the world, to save all that should believe in, and obey Christ, unless he had absolutely decreed that salvation should be provided, and effectually wrought out by Christ. And since . . . a decree of God infers necessity; hence it became necessary that Christ should persevere, and actually work out salvation for us, and that he should not fail by the commission of sin."[67]

Eighth, God made a promise to the Son before the ages that through the Son, salvation would come to people (cf. Titus 1:2). It would be inconsistent with this promise for the Son to fail in holiness.

Ninth, in a related way, it would be inconsistent for the Son to fail to do the will of the Father on account of the Father's promise to the Son. Edwards explains, "If the *Logos*, who was with the Father, before the world, and who made the world, thus engaged in covenant to do the will of the Father in the human nature, and the promise, was as it were recorded, that it might be made sure, doubtless it was *impossible* that it should fail; and so it was *impossible* that Christ should fail of doing the will of the Father in the human nature."[68] Thus, Christ says, "Behold, I have come to do your will, O God, as it is written of me in the scroll of the book" (Heb 10:7; cf. Ps 40:7–8).

Tenth, Edwards argues that if it were possible that Christ should fail in holiness, then "the salvation of all the saints, who were saved from the beginning of the world, to the death of Christ, was not built on a firm foundation."[69] He continues, "If Christ's virtue might fail, [David, and by extension the saints of old,] was mistaken: his great comfort was not built so sure, as he thought it was, being founded entirely on the determinations of the free will of Christ's human soul: which was subject to no necessity, and might be determined either one way or the other."[70]

Eleventh, Christ, himself, was confident in his future glory even in the midst of trial and temptation. If Christ could have failed in holiness, he "would have been guilty of presumption, in so abounding in peremptory promises of great things, which depended on a mere contingence; viz. the determinations of his free will, consisting in a freedom *ad utrumque*, to

66. Edwards, *Freedom of the Will*, 286.

67. Edwards, *Freedom of the Will*, 286.

68. Edwards, *Freedom of the Will*, 287.

69. Edwards, *Freedom of the Will*, 287.

70. Edwards, *Freedom of the Will*, 288.

either sin or holiness, standing in indifference, and incident, in thousands of future instances, to go either one way or the other."[71]

2c.ii. *Jesus' Acts Were Morally Praiseworthy*

Having shown that it would be impossible for Christ to have failed in holiness, Edwards proceeds to show that Christ's acts are indeed morally praiseworthy. Edwards poignantly states, "If there be any truth in Christianity or the holy Scriptures, the man Christ Jesus had his will infallibly, unalterably and unfrustrably determined to good, and that alone; but yet he had promises of glorious rewards made to him, on condition of his persevering in, and perfecting the work which God had appointed (Is. 53:10, 11, 12; Ps. 2 and 110; Is. 49:7, 8, 9)."[72] Christ was promised success and reward for his obedience, and his future success and reward were themselves motivation for his obedience (Heb 12:1–2; Rev 3:21).

Edwards finds it absurd to deny Christ's virtue on account of his not having liberty of indifference. He writes:

> And how strange would it be to hear any Christian assert, that the holy and excellent temper and behavior of Jesus Christ, and that obedience which he performed under such great trials, was not virtuous or praiseworthy; because his will was not free *ad utrumque*, to either holiness or sin, but was unalterably determined to one; that upon this account, there is no virtue at all, in all Christ's humility, meekness, patience, charity, forgiveness of enemies, contempt of the world, heavenly-mindedness, submission to the will of God, perfect obedience to his commands (though he was obedient unto death, even death of the cross), his great compassion to the afflicted, his unparalleled love to mankind, his faithfulness to God and man, under such great trials; his praying for his enemies, even when nailing him to the cross; that "virtue," when applied to these things, "is but an empty name"; that there was no merit in any of these things; that is, that Christ was "worthy" of nothing at all on account of them, worthy of no reward, no praise, no honor or respect from God or man; because his will was not indifferent, and free either to these things, or the contrary; but under such a strong inclination or bias to the things that were excellent, as made it impossible that he should choose the contrary.[73]

71. Edwards, *Freedom of the Will*, 288–89.
72. Edwards, *Freedom of the Will*, 289–90.
73. Edwards, *Freedom of the Will*, 290–91.

And if Christ is not virtuous, then we ought not to imitate him. Yet, Scripture urges us to imitate Christ in his obedience and suffering in order to share in his reward (e.g., John 15:10; Rom 8:17; 2 Tim 2:11–12; 1 Pet 4:13).

Scripture teaches that God was pleased with the righteousness of Jesus. "The sacrifices of old are spoken of as a sweet savor to God, but the obedience of Christ is far more acceptable than they."[74] In addition to Isaiah 42:21, Psalm 40:6–8, and Matthew 17:5, Edwards partially quotes John 10:17–18, which I provide here in full in a modern translation: "For this reason the Father loves me, because I lay down my life that I may take it up again. No one takes it from me, but I lay it down of my own accord. I have authority to lay it down, and I have authority to take it up again. This charge I have received from my Father." Edwards explains that in this text, "Christ tells us expressly, that the Father loves him for that wonderful instance of his obedience, his voluntarily yielding himself to death, in compliance with the Father's command."[75]

If Christ's acts were not praiseworthy, then the heavenly hosts were mistaken. Edwards cites Revelation 5:8–12:

> The four beasts and the four and twenty elders fell down before the Lamb, having everyone of them harps, and golden vials full of odors . . . and they sung a new song, saying, thou art *worthy* to take the book, and to open the seals thereof; for thou wast slain . . . and I beheld, and I heard the voice of many angels round about the throne, and the beasts, and the elders, and the number of them was ten thousand times then thousand, and thousands of thousands, saying with a loud voice, *worthy* is the Lamb that was slain, to receive power, and riches, and wisdom, and strength, and honor, and glory, and blessing.[76]

God rewards Jesus "far above all his other servants" (e.g., Phil 2:7–9; Ps 45:7).[77] And there is no doubt that Jesus' reward is a true reward, i.e., "a benefit bestowed in consequence of something morally excellent in quality or behavior, in testimony of well-pleasedness in that moral excellency, and respect and favor on that account."[78]

Finally, in the same way that Adam was in a state of trial in the Garden of Eden, Jesus, too, was in a state of trial. "The last Adam, as Christ is called (1 Cor. 15:45; Rom. 5:14), taking on him the human nature, and so the form

74. Edwards, *Freedom of the Will*, 291–92.
75. Edwards, *Freedom of the Will*, 292.
76. Edwards, *Freedom of the Will*, 292.
77. Edwards, *Freedom of the Will*, 293.
78. Edwards, *Freedom of the Will*, 293.

of a servant, and being under the law, to stand and act for us, was put into a state of trial, as the first Adam was."[79] Jesus' situation satisfied the conditions in which subjects are rightly considered to be in a state of trial, "namely, their afflictions being spoken of as their trials or temptations, their being the subjects of promises, and their being exposed to Satan's temptations."[80]

2d. Summary of Historical Arguments

Compatibilism is the dominant position in the Reformed tradition regarding free will.[81] Reformed Protestants, with Calvin, typically see a three-tier determinism: a robust divine providence (theological determinism), a view of the soul that considers the will to be dependent on the final dictate of the intellect (psychological determinism), and a moral necessity initiated by original sin toward evil and regeneration toward good (bondage of the will). Despite determinism, these Protestants see human beings as significantly free moral agents—worthy of praise or blame.

Christological arguments for compatibilism are common in the Reformed tradition. These arguments come in three forms: (1) appeals to the teachings of Jesus Christ, (2) appeals to Christ's wills and impeccability, and (3) appeals to the necessity of the incarnation and atonement.[82] I have shown that Calvin appeals to the teachings of Jesus Christ to support his view of humanity's inability to do good apart from the grace of God, and yet, humans are morally responsible agents. I have shown that Turretin and Edwards appeal to the necessity of the incarnation and atonement while simultaneously affirming Christ's willing obedience. I have also shown how both Turretin and Edwards reject the notion that freedom requires indifference by appealing to Christ's impeccability and volitional non-contrariety.

79. Edwards, *Freedom of the Will*, 293.

80. Edwards, *Freedom of the Will*, 293.

81. For example, see Berkhof, *Systematic Theology*, 106–8, 247–48; Horton, *Christian Faith*, 355–62, 431–34; Frame, *Systematic Theology*, 148–68, 809–44.

82. Each of these christological arguments may be found in contemporary Reformed theology. For the first appeal, see Ware, *God's Greater Glory*, 79–81; Frame, *Doctrine of God*, 142; Grudem, *Systematic Theology*, 434. For the second appeal, see Carson, *Divine Sovereignty and Human Responsibility*, 157–60; Ware, "Gospel of Christ," 320–33; Ware, *God's Greater Glory*, 94–95. For the third appeal, see Helm, *Providence of God*, 213–16; Carson, *Divine Sovereignty and Human Responsibility*, 157–60; Feinberg, *No One Like Him*, 518, 766–67; Ware, *God's Greater Glory*, 89–90; Grudem, *Systematic Theology*, 433.

3. The Formal Argument

My project is not a rejection of previous christological arguments for compatibilism but a continuation, clarification, and supplementation of the Reformed tradition. The freewill debate has evolved since the times of Calvin, Turretin, and Edwards. New challenges have arisen. New terms have been coined. New models of freedom, action, and moral responsibility have been formed. Therefore, the christological case for compatibilism must be revitalized and updated.

At least one of four propositions is true: (1) PAP libertarianism is true; (2) sourcehood libertarianism is true; (3) hard determinism is true; (4) compatibilism is true.[83] Propositions 1 and 2 are not mutually exclusive, but if 3 or 4 are true, then all others are false. I intend to show that if we assume the truth of classical Christology, we are able to rule out propositions 1–3, and affirm 4. In the following chapters, I shall assume classical Christology and assess whether it is consistent with any of the four propositions above. In chapter 4, I demonstrate that classical Christology is inconsistent with PAP libertarianism. Christ willingly submitted to the Father's will, and yet, he could not have done otherwise. In chapter 5, I argue that classical Christology is inconsistent with sourcehood libertarianism. The ultimate source of Christ's actions is not found in his human nature or psychology but in the Godhead. In chapters 6 and 7, I show that classical Christology is inconsistent with hard determinism. Although God's causality is determinative, Christ is morally praiseworthy for his actions. In chapters 8–10, I provide positive reasons to believe that compatibilism is consistent with classical Christology. I utilize the three forms of christological argument for compatibilism: (1) an appeal to Christ's volitional non-contrariety and impeccability, (2) an appeal to the necessity of Christ's incarnation and atonement according to divine decree and promise, and (3) an appeal to Christ's teaching about himself and human nature.

The formal argument of Part 2 of this book may be expressed as follows. Let "J" stand for Classical Christology; "P" for PAP Libertarianism; "S" for Sourcehood Libertarianism; "D" for Hard Determinism; and "C" for Compatibilism.

1. Either P or S or D or C.	Premise
2. If J then not P.	Chapter 4
3. If J then not S.	Chapter 5
4. If J then not D.	Chapter 6–7

83. Semi-compatibilism may be included in this option. See chapter 1.

5. Therefore, if J then C. Derived from 1, 2, 3, and 4

In other words, either PAP libertarianism or sourcehood libertarianism or hard determinism or compatibilism is true. Because classical Christology is inconsistent with PAP libertarianism, sourcehood libertarianism, and hard determinism, then it must be consistent with compatibilism.

Part II:

The Negative Christological Case for Compatibilism

4

Christ and the Principle of Alternative Possibilities

1. Introduction

Classical Christology provides reason to reject the categorical reading of the principle of alternative possibilities (PAP).[1] The Gethsemane prayer highlights an instance in which Jesus Christ performs a voluntary and morally significant action which he could not have done otherwise, namely, his submission to God's will. The classical christological doctrine of volitional non-contrariety (VNC) undermines PAP. Classical Christology teaches that Christ's human will could not be contrary to his divine will. Yet, classical Christology also teaches that Christ's death is voluntary and morally praiseworthy. First, I present classical Christology and VNC. Second, I define and disambiguate varieties of PAP. Third, I show that Christ's prayer in Gethsemane disproves the categorical reading of PAP. Then, I spend the second half of the chapter responding to objections.

2. Classical Christology and Volitional Non-Contrariety

Classical Christology gives us reason to reject the categorical reading of PAP. In this section, I highlight that element of classical Christology that leads to the rejection of the categorical reading of PAP: VNC.

1. A version of this chapter appears in Johnson, "Christ and the Principle of Alternative Possibilities," 314–21.

Classical Christology posits two wills in Christ.[2] As the Chalcedonian logic goes, God the Son is one person in two natures: "Our Lord Jesus Christ is one and the same Son, the same perfect in Godhead and the same perfect in manhood, truly God and truly man, the same of a rational soul and body."[3] Chalcedon was at pains to deny a union of Logos and mere flesh. Rather, the Logos took to himself a complete human nature—body *and* rational soul. What was implicit at Chalcedon was made explicit at Constantinople III: "And we proclaim equally two natural volitions or wills in him and two natural principles of action which undergo no division, no change, no partition, no confusion, in accordance with the teaching of the holy fathers."[4] Thus, dyothelitism is the position of conciliar orthodoxy; Christ has two wills: one human and one divine.

An important distinction must be made between the *faculty* of the will and the *object* of the will. Dyothelitism teaches that Christ has two faculties of will, i.e., two natural wills: human and divine. Christ's divine faculty of will is the numerically identical faculty of will of the whole Godhead; Father, Son, and Spirit share the one divine will. The object of the will, however, is the thing (or state of affairs) willed. This distinction can be seen in Jesus' prayer in Gethsemane in which he resolves to conform the object of his human will to the object of his divine will: "My Father, if it be possible, let this cup pass from me; nevertheless, not as I will, but as you will" (Matt 26:39).[5]

Christ's human will could never have been contrary to—but was always in conformity with—the divine will according to its object.[6] The doctrine of VNC is codified in Constantinople III which reads: "And the two natural wills not in opposition, . . . but his human will following, and not resisting or struggling, rather in fact subject to his divine and all powerful will. For the will of the flesh had to be moved, and yet to be subjected to the divine will."[7] That Christ's humanity is subject to his divinity does not entail that Christ,

2. For expedience, I use the names "Christ," "Jesus," and "Son," interchangeably.

3. Kelly, *Early Christian Doctrines*, 339. For more on Chalcedonian Christology, see Grillmeier, *Christ in Christian Tradition*.

4. Tanner, *Decrees of the Ecumenical Councils*, 128.

5. Because wills are natural rather than personal, the Father's will is the very same divine will of the Son.

6. For exegetical support of VNC, consider what Jesus says in John 5:19: "Truly, truly, I say to you, the Son can do nothing of his own accord, but only what he sees the Father doing. For whatever the Father does, that the Son does likewise"; and 8:28–29: "When you have lifted up the Son of Man, then you will know that I am he, and that I do nothing on my own authority, but speak just as the Father taught me. And he who sent me is with me. He has not left me alone, for I always do the things that are pleasing to him."

7. Tanner, *Decrees of the Ecumenical Councils*, 128.

in his humanity, lacked deliberation or even competing desires.[8] Christ could have competing desires (or objects of the will) as long as (1) the desire upon which Christ acted was conformed to the divine will as to its object, and (2) none of the competing desires were sinful in themselves.[9] There is a real sense in which Christ did not want to die, but that desire to avoid death was overridden by his greater desire to obey his Father.[10]

8. Theologians of the Middle Ages went to great lengths to show the complexity of Christ's human will in relation to his divine will. Especially noteworthy are Maximus the Confessor and Thomas Aquinas. See Bathrellos, *Byzantine Christ*, and Barnes, *Christ's Two Wills in Scholastic Thought*, for expositions of Maximus and Aquinas, respectively.

9. Consider Kane's definition for "wills": "(W) An agent *wills* to do something at time t just in case the agent has reasons or motives at t for doing it that the agent wants to act on more than he or she wants to act on any other reasons (for doing otherwise)." Kane, *Significance of Free Will*, 30.

10. I have provided only a sketch of VNC—enough to suit the purpose of this chapter. VNC is an especially crucial doctrine whose complexity is multiplied by theological, metaphysical, and psychological considerations. Perhaps the most sophisticated explanation of VNC comes from Thomas Aquinas. I provide a summary of Aquinas' teaching in what follows: Christ has two wills, one according to each nature. The divine will is the numerically identical will of the Father and the Spirit. The human will, itself, can be divided into the will of reason and the will of sensuality. The will of reason can be further divided into the *will as reason* (or rational will) and the *will as nature* (or natural will). Barnes explains, "The *thelēsis*, or natural will, regards the good taken absolutely, while the *boulēsis*, or rational will, regards the good in terms of means." Barnes, *Christ's Two Wills in Scholastic Thought*, 137. Barnes further explains, "The will as reason exercises dominion in matters ordered to an end and so governs the will as nature when it is carried to an end. . . . The will as nature can only regard the inherent value of something and so cannot account for the instrumental good or ill of that thing." Barnes, *Christ's Two Wills in Scholastic Thought*, 149. Aquinas summarizes:

> It is clear therefore that *according to the will of reason* [Christ's human will] was conformed to the divine will in the thing willed with respect to everything it willed perfectly and absolutely, but not with respect to what it willed imperfectly. Similarly, the *will of sensuality* was also not conformed to the divine will in the thing willed in those things injurious to nature; because it does not pertain to sensuality to order something to an end, but those things injurious to nature were good and acceptable to God from their order to an end. Yet the will of sensuality and the will of reason were conformed to the divine will in the act of willing; although not in the thing willed; because, although God might not will what Christ's will of sensuality or will as nature willed, nevertheless God willed the very act of each . . . . (Aquinas, *In* III, d.17, a.2, solution I [*Scriptum* 3:536–38], cited in Barnes, *Christ's Two Wills in Scholastic Thought*, 146).

3. The Principle of Alternative Possibilities

PAP, according to Harry G. Frankfurt, "states that a person is morally responsible for what he has done only if he could have done otherwise."[11] According to PAP, my having said a kind word to my daughter was a moral act only if I could have chosen not to say that kind word to my daughter. Frankfurt himself was critical of PAP, so he produced thought experiments that portended to contradict PAP. Frankfurt-style counterexamples are received with mixed approval.[12]

One difficulty with PAP and the phrase "could have done otherwise" is that it is ambiguous between a categorical and a conditional reading. Following Guillaume Bignon, I shall distinguish between PAP_{ALL} and PAP_{IF}. Bignon stipulates, "Let PAP_{ALL} be the principle that 'a person is morally responsible for what he has done only if, *all things inside and outside the person being just as they are at the moment of choice*, he could have done otherwise.' Let us name this sort of ability a *categorical ability*."[13] On PAP_{ALL}, if we were to rewind time to the moment just before I say that kind word to my daughter, with all else being the same, I could have done otherwise.

PAP_{IF}, according to Bignon, is "the principle that 'a person is morally responsible for what he has done only if he could have done otherwise, *had his inner desires inclined him to do so at the moment of choice*.'"[14] This sort of ability is a *conditional ability*. On PAP_{IF}, if we were to rewind time to the moment just before I say that kind word to my daughter, with all else being the same, I could *not* have done otherwise. But I *could* have done otherwise, *if* my beliefs or desires were different at the moment just before the action.

Compatibilists often hold PAP_{IF} to be true and PAP_{ALL} to be false.[15] Many incompatibilists, however, hold PAP_{ALL} to be true but deny that the conditional ability of PAP_{IF} is sufficient for moral responsibility.[16] This chap-

11. Frankfurt, "Alternative Possibilities and Moral Responsibility," 1.

12. The literature on Frankfurt-style counterexamples and PAP is enormous. See chapter 1.

13. Bignon, *Excusing Sinners and Blaming God*, 72.

14. Bignon, *Excusing Sinners and Blaming God*, 72.

15. Dispositional compatibilists argue that the ability to do otherwise is still necessary for freedom. On this view, I must have those intrinsic properties that underlie the power, for example, to say a kind word to my daughter. Because those properties are intrinsic to me, I have the ability to say a kind word to my daughter whether or not I have the opportunity or desire to do so. Christ certainly had the relevant natural (human) powers or dispositions to act otherwise, but natural powers or dispositions do not give Christ the categorical ability to do otherwise.

16. Indeed, many compatibilists will deny that the conditional ability of PAP_{IF} is *sufficient* for moral responsibility. The key difference is that most compatibilists view

ter is concerned with PAP_{ALL}, the categorical reading of PAP. The freewill literature in contemporary analytic philosophy is full of Frankfurt-style counterexamples. What is missing from the literature is an *actual* counterexample. If there is an act performed by some agent that is voluntary, morally significant, and one that the agent categorically could not have done otherwise, then PAP_{ALL} is false. I argue, below, that Jesus' resolution to go to the cross, his submission to God's will, exhibited in his prayer at Gethsemane, is an actual example of an act that is voluntary, morally significant, and one that he categorically could not have done otherwise.

One further clarification is necessary. Christ is one person subsisting in two natures. The person, Christ, is the one subject of both his human and divine actions—each of which is a principle of action. How PAP relates to Christ's divine freedom is beyond the scope of this book. Rather, my aim is to show that Christ *according to his human nature* performed an action that disproves PAP_{ALL}.[17] The nature–person distinction, therefore, requires us to provide a formula of PAP_{ALL} that fits both persons with one nature and persons with multiple natures:

> PAP_N: A person *P* is morally responsible for an action only if *P* could have done otherwise solely via the nature by which *P* performed that action, all things just as they are at the moment of choice.

PAP_N is a categorical formulation of PAP that affirms that natures are principles of action; yet persons, not natures, are moral agents. In what follows, I show that classical Christology provides reason to reject PAP_N.

4. PAP at Gethsemane

The Gethsemane prayer has a unique perspicuity on the matter of PAP. Jesus' prayer in the garden is not only a key event in the biblical storyline but also the juncture of multiple christological doctrines and themes. In his prayer, Jesus Christ, the Son of God incarnate, submits his will to the will of God the Father. Thus, he resolves to volunteer his life—to be put to death for the sins of many: "nevertheless, not as I will, but as you will" (Matt 26:39).[18]

the categorical ability of PAP_{ALL} as unnecessary but the conditional ability of PAP_{IF} as necessary—if not sufficient—for moral responsibility.

17. I take Christ's human nature to be concrete rather than abstract. For more on Christ's human nature as concrete, see Hill's introduction to *The Metaphysics of the Incarnation*, 11–12; Crisp, *Divinity and Humanity*, 34–71; Pawl, *In Defense of Conciliar Christology*, 34–39.

18. Compare Mark 14:36 and Luke 22:42.

In this section, I consider Jesus' prayer as a voluntary, morally significant act in light of VNC.

God sent his Son to save humanity (John 3:16–17). Jesus knew that his mission included his own death; and he knew the time and manner of his death (Matt 16:21; 17:22–23; 20:17–19; 26:2). Indeed, he was *commanded* to lay down his life willingly and to take it up again: "No one takes it [my life] from me, but I lay it down of my own accord. I have authority to lay it down, and I have authority to take it up again. This charge [ταύτην τὴν ἐντολὴν] I have received from my Father" (John 10:18).[19] Furthermore, the phrase "of my own accord" and the use of the noun "authority" imply both willingness and immunity to coercion or compulsion.[20] Jesus was commanded to volunteer his life. Because the Father commanded the Son to die—and to die *in this way*—it would have been a sin, a moral failure, not to volunteer his life.

The narrative leading up to and including Gethsemane indicates that Jesus viewed this moment—this very prayer—as pivotal. In Matthew 26, Jesus foretells his death by crucifixion (v. 2), acknowledges his upcoming burial (v. 12), discloses that Judas will soon betray him (vv. 20–25), institutes the Lord's Supper, symbolizing his impending death (vv. 26–29), predicts Peter's denial with remarkable accuracy, and tells his disciples to watch and pray as he prays to the Father. Jesus was fully cognizant of what was happening. Jesus' prayer in Gethsemane was his last moment alone with the Father. Would he shirk his mission—run or hide or deny his identity? Or would he submit to the will of God—to be obedient unto death—even death on a cross (Phil 2:8)?

According to VNC, Christ could not have shirked his mission. He had to submit to God's will, and he could not have done otherwise. Yet, this submission was both voluntary and morally praiseworthy. The act's voluntariness is clear from Christ's own words: "I lay it down of my own accord" (John 10:18). The moral significance of this act is supported throughout Scripture.[21] Christ is praised for his obedience (Rom 5:18–19); he is called "righteous' (Acts 3:14), "good" (Titus 3:4), "worthy" (Heb 3:3), and "faithful" (Heb 2:17). Christ is rewarded for his obedience (Phil 2:9). And we are exhorted to imitate Christ's humility and obedience (Phil 2:5–11). Christ did the morally right thing: he obeyed God. Therefore, PAP_N is false. At the

19. All Greek text is taken from the *Greek New Testament: SBL Edition* (SBLGNT), edited by Michael Holmes.

20. Consider Kane's definition of "voluntary": "(V) An agent acts *voluntarily* (or *willingly*) at t just in case, at t, the agent does what he or she wills to do (in the sense of W), for the reasons he or she wills to do it, and the agent's doing it and willing to do it are not the result of coercion or compulsion." Kane, *Significance of Free Will*, 30.

21. See chapter 5 for a fuller defense of Christ's status as a moral agent.

moment of choice—his prayer at Gethsemane—Jesus was willing and morally responsible for his action despite not being able to do otherwise. At the moment of Christ's greatest temptation, he willingly submitted to God's will.

5. Objections

Having argued that classical Christology provides reason to reject PAP, I now consider several objections. The objections and my responses are more complicated than the central argument of this chapter, so they take up significantly more space and even flow into the following chapters.

5a. Objection About Moral Responsibility

Although I have shown that Christ's submission was a morally relevant act, one might argue that I have merely demonstrated that alternative possibilities are unnecessary in the case of moral *praise*, but I have not proven anything about moral *blame*. According to this objection, the conditions for praise and blame are asymmetrical. In order to deem an agent to be morally blameworthy, the agent must have been able to do otherwise.[22]

In response, first, because Christ's human will always concurs with his divine will, there simply are no cases in which Christ deserves moral blame. But, insofar as a morally praiseworthy action is a morally significant action, I have defended my thesis. The Gethsemane prayer is a concrete example in which a person performs a voluntary and morally significant action despite lacking the categorical ability to do otherwise.

Second, the claim that moral praiseworthiness and blameworthiness are asymmetrical is a claim typically made by certain compatibilists, not incompatibilists. Thus, those who make this distinction do not think moral blameworthiness requires the *categorical* ability to do otherwise, but, rather, it requires some general ability or dispositional capacity to do otherwise.[23] In this chapter, I have argued that the categorical ability to do otherwise is not a necessary condition for moral responsibility. I have neither addressed the sufficient conditions for moral responsibility nor proposed a mechanism

22. For example, Wolf, *Freedom Within Reason*, argues that when moral agents act in accordance with reason, they are morally praiseworthy even if they could not have done otherwise. But when moral agents are able to act according to reason but act contrary to reason, they are morally blameworthy. Therefore, PAP holds in the case of blame but not praise. See also Nelkin, *Making Sense of Freedom and Moral Responsibility*.

23. For a critique of Nelkin's dispositional compatibilism, see McKenna, "Source Compatibilism and That Pesky Ability to Do Otherwise," 105–16.

for free action. Whether the ability of *any* sense of PAP is necessary for moral responsibility is beyond the scope of this chapter—as is whether the necessary conditions for praise differ from blame.

5b. Objection About PAP_N

Although classical Christology provides reason to reject PAP_N, one might deny that PAP_N is the relevant formulation of PAP_{ALL}. Rather, the relevant formulation of PAP_{ALL} is PAP_P,

> PAP_P: A person *P* is morally responsible for an action only if *P* could have done otherwise via the nature by which *P* performed that action, all things just as they are at the moment of choice.

PAP_P removes the adverb "solely" from PAP_N, which results in Christ *indeed* being able to act otherwise. As the objection goes, the Son *qua* divinity has the categorical ability to act otherwise; nothing determines or necessitates divine action one way or another. Therefore, according to PAP_P, there *is* something Christ could have done otherwise than he did: he could have divinely willed that his humanity do otherwise than it did. So, even if Christ could not do otherwise in his humanity *simpliciter*, the theandric person could have done otherwise by divinely willing otherwise, thereby changing what he does *qua* humanity.

I maintain, however, that PAP_P is not preferable to PAP_N, and even if it were, classical Christology still provides reason to reject it. Here are three reasons to prefer PAP_N.

First, PAP_N is preferable to PAP_P because the question at hand is whether Christ *according to his humanity* could do otherwise. PAP_N is able to eliminate all factors outside his humanity, whereas PAP_P is not. For that reason, it seems more relevant to our own freedom and moral responsibility (and the focus of PAP generally).

Second, PAP_P makes the nature–person distinction superfluous with respect to PAP. The ability to do otherwise ought to be found in the same principle of action, the nature, by which the action was performed. The following analogy illustrates this problem with PAP_P. Suppose my right hand is numb and my physical therapist asks me if I am able to make a fist with my right hand. If I responded, "Sure, I can. I just need to use my left hand to close my right hand," the physical therapist would not be satisfied with my answer.

Third, the result of PAP_P looks suspiciously like a conditional, rather than a categorical result. Christ *qua* humanity could have willed otherwise *only if* Christ *qua* divinity had willed otherwise.

But, for the sake of argument, let us assume PAP_P is the relevant formulation. The objection, then, can be articulated as such: God the Son could have actualized a world (W_1) exactly similar to the actual world (α) up to the moment of choice (t), but the Son *qua* humanity did otherwise in W_1 than in α at t.[24]

Can PAP_P hold in the case of Jesus' prayer in Gethsemane? No; it cannot because God could not have willed his humanity to do otherwise *at the moment of choice*. First, as shown above, Jesus had certain beliefs about Gethsemane and his impending betrayal and death. He believed this prayer was a pivotal moment in the expression of his obedience—and he believed he would indeed make the ultimate expression of his obedience at that moment. If he were to do other than to submit to God's will, we would have to admit that Jesus held false beliefs about what he, himself, would do.

Second, perhaps we could forbear Christ holding false beliefs *qua* humanity, but PAP_P implies that God is possibly deceptive. Jesus believed he was fulfilling Scripture and God's command and purpose up to the moment of prayer. But if PAP_P were right, it would be possible for God to deceive Jesus: to lead him to believe certain things about the event in Gethsemane that were not true.

5c. *Objection About Alternative Possibilities*

One might object by arguing that Jesus did, indeed, have alternative possibilities. For example, he could have whispered or yelled his prayer of submission; he could have spoken his prayer in Aramaic or Greek or Latin or Hebrew. None of these alternative possibilities seem to violate VNC. As Aquinas said, "The will of Christ, though determined to good, is not determined to this or that good. Hence it pertains to Christ, even as to the blessed, to choose with a free-will confirmed in good."[25] In other words, we can grant that Jesus had to submit, but *how* he would submit was not determined.

24. It is not obvious how to interpret "at the moment of choice" in a discussion about God. Is the divine willing occurring at the moment of choice? Or is just the alternative human action occurring at the moment of choice? The answer may depend on God's relation to time. If God is temporal, then the objection might be interpreted in this way: At the moment when Jesus prays in the Garden of Gethsemane, he could have acted *via* his divine nature to bring about a different response in his humanity than he actually did. But whether God is temporal or atemporal, PAP_P succumbs to the same criticisms.

25. *ST* III, q. 18, a.4, ad 3.

Bignon points out, however, that because actions can be described at different levels of granularity, "the action for which one is morally responsible must be described at the same level of granularity, when asserting of it that the person 'could have done otherwise.' He could have done otherwise than *that very action, thus described, at that level of granularity*."[26] The *morally* relevant action considered at Gethsemane is Jesus' submission to God's will. "Jesus' submission to God's will" is a coarse-grained description, which requires a coarse-grained alternative, e.g., "Jesus' defiance to God's will." Jesus could not have defied God's will. Whether or not Jesus could have used different words in his prayer of submission is irrelevant to the issue of VNC and PAP_N because every way in which Jesus could have submitted to God's will is a fine-grained species of Jesus' submission to God's will. Let us grant, for the moment, that Jesus could have whispered his prayer of submission. The fine-grained corollary to whispering a prayer of submission to God's will is whispering a prayer of defiance to God's will. Jesus could not have whispered a prayer of defiance to God's will.

The recalcitrant objector might insist that the agent need not have alternative *moral* possibilities but alternative *token* possibilities of the same moral act-type. In other words, the agent must have some leeway freedom for the act to be morally significant—even if there are no possible alternatives that result in a different moral value. In essence, this objection claims that unless Christ is determined to one token action—one particular action—then he does have the power to do otherwise.

This objection concerns the very nature of the relationship between Christ's divinity and humanity, and thus, it is beyond the scope of this chapter. In chapters 7 and 8, I consider whether Christ *qua* humanity was determined. If so, then he certainly had no alternative token possibilities.

5d. Objection About Impeccability and Temptation

One final objection concerns an apparent result of denying PAP. If Christ could not do otherwise than follow the divine will, then certainly he could not have sinned. But if Christ could not have sinned, then he must never have been truly tempted. And if his temptations were not real, then we ought to question either his true humanity or the moral worth of his actions.

Classical Christology, however, affirms both that Christ was impeccable—even during his earthly ministry—and that he was truly human. Furthermore, I have demonstrated that Christ was a morally responsible agent. Therefore, the objection that Christ's temptations were not real is

26. Bignon, *Excusing Sinners and Blaming God*, 112 (emphasis his).

mistaken. Indeed, the objection begs the question by presupposing that the categorical ability to do otherwise is necessary for moral responsibility. A closer look at Christ's impeccability will satisfy this objection.

Classical Christology maintains not only that Christ was sinless in his human life but that he was impeccable; he was unable to sin. Three clarifications are in order. First, when we attribute impeccability to Christ, we are attributing impeccability to Christ according to his humanity.[27] The question is not "Could *God* sin?" (of course, not) but "Could God sin *as man*?" Classical Christology says, "No."[28]

Second, there is a distinction between (1) Christ wanting to sin and (2) Christ wanting to do *x* such that if he were to do *x*, he would be sinning. Christ never wanted or desired to sin. For example, during his temptation in the wilderness, he was hungry. "The devil said to him, 'If you are the Son of God, command this stone to become bread'" (Luke 4:3). Jesus did not desire to sin; rather, he desired bread (he was hungry), but if he were to have commanded the stone to become bread, he would have sinned. *Wanting to sin* seems to be a sin itself. So, Christ's impeccability entails that he was unable to want to sin.

Third, impeccability is the *categorical* impossibility of sinning. Because Christ is God, necessarily, he could not sin. In other words, there is no possible world in which Christ sins. A *conditional* reading of impeccability might look like, "If Christ wanted to sin, he could have sinned." But Christ's impeccability entails that he could never *want* to sin, so the antecedent is false. When the antecedent of a conditional is false, the conditional itself is true but vacuously so; it is also true that "If Christ wanted to sin, he could not have sinned."

Jesus' prayer of submission is his victory over temptation. The episode in the Garden of Gethsemane recalls Adam's temptation in the Garden of Eden. Here, Jesus, the new and better Adam, is tempted—not with *sin* but with escape from suffering and death.[29] Jesus endured the temptation to its full extent. And this temptation was itself excruciating: "And being in agony he prayed more earnestly; and his sweat became like great drops of blood

27. Calvin writes, "And this remains for us as an established fact: whenever Scripture calls our attention to the purity of Christ, it is to be understood of his true human nature, for it would have been superfluous to say that God is pure." Calvin, *Institutes* 2.13.4.

28. I am not suggesting that Christ's human nature *as nature* is impeccable. Rather, because the human nature is assumed by Christ, Christ is impeccable according to that nature; i.e., Christ could not commit a sinful human act. See Pawl's discussion of impeccability in *In Defense of Extended Conciliar Christology*, 132–64.

29. Likewise, Adam was not tempted with *sin* but with the apparent opportunity to become like God—knowing both good and evil; but to eat of the tree would be sin because God forbade it.

falling to the ground" (Luke 22:44). For this reason, "we do not have a high priest who is unable to sympathize with our weakness, but one who in every respect has been tempted as we are, yet without sin" (Heb 4:15). Impeccability, then, is compatible with Christ's temptations.[30] Christ truly had to overcome those desires the satisfaction of which would result in sin. And he did so with the psychological processes common to humanity and support from divine grace. The fact that Christ could not have done otherwise undermines neither Christ's experience of temptation nor the moral worth of his success.[31] He is praiseworthy for what he has done.

6. Conclusion

I have argued that classical Christology provides reason to reject the categorical reading of PAP. After I reviewed an essential element of classical Christology (VNC) and formulated a version of PAP that accounts for persons with one or more natures (PAP_N), I demonstrated that Christ's submission to God at Gethsemane was voluntary, morally significant, and yet, he could not have done otherwise. Therefore, PAP_N is false.

30. See Feinberg's compatibilist interpretation of Christ's impeccability in "Incarnation of Jesus Christ," 241–45.

31. Herman Bavinck is helpful on the matter of Christ's impeccability and temptations:

> Still, this is not to cancel the essential distinction between the holiness of God and the holiness of Christ as a human being. With reference to this distinction, Jesus could say that no one is good, no one is goodness itself but God alone (Matt. 19:16–17; Mark 10:17–18; Luke 18:18–19). The goodness or holiness of Christ, according to his human nature is not a divine original goodness but one that has been given, infused, and for that reason it must also—in the way of struggle and temptation—reveal, maintain, and confirm itself. The latter presupposes the former; good fruit grows on a good tree, but the soundness of the tree still has to be shown in the soundness of the fruit. Similarly, Christ had to manifest his innate holiness through temptation and struggle; this struggle is not made redundant or vain by virtue of the inability to sin (*non posse peccare*). For although real temptation could not come to Jesus from within but only from without, he nevertheless possessed a human nature, which dreaded suffering and death. Thus, throughout his life, he was tempted in all sorts of ways—by Satan, his enemies, and even by his disciples (Matt. 4:1–11; Mark 1:13; Luke 4:1–13; Matt. 12:29; Luke 11:22; Matt. 16:23; Mark 8:33). And in those temptations he was bound, fighting as he went to remain faithful; the inability to sin (*non posse peccare*) was not a matter of coercion but ethical in nature and therefore had to be manifested in an ethical manner. (Bavinck, *Reformed Dogmatics*, 3:314–15)

The implication of this chapter is that classical Christology entails the falsity of PAP libertarianism. If PAP is inconsistent with classical Christology, then PAP libertarianism is inconsistent with classical Christology. In this chapter, I have assumed neither determinism nor indeterminism; nor have I tried to explain *how* Christ's two wills always concur. I have merely shown that alternative possibilities—in the categorical sense—are not necessary for moral responsibility. It remains to be shown whether incompatibilism or compatibilism is true. For example, sourcehood incompatibilists "hold that, although moral responsibility is incompatible with determinism, moral responsibility does not require that the agent could have avoided acting as he did. On this view, what moral responsibility requires is that the agent was the ultimate originator of his act, that is, he performed the act without being in any way caused or nomically determined to perform it."[32] And, of course, compatibilists believe that freedom and moral responsibility are compatible with divine determinism.

In the next chapter, I consider whether classical Christology is consistent with Christ being ultimately responsible for his actions. In other words, I consider the sourcehood condition for libertarianism. In the following two chapters, I address the nature of VNC in order to ascertain the mechanism by which the human will is moved by the divine will.

32. Widerker, "Frankfurt-Friendly Libertarianism," 283.

5

Christ and Sourcehood

1. Introduction

In the previous chapter, I showed that classical Christology is inconsistent with a categorical reading of the principle of alternative possibilities (PAP). What I have called "PAP libertarianism," then, is ruled out if classical Christology is true. Some libertarians, however, deny that alternative possibilities are necessary for free will. Rather, they insist that free will and moral responsibility require an agent's being the ultimate source of his or her action. In this chapter, I argue that if classical Christology is true, then sourcehood libertarianism is false. The ultimate source of Christ's actions is not found in his human psychology or human nature but in God—in the divine will and decree. First, I discuss sourcehood libertarianism and the conditions needed for ultimate sourcehood. Second, I provide a definition of ultimate sourcehood that accounts for persons with one or more natures. Third, I argue that Christ is a moral agent who deserves moral praise; yet he is not the ultimate source of his actions; therefore, sourcehood libertarianism is false. Finally, I respond to three objections.

2. Sourcehood Libertarianism

Sourcehood libertarians argue that free will and moral responsibility require that the agent be the ultimate source of his or her actions. Recall that sourcehood libertarianism comes in wide and narrow varieties.[1] Wide sourcehood

1. See Timpe, *Free Will*, 141–61. Stump writes, "There are at least two species of libertarianism. Each accepts that people are responsible and that 'the past does not determine a unique future,' but one accepts and the other rejects PAP." Stump, "Alternative Possibilities and Moral Responsibility," 321.

libertarians believe that, although there is some sense in which free agency requires alternative possibilities (i.e., PAP), ultimate sourcehood is more fundamental. Narrow sourcehood libertarians deny wholesale that alternative possibilities are necessary for free agency. Although the focus of this chapter will be on narrow sourcehood libertarianism, the thesis affects all accounts of ultimate sourcehood. If it can be shown that Christ cannot meet the requirements for ultimate sourcehood, then sourcehood libertarianism is inconsistent with classical Christology. In this section, I provide an overview of sourcehood libertarianism.

2a. Freedom Without PAP

William Lane Craig is a libertarian who is convinced by Frankfurt-style counterexamples (FSCs) that the ability to do otherwise is not necessary for freedom and moral responsibility.[2] He argues that "what is essential to libertarian freedom is not the possibility of choosing otherwise but rather the absence of causal constraints outside oneself that determine how one chooses."[3] In fact, Craig believes that Christ did not have the categorical ability to do otherwise: "This understanding of libertarian freedom [i.e., sourcehood libertarianism] has the advantage that it enables us to ascribe libertarian freedom to God himself and to Christ in resisting temptation, which Boyd [i.e., the PAP libertarian, Gregory A. Boyd] cannot."[4]

Eleonore Stump is also convinced by FSCs to reject PAP. She locates ultimate sourcehood in the intellect and will. She develops a thought experiment in which the reader offers her a nickel to cut her "daughter up into little pieces."[5] She cannot imagine accepting the offer. She writes, "But that's because I can see that it's such a bad offer. I lose what is infinitely valuable to me and gain what I value almost at nothing. As long as I have these beliefs and desires, I *couldn't* accept your offer. And yet I see no reason to suppose I'm not responsible for my act of refusing it."[6] She explains that in this thought experiment and others, "The ultimate source of her action is found in her intellect and will; she does what she does only because of her own beliefs and desires, and there is no other cause of what she does. She is

2. See chapters 1 and 4 for more on FSCs and the principle of alternative possibilities (PAP).

3. Craig, "Response to Gregory A. Boyd," 225.

4. Craig, "Response to Gregory A. Boyd," 225. See Bignon's discussion in *Excusing Sinners and Blaming God*, 120–29.

5. Stump, "Alternative Possibilities and Moral Responsibility," 323.

6. Stump, "Alternative Possibilities and Moral Responsibility," 323.

therefore ultimately responsible for what she does."[7] Alternative possibilities are unnecessary. "Her intellect and will might be such that all options but one are unthinkable for her."[8]

Stump adopts Frankfurt's identification model of persons with its hierarchical structure of desires.[9] She applies this model to Jesus' prayer in Gethsemane: "Christ had a first-order desire not to die, but he also had a second-order desire for a will that willed what God willed as regards his crucifixion. His first-order desire was in opposition to God's (consequent) will. But his will was nonetheless in harmony with God's will, insofar as Christ had a second-order desire to will the good that God willed."[10] Jesus, then, "formed a first-order desire for the crucifixion" and acted upon it.[11]

Compatibilists agree with Craig and Stump that Jesus could not have done otherwise in the Garden of Gethsemane, that his action was voluntary and the product of a complex psychology, and that Jesus was responsible for his action. Compatibilists will even agree that Jesus was the source of his actions. For compatibilists, an agent can be the source of the action if, for example, the action is the one the agent wanted to perform or if the action is done for the agent's reasons.[12] We may call this "local sourcehood" or "proximate sourcehood" as opposed to ultimate sourcehood. But sourcehood libertarians, like Craig and Stump, argue further that an agent is free and morally responsible with respect to some act only when the agent is the *ultimate* source of the act.

2b. Ultimate Sourcehood and Responsibility

Ultimacy is the nonnegotiable core of sourcehood libertarianism. Free and moral action must ultimately be up to the agent. Robert Kane explains:

> *Free will*, in the traditional sense I want to retrieve . . . is *the power of agents to be the ultimate creation (or originators) and sustainers of their own ends or purposes*. . . . [T]o will freely, in this traditional sense, is to be the ultimate creator (prime mover, so to speak) of your own purposes. Such a notion of *ultimate*

7. Stump, "Alternative Possibilities and Moral Responsibility," 324.

8. Stump, "Alternative Possibilities and Moral Responsibility," 324.

9. See Frankfurt, *Importance of What We Care About*. See also my discussion in chapter 2.

10. Stump, *Atonement*, 191.

11. Stump, *Atonement*, 191.

12. See Timpe's discussion of two compatibilist accounts of sourcehood in *Free Will*, 119–40.

> creation of purposes is obscure, to be sure—many would say it is unintelligible—but there is little doubt that it has fueled intuitions about free will from the beginning. Its meaning can be captured initially by an image: when we trace the causal or explanatory chains of action back to their sources in the purposes of free agents, these causal chains must come to an end or terminate in the willings (choices, decisions, or efforts) of the agents, which cause or bring about their purposes. If these willings were in turn caused by something else, so that the explanatory chains could be traced back further to heredity or environment, to God, or fate, then the ultimacy would not lie with the agents but with something else.[13]

Determinism is incompatible with an agent's being the ultimate source of her actions because it entails that the ultimate source of the agent's actions are conditions outside herself. Linda Zagzebski explains:

> According to causal determinism the chain of causes of an act leads backwards in time to something completely outside the agent. What bothers libertarians is that it seems to follow that something outside the agent is the ultimate cause of the act, what makes it happen. And if what ultimately makes an act happen is what ultimately is responsible for it, then causal determinism seems to imply that no one is ultimately responsible for his acts.[14]

But moral responsibility, according to sourcehood libertarians, requires that the agent is the ultimate source of her actions. Michael Bergmann and J. A. Cover argue that "to be responsible for A involves being the front end of the causal chain issuing in A: S is responsible for her act A so long as the causal buck for A stops with S."[15] Kane offers a more detailed account of ultimate responsibility (UR):

> (UR) An agent is *ultimately responsible* for some (event or state) E's occurring only if (R) the agent is personally responsible for E's occurring in a sense which entails that something the agent voluntarily (or willingly) did or omitted, and for which the agent could have voluntarily done otherwise, either was, or causally contributed to, E's occurrence and made a difference to whether or not E occurred; and (U) for every X and Y (where X and Y represent occurrences of events and/or states) if the agent

13. Kane, *Significance of Free Will*, 4.

14. Zagzebski, "Does Libertarian Freedom Require Alternative Possibilities?," 231.

15. Bergmann and Cover, "Divine Responsibility Without Divine Freedom," 392.

> is personally responsible for X, and if Y is an *arche* (or sufficient ground or cause or explanation) for X, then the agent must also be personally responsible for Y.[16]

2c. *Sourcehood and Contingency*

The greatest challenge for sourcehood libertarianism is explaining how an agent's actions can be free and morally significant without alternative possibilities. PAP libertarians worry that, without alternative possibilities, an agent's choices and actions are determined or even necessary. Alternative possibilities, they argue, account for the contingency of an agent's choices and actions. Sourcehood libertarians still want to affirm that an agent's actions are contingent, but they do not appeal to alternative possibilities. Zagzebski, for example, argues that, although an agent's action may not be temporally contingent, it may be causally contingent—and causal contingency is what safeguards ultimate sourcehood, freedom, and moral responsibility. Zagzebski offers two theses: the libertarian thesis on responsibility (LTR) and the principle of causal contingency (PCC):

> LTR: An agent is morally responsible for her act only if the act is causally contingent.[17]
>
> PCC: An act A is non-determined (causally contingent) if and only if there is a possible world W in which all the events in the causal history of A in the actual world occur and in which A does not occur.[18]

Zagzebski explains, "Temporal contingency entails that the agent had alternative possibilities at the time of the act. If it is compatible with the entire past history of the world that the agent does either A or not A, then when the agent does A she could have done otherwise. Causal contingency as defined by PCC does not entail alternate possibilities."[19] She appeals to divine foreknowledge as an example that makes an action temporally necessary but causally contingent: "God's foreknowledge of my act might make it the case that I cannot do otherwise even though God's foreknowledge does not cause my act, and if my act has other determining causes, it is causally

16. Kane, *Significance of Free Will*, 35.
17. Zagzebski, "Does Libertarian Freedom Require Alternative Possibilities?," 233.
18. Zagzebski, "Does Libertarian Freedom Require Alternative Possibilities?," 232.
19. Zagzebski, "Does Libertarian Freedom Require Alternative Possibilities?," 233.

contingent."[20] Thus, on sourcehood accounts of freedom, an agent's action must not be caused by anything external to the agent for the action to be contingent.

3. Christ and Ultimate Sourcehood

The statement "Jesus Christ is the ultimate source of his own free and morally significant actions" is ambiguous because Jesus is one person with two natures: one agent with two principles of action. The nature–person distinction reminds us that the *person* is the acting subject—the agent, or the *who*. The *nature* is that which makes the thing the thing that it is—the *what*. Recall that in the previous chapter, we had to produce a formulation of PAP that accounts for persons with one or more natures:

> PAP_N: A person *P* is morally responsible for an action only if *P* could have done otherwise solely via the nature by which *P* performed that action, all things just as they are at the moment of choice.

It is necessary, therefore, to produce a formulation of ultimate sourcehood (US) that accounts for persons with one or more natures. A standard formulation of US is:

> US: A person *P* is morally responsible for an action only if *P* is the ultimate source of the action.[21]

The uniqueness of the incarnation necessitates a revised version of US that accounts for persons with one or more natures:

> US_N: A person *P* is morally responsible for an action only if the ultimate source of the action is found in the nature by which *P* performed the action.

Note that the traditional concept of a nature includes the material and/or immaterial constituents, faculties, dispositions, and powers of the object. For persons of rational natures, the thoughts, desires, intentions, and volitions belong to the person, but they occur *in* and *by* (or *through*) the nature. Thus, the thoughts of Jesus *qua* humanity are produced *by* his human nature (i.e., by his human intellect and will) and *in* his human nature (i.e., in his temporally and spatially located human mind). Timothy Pawl affirms, "Agents make volitions in virtue of their rational faculties, much

20. Zagzebski, "Does Libertarian Freedom Require Alternative Possibilities?," 233.

21. See McKenna, "Incompatibilism, Ultimacy, and the Transfer of Non-Responsibility," 40; cf. Shabo, "Uncompromising Source Incompatibilism," 365.

as it is agents that see in virtue of their eyes, optic nerves, and relevant portions of their brains."[22] Because Christ has two sets of rational faculties (i.e., human and divine), we need to isolate his human rational faculties. US_N is a superior formulation than US because, in this case, it eliminates all factors outside the humanity of Christ—which is the subject in question.

In the following section, I argue that if US_N is true, then Christ is not morally responsible for his actions because Christ is not the *ultimate* source of his actions. The ultimate source of Christ's human actions is God—his divine will and decree. But Christ is, indeed, morally responsible for his actions; therefore, US_N is false. Ultimate sourcehood is not necessary for moral responsibility. And, therefore, sourcehood libertarianism is false.

I shall begin by considering the biblical witness to the human agency of Jesus Christ and to the moral significance of his choices and actions. Then, I argue that the ultimate source of Jesus' actions is the divine will. Of course, Jesus Christ is God, so he *is* the ultimate source of his human actions in the broader sense. But we are concerned with the narrower sense—Christ according to his humanity. I respond to this difficulty and other objections in the last section of the chapter.

4. Christ the Moral Agent and Exemplar

In the previous chapters, I have taken Christ's status as a moral exemplar for granted, more or less. I have presupposed that anyone who holds to classical Christology would also hold to Christ's moral agency and character. This presupposition is common to the Reformed tradition. For example, Jonathan Edwards writes, "If there be any truth in Christianity or the holy Scriptures, the man Christ Jesus had his will infallibly, unalterably and unfrustrably determined to good, and that alone; but yet he had promises of glorious rewards made to him, on condition of his persevering in, and perfecting the work which God had appointed (Is. 53:10, 11, 12; Ps. 2 and 110; Is. 49:7, 8, 9)."[23] Here, I provide a fuller treatment of Christ's moral praiseworthiness.

4a. *Christ* Qua *Humanity Is Free and Morally Praiseworthy*

Remember that we are concerned with Christ *qua* humanity, i.e., Christ according to his choices and actions in and through his human nature. To say

22. Pawl, *In Defense of Extended Conciliar Christology*, 124.
23. Edwards, *Freedom of the Will*, 289–90.

that Christ *qua* divinity is morally responsible is true only by analogy.[24] For one to be morally responsible requires that one has someone or something *to which* one is responsible. In the case of human creatures, they are morally responsible and accountable to God. In the case of God, however, there is no one or thing to which God is responsible or held accountable. Likewise, in the case of human creatures, they are given moral laws by a higher moral authority—a Lawgiver. But in the case of God, there is no higher moral authority; he is the Lawgiver. Therefore, to say that God or Christ *qua* divinity is morally responsible *by analogy* is to say that God is a good and ethical being. He acts consistently with objective morality (because he, himself, is the source and standard of morality). And, if he were a human creature, he would act in such a way as to be morally praiseworthy in a univocal sense—and that is exactly the case with Christ *qua* humanity. Because Jesus is the perfect image of God in creation, what is true of God's morality *analogically* is true of Christ's morality *univocally*.

4b. Christ Is a Moral Agent

Christ had significant freedom during his earthly life. He was the local (but not ultimate) source of his actions, and he engaged in the intellectual and volitional activity we associate with freedom. Jesus had wisdom and knowledge (Matt 9:4; Luke 2:52). He reasoned and made arguments (Mark 12:24–27). The Bible says Jesus desired (Mark 9:30), chose (John 6:70), decided (John 1:43), willed (Matt 8:3), and made plans for the future (Matt 26:17–19).[25] His prayer in Gethsemane revealed that he has a complex set of desires (Matt 26:36–46).[26] Jesus willingly does the will of his Father; he

24. See Morris, *Anselmian Explorations*, 26–41.

25. Most of these references contain the root verbs θέλω or ἐκλέγομαι.

26. Stump interprets Jesus' experience in Gethsemane on a Frankfurtian hierarchy of desire:

> We can see Aquinas' point here by understanding Christ's will during his prayer in terms of the hierarchical structure of the will. On this understanding, Christ had a first-order desire not to die, but he also had a second-order desire for a will that willed what God willed as regards his crucifixion. His first-order desire was in opposition to God's (consequent) will. But his will was nonetheless in harmony with God's will, insofar as Christ had a second-order desire to will the good that God willed.
>
> If, contrary to the story in the Gospels, Christ had let his first-order desire override his second-order desire, then his will would not have been in conformity with God's will. In that case, Christ's first-order desire not to die would have been the will on which he acted; and his

says, "For this reason the Father loves me, because I lay down my life that I may take it up again. No one takes it from me, but I lay it down of my own accord. I have authority to lay it down, and I have authority to take it up again. This charge I have received from my Father" (John 10:17–18). Far from being unfree, Jesus is the very source of freedom. Those who practice sin are slaves to sin, but Jesus teaches: "The slave does not remain in the house forever; the son remains forever. So if the Son sets you free, you will be free indeed" (John 8:35–36).

For this and similar reasons, the church has taught that Christ's human nature was a composite of body and rational soul—a rational soul distinct from the divine Logos. Moreover, the church has taught that Christ's human nature was complete with its own volition and operation. The Son was like us yet without sin. In whatever way humans were created such that they have the faculties and conditions for freedom, the Son was made in that same way.

4c. Christ Is Praised for His Obedience

Christ was perfectly obedient in his life and death (Phil 2:8; Heb 2:10; 5:8–9; 7:26–28). Christ's obedience is considered righteousness. For example, "Therefore, as one trespass led to condemnation for all men, so one act of righteousness leads to justification and life for all men. For as by the one

---

> second-order desire, that God's will take precedence over his own, would have remained ineffectual. While he would have desired to have a will that willed what God wills, the will that was effectual in him and on which he acted would have been his first-order desire, which was in opposition to what God wills. In the case in the story as it actually is in the Gospels, however, Christ let his will be governed by his second-order desire that God's will be done. In the course of his praying, in the story it became clear to Christ that God's will then was that Christ be crucified. Given this recognition and the second-order desire for a will to will what God wills, Christ formed a first-order desire for the crucifixion. When Christ finished his prayer, he acted on that first-order desire; and so Christ acted in accordance with God's will. In the struggle with his first-order desire not to be crucified, Christ's will was in conformity with God's will. This is so even though Christ continued to have a first-order desire not to be crucified. That first-order desire was present but ineffective to govern Christ's subsequent actions. Although Christ continued to want not to be crucified, that desire was not the one on which Christ acted. (Stump, *Atonement*, 191)

That Stump's Frankfurtian reading of Christ's human psychology seems plausible is evidence that Christ is a moral agent and that he meets the requirements of (at least local) sourcehood: Christ *qua* humanity identifies with his own will.

man's disobedience the many were made sinners, so by the one man's obedience the many will be made righteous" (Rom 5:18–19). The Bible repeatedly calls Jesus "righteous" and "just" (δικαιος) (Acts 3:14; 2 Tim 4:8; 1 Pet 3:18). He is also called "holy" (ὅσιος; ἅγιος) (Acts 2:27; 3:14; 1 Pet 3:15), "pure" (ἁγνός) (1 John 3:3), "good" (χρηστός) (Titus 3:4; 1 Pet 2:3), "worthy" (ἄξιος) (Heb 3:3; Rev 4:11; 5:9–12), "true" (ἀληθινός) (1 John 5:20; Rev 19:11), and "faithful" (πιστὸς) (2 Thess 3:3; Heb 2:17; Rev 19:11). Jesus fulfilled the law (Matt 5:17) and always did what is *pleasing* to the Father (ἀρεστός) (John 8:29).

4d. Christ Is Rewarded for His Obedience

Jesus Christ is rewarded for his obedience. He is the Son of God from all eternity. It was fitting that he, as Son, should be sent into the world to succeed where others of God's "sons" had failed. Adam, the first son of God (Luke 3:38), made in God's image (Gen 1:26–27), disobeyed (Gen 3:1–7). The nation Israel was God's son (Hos 11:1), but Israel repeatedly went after other gods. King David was the son of God (2 Sam 7:14), yet he failed, too. Jesus, the new and better Adam (Rom 5:12–21), the true Israel (Hos 11:1; Matt 2:15), the Davidic king (Rom 1:3), the perfect image (Col 1:15; Heb 1:3) succeeds in perfect obedience. Because of his obedience, "God has highly exalted him" (Phil 2:9; cf. Acts 2:33; 5:30–31). He earned his name, title, and role as the incarnate Son of God by his obedience: "[he] was descended from David according to the flesh and was declared to be the Son of God in power according to the Spirit of holiness by his resurrection from the dead, Jesus Christ our Lord" (Rom 1:3–4) and was given "the name that is above every name" (Phil 2:9). His obedience unto death made him worthy: "Worthy are you to take the scroll and to open its seals, for you were slain" (Rev 5:9).

4e. Christians Are Commanded to Imitate Christ

Christians are commanded to imitate Christ. The christological hymn in Philippians 2:6–11 is preceded by Paul's exhortation that we be like Christ: "Have this mind among yourselves, which is yours in Christ Jesus" (Phil 2:5). We are to imitate Christ's humility and obedience. Elsewhere, Paul writes, "Be imitators of me, as I am of Christ" (1 Cor 11:1). Jesus, himself, taught us to follow him (Matt 19:21; Mark 1:17; John 8:12). And he said, "It is enough for the disciple to be like his teacher, and the servant his master" (Matt 10:25). Indeed, it was God's plan from all eternity that we might be "conformed to the image of his Son" (Rom 8:29) and that we should be like him in his death and resurrection (Rom 6:5; Phil 3:10–11; 1 John 3:2).

5. Christ and the Ultimate Source

I have shown that Christ *qua* humanity is a moral agent that, at least, has the faculties required for local sourcehood, namely, an intellect and will. Christ is praised and rewarded for his obedience, and Christians are called to imitate him in his obedience. Classical Christology holds that Christ is a morally responsible agent. But Christ, *qua* humanity, is not the *ultimate* source of his actions. We know that Jesus according to his humanity is not the ultimate source of his actions from his own teaching, the definite plan of God, and the relationship between the two wills of Christ.

I argue that if classical Christology is true, then sourcehood libertarianism is false. Because Jesus according to his humanity is a true moral agent but not the ultimate source of his actions, being the ultimate source of one's actions is not necessary for moral responsibility.

Jesus affirms that he is not the ultimate source of his actions when he says, "Truly, truly, I say to you, the Son can do nothing of his own accord, but only what he sees the Father doing. For whatever the Father does, the Son does likewise" (John 5:19); "For I have come down from heaven, not to do my own will but the will of him who sent me" (John 6:38); "I do nothing on my own authority, but speak just as the Father taught me. And he who sent me is with me. He has not left me alone, for I always do the things that are pleasing to him" (John 8:28–29).

Jesus recognized that his earthly life was sustained and directed by God. For example, when he was tempted by Satan to turn stones into bread, Jesus responded by saying that it is God who preserves life: "Man shall not live by bread alone, but by every word that comes from the mouth of God" (Matt 4:4). He knew that his life and ministry were ordained by God. After reading from the scroll of Isaiah in the synagogue, knowing that he is the prophesied Messiah, he said, "Today this Scripture has been fulfilled in your hearing" (Luke 4:21). Likewise, when Jesus was betrayed, he said, "But all this has taken place that the Scriptures of the prophets might be fulfilled" (Matt 26:56). Jesus' life was prepared beforehand and governed by divine providence.

Jesus also taught the principle that a son does what his father does. The Pharisees are slaves to sin because their father is the devil—a liar and murderer. Jesus explains, "I speak of what I have seen with my Father, and you do what you have heard from your father" (John 8:38). Jesus is so identified with the work of the Father that Jesus can say, "If God were your Father, you would love me, for I came from God and I am here. I came not of my own accord, but he sent me" (John 8:42). Indeed, "I and the Father are one" (John 10:30). Jesus' works are ultimately the works of the Father: "If I am not doing the works of my Father, then do not believe me; but if I do them, even though you do not believe me, believe the works, that you may know and understand the Father is in me and I am in the Father" (John 10:37–38).

The Bible teaches that the life, death, and resurrection were part of God's plan from eternity. For example, "this Jesus, delivered up according to the definite plan and foreknowledge of God, you crucified and killed by the hands of lawless men" (Acts 2:23). Paul was given the grace to preach "and to bring to light for everyone what is the plan of the mystery hidden for ages in God, who created all things. . . . This was according to the eternal purpose that he realized in Christ Jesus our Lord" (Eph 3:9, 10). Notice that this plan constituted an eternal purpose *in God* and realized in Jesus.

For these reasons and more, the church has taught that Christ is one person subsisting in two natures. And Christ's human nature is a composite of body and rational soul. And Christ's rational soul is complete with an intellect and will. And, thus, in Christ, there are

> two natural volitions or wills in him and two natural principles of action which undergo no division, no change, no partition, no confusion, in accordance with the teaching of the holy fathers. And the two natural wills not in opposition, as the impious heretics said, far from it, but his human will following, and not resisting or struggling, rather in fact subject to his divine and all powerful will. For the will of the flesh had to be moved, and yet to be subjected to the divine will, according to the most wise Athanasius.[27]

Christ's human will is not ultimate; his divine will is ultimate. The human will was moved by the divine will. Christ *qua* humanity cannot satisfy the conditions of US_N. Therefore, Christ *qua* humanity is not the ultimate source of his actions.

6. Objections

I have argued that if classical Christology is true, then sourcehood libertarianism is false. Because Jesus is a true moral agent but not the ultimate source of his actions, being the ultimate source of one's actions is not necessary for moral responsibility. Now, I consider three objections.

27. Tanner, *Decrees of the Ecumenical* Councils, 128.

6a. Objection About US_N

One might deny that US_N is the relevant formulation of US. Because Jesus Christ is one person, he is one moral agent. Whenever the Son acts *qua* humanity, it is still the Son acting. The ultimate source of all of Jesus' choices and actions is Jesus himself. Therefore, according to this objection, the relevant formulation of US is simply US: a person *P* is morally responsible for an action only if *P* is the ultimate source of the action.

I gladly affirm that the Son is the ultimate source of the Son's human actions. Scripture and historical orthodoxy affirm it, too. But to appeal to US rather than US_N in the context of Jesus' human freedom is infelicitous. Although the Son is true God, eternally generated from the Father, his humanity is created. Thus, his human nature and human life are on the creature side of the Creator–creature distinction. His humanity is ruled by divine purpose and providence. Therefore, the matter of Christ's human freedom must be considered *under* divine purpose and providence—not *over* it.

Furthermore, US_N is appropriate because even incompatibilists affirm it. Indeed, all the ink spilled attempting to defend a libertarian account of Christ's freedom is proof that US_N is appropriate. For example, Iesu Solano and J. A. Aldama defend the thesis that "The human will of Christ, even in suffering death, was free from necessity."[28] And Timothy Pawl defends "The Human Freedom Thesis," which states, "Christ, by virtue of his assumed human will, was free."[29] There is no doubt that these theologians and philosophers would say that God himself is free in a libertarian sense. The fact that these incompatibilists have to make the additional point that Christ *qua* humanity is free warrants the isolation of Christ's humanity in US_N.

6b. Objection About Nestorianism

The next objection is also related to US_N. Someone might charge US_N with Nestorianism because it bifurcates Christ into two persons by applying freedom to the natures rather than the person. If we have to consider Christ's human nature and freedom apart from his person, so the objection goes, then we are treating Christ's human nature as its own person—which is Nestorianism.

28. Solano and Aldama, *On the Incarnate Word*, 193.

29. Pawl, *In Defense of Extended Conciliar Christology*, 123. Interestingly, Pawl's definition of free will does not appeal to alternative possibilities. For Pawl, free will is "the set of capacities an agent has which allow her to control her volitions, the exercise of which is necessary for the agent to be morally responsible for those volitions." Pawl, *In Defense of Extended Conciliar Christology*, 124.

I deny that US_N or anything I have argued is Nestorian. I have argued that the one person is the acting subject—the agent—who deserves moral praise or blame. There is one person—Jesus Christ, the Son of God—who acts through two natures: human and divine. I have argued that Christ *qua* humanity (or "Christ's humanity" as a shorthand) is not the ultimate source of his actions. The *communicatio idiomatum* teaches that the predicates of Christ according to either nature is rightly applied to the person of Christ. Therefore, it is right to say both that Christ is and is not the ultimate source of his human actions. He is the ultimate source of his human actions *qua* divinity, but he is not the ultimate source *qua* humanity.

In fact, my position preserves Chalcedonian Christology better than the incompatibilist alternative. To deny that Christ *qua* humanity is the ultimate source of his human actions is further from Nestorianism than to affirm it. My position is that the ultimate source of Christ's human action is found in the Godhead, but the incompatibilist must say that the ultimate source of Christ's human action is found outside the Godhead and in creation. The incompatibilist must say that Christ has two ultimate sources—one for his divine actions and one for his human actions—and this concession seems more in danger of making Christ two persons.[30]

6c. *Objection About Cause*

One might object that I have not provided sufficient evidence that Jesus' choices and actions were *caused* by the divine will and decree. There may have been causal contingency in Jesus' life. If Jesus' choices and actions were not caused by external factors, including the divine will, then, perhaps, he is the ultimate source of his actions after all.

Although I have provided much evidence that Christ *qua* humanity is not the ultimate source of his actions, I have not proven that his actions were caused by the divine will—only subject to and directed by it. The matter of the precise relation between Christ's human and divine wills is complex and too large for this chapter. In the next chapter, I shall argue that Christ's human will is, indeed, caused by the divine will. Because his human will is caused by the divine will, there is no causal contingency in the sense that Zagzebski describes. Thus, Christ *qua* humanity is not the ultimate source of his human actions.

30. I shall discuss the unity of Christ's person on incompatibilist and compatibilist models in further detail in the next chapter.

7. Conclusion

In this chapter, I have argued that if classical Christology is true, then sourcehood libertarianism is false. In the previous chapter, I argued that if classical Christology is true, then PAP libertarianism is false. Therefore, if classical Christology is true, then libertarianism *simpliciter* is false. I have not shown, however, that Christ's human will was caused by the divine will; and I have not shown that Christ's human will was determined in any sense. In the following two chapters, I consider the matter of causation and determinism more closely.

6

Christ, Movement, and Causation

1. Introduction

In the previous two chapters, I considered the elements undergirding the two prominent varieties of libertarianism: alternative possibilities and sourcehood. I have shown that libertarianism is inconsistent with classical Christology. I have done so without an appeal to theological determinism or divine causality, though I have appealed to the priority of the divine will over the human will of Christ. In this and the next chapter, I consider the matters of determinism and divine causality more closely.[1] Recall that hard determinism is the thesis that (1) freedom and moral responsibility are incompatible with determinism, and (2) determinism is true. I argue that hard determinism is inconsistent with classical Christology.

This chapter is split into two main sections. In the first section, I examine the nature of the harmony between Christ's two wills, i.e., the doctrine of volitional non-contrariety (VNC). I assess what it means for Constantinople III to claim that Christ's human will had to be *moved*. A survey of Maximus the Confessor's teaching demonstrates that Christ's human will being moved is consistent with his human self-determination. If being moved by God amounts to being determined by God, then hard determinism is false.

In the second section, I evaluate several models of concurrence between Christ's wills, including the Parameter Model, the Molinist Model, the Beatific Vision Model, and the Causal Model. I argue that the Causal Model is best; the way in which Christ's human will was moved was by divine causation.

In the following chapter, I consider whether that causal movement of Christ's human will should be understood deterministically. I evaluate

1. A version of this chapter appears in Johnson, "On the Harmony of Christ's Wills."

a model of divine causation that affirms divine universal causality without determinism. I argue, however, that when God causes something, it is determined. Thus, when God *moves* Jesus to act in a particular way, Jesus is determined to act in that way.

2. To Be Moved and Self-Determined

Classical Christology maintains that Christ has two wills and that his two wills are never contrary to each other according to their object. There is debate, however, over the nature of their harmony.[2] It seems either the two wills are parallel—terminating on the same object (merely) by virtue of being hypostasized by the one divine Logos; or, the wills are subordinated—the divine will causing (or *moving*) the human will to terminate on the same object. In this section, I interpret Constantinople III in light of the theology of Maximus the Confessor, the champion of dyothelitism during the monothelite controversy in the AD 600s.[3] I argue that Christ's having self-determination is compatible with his being moved and subject to the divine will.

2a. The Third Council of Constantinople

The Third Council of Constantinople teaches that Christ's two wills are not "in opposition, as the impious heretics said, far from it, but his human will following, and not resisting or struggling, rather in fact subject to his divine and all powerful will."[4] The most contentious passage proceeds: "For the will of the flesh had to be moved, and yet to be subjected to the divine will (ἔδει γὰρ τὸ τῆς σαρκὸς θέλημα κινηθῆναι, ὑποταγῆναι δὲ τῷ θελήματι τῷ θεϊκῷ; *Oportebat enim carnis voluntatem moveri, subiici vero voluntati divinae*)."[5] The verb "κινηθῆναι" ("to be moved") is the first aorist passive infinitive, and its translation is debated. If it is translated in the passive voice, then it asserts that God had to move the human will. A passive voice translation is harder to reconcile with libertarianism. If, however, the verb is translated in the middle voice, then it asserts that the human will had to move itself. A middle voice translation is more amenable to libertarianism.

2. See Bathrellos' overview of this debate in *Byzantine Christ*, 162–74.

3. For a history of the monothelite controversy leading up to the Third Council of Constantinople, see Davis, *First Seven Ecumenical Councils*, 258–89.

4. Tanner, *Decrees of the Ecumenical Councils*, 128.

5. Tanner, *Decrees of the Ecumenical Councils*, 128.

2b. The Middle Voice Sense

Iesu Solano and J. A. de Aldama argue that "the sense of the middle voice is both grammatically permitted and from its opposition to the following verb ὑποταγῆναι δὲ it is required. Therefore the exact version is: for it was necessary that the will of the flesh move itself, but also that it be submitted to the divine will . . . ."[6] Timothy Pawl, commenting on the conclusions of Aldama and Solano, writes, "If that's the case, if the will is moving itself, and not merely being moved—that takes most of the steam out of the argument that this passage implies that Christ's human will was not free due to its being pulled around by the divine will."[7]

Aldama and Solano are correct that "κινηθῆναι" may be translated in the sense of the middle voice. But when it is so understood, it is not reflexive but used "As an expression of being a living being [e.g.,] ἐν αὐτῷ ζῶμεν καὶ κινούμεθα καὶ ἐσμέν *in him we live and move and have our being* **Ac 17:28**."[8] Indeed, Athanasius, the one to whom this teaching about movement is attributed, cites Acts 17:28 in the context of the Logos moving both the universe and his humanity: "Therefore it is not at all unfitting for the Word to be in a human being, and that by him and in him all things are illumined and move [κινεῖσθαι] and live."[9] And according to Maximus, all creatures

6. Solano and Aldama, *On the Incarnate Word*, 183.

7. Pawl, *In Defense of Extended Conciliar Christology*, 131.

8. "κινέω," *BDAG* (bold in the original).

9. Athanasius, *On the Incarnation*, 42. It is important to note that Constantinople III appeals to the teachings of "the most wise Athanasius" for the claim that "the will of the flesh had to be moved, and yet to be subjected to the divine will." Tanner indicates that the fathers referred to a now-lost tract on the text "now my spirit is troubled," in *Decrees of the Ecumenical Councils*, 128. Of course, appealing to Athanasius is difficult because he did not have as developed a Christology as Maximus. Athanasius maintained a Word–flesh model of the incarnation which obscured the will issue. For example, Athanasius writes, "For he was not enclosed in the body, nor was he in the body but not elsewhere. Nor while he moved [ἐκίνει] that [body] was the universe left void of his activity and providence." Athanasius, *On the Incarnation*, 17. And later, he writes,

> For if it were completely absurd for him to be in a body, it would be absurd for him to come into the whole, and illumine and move [κινεῖν] all things by his own providence, for the universe is also a body. But if it is fitting for him to come into the cosmos and to be made known in the universe, it would also be fitting for him to appear in a human body and that it should be illumined and moved [ἐνεργεὶν] by him. For the human race is part of the whole, and if the part is unsuitable to be his instrument towards the knowledge of his divinity, it would be most absurd that he should be made known even through the whole cosmos. . . . [O]ne who grants and believes the Word of God to be in all, and that all is illumined and moved [κινεῖσθαι] by him, should not think it absurd that a single

move and are moved. He defines "motion as that which manifesteth," and "passion as that which is moved."[10] He explains, "For all things that are from God and after God change by motion, for they are not self-moved beings of omnipotent power."[11] Therefore, the middle sense would be "move" not "move itself."

Aldama and Solano provide further support for their "move itself" translation. They appeal to a discourse read at Constantinople III which confirmed that Christ, according to his humanity, has an essential will by which he has the power of free will. Aldama and Solano comment, "The human will of Christ is defined by the Fathers to be so *voluntary* that it is also understood as *free*."[12] Because Aldama and Solano presuppose that "to be moved" is incompatible with free will, they beg the question. This evidence, then, is no more reason for affirming their translation ("move itself") than for affirming the passive translation ("to be moved").

Finally, even if somehow "to be moved" is the best translation, the burden shifts to translating both "ὑποταγῆναι" and "κινηθῆναι" under the constraint of "ἔδει." The passive tense of "ὑποταγῆναι" could have the traditional passive sense of "to become subject," or the middle sense of "to subject oneself" or even "to obey."[13] Again, the middle sense seems more amenable to libertarianism. But even if "to obey" is the best translation, this obedience is constrained by necessity (ἔδει). Christ *had* to obey.

2c. The Passive Voice Sense

Many interpreters of Maximus, however, follow the passive ("to be moved") translation. For example, Demetrios Bathrellos interprets Maximus as teaching that the human will had to be moved by the divine will—but first,

---

> human body should be moved [κινεῖσθαι] and illumined by him. (Athanasius, *On the Incarnation*, 41)

Because Athanasius does not have a clear distinction between the divine and human wills of Christ, his language of "movement" seems to pertain to the Logos moving the human body, not the human will.

10. Maximus, *Disputation with Pyrrhus*, 214.

11. Maximus, *Disputation with Pyrrhus*, 214.

12. Aldama and Solano, *On the Incarnate Word*, 183. They cite J. D. Mansi, *Sacrorum Conciliorum nova et amplissima collection*, 11,663, for the following quotation: "For if we were to say that the human nature of the Lord is without a will and without activity, how can the perfection of his humanity be saved? For nothing else constitutes the integrity of the human substance, except the essential will, by which the power of free will in us is designated; also the same is said of his substantial operation."

13. See "ὑποτάσσω," *BDAG*.

Christ consented to be moved. He sees an analogy in Maximus's writing about the wills of the saints and Christ's human will. He writes, "the movement of the saints by God presupposes the personal consent of those who are moved. God does not move the saints without their personal consent."[14] He summarizes, "By obeying the Father, Christ did something similar to what the saints also do, by allowing themselves to be moved by God in imitation of Christ."[15] It is possible for saints and Christ to be subject to the divine will "because they will have handed over their self-determinative power (αὐτεξούσιον) willingly to God, and they will will nothing but what God wills."[16] Jesus' prayer in Gethsemane is the paragon of Christ's human obedience:

> The acceptance of the cup is the apex of the soteriologically indispensable human obedience of the Son to the divine will of the Father, which is identical with his own divine will. To say in this context that the human will of Christ was moved by the divine will would invalidate the whole point. For it goes without saying that obedience presupposes as a *conditio sine qua non* the self-determining personal acceptance on the part of him who obeys—that is, on the part of Christ as man—of the desire of the will which is obeyed.[17]

According to Bathrellos's interpretation, Christ's obedience at Gethsemane is first and foremost Christ's self-determined consent to the will of the Father because obedience presupposes that his human will was not moved by the divine will.

Although Bathrellos accepts a passive translation ("to be moved"), he also begs the question by assuming the truth of incompatibilism in his interpretation of Maximus. For Bathrellos, Christ's human obedience (i.e., moral responsibility) and self-determination (i.e., free agency) are incompatible with God moving his human will. He writes, "Maximus's claim that Christ obeyed the Father to the point of death, . . . by willing whatever God wills, makes sense only if this obedience of Christ to the Father was self-determiningly undertaken by him as man."[18] For Bathrellos, then, self-determination is tantamount to libertarianism.

14. Bathrellos, *Byzantine Christ*, 170.
15. Bathrellos, *Byzantine Christ*, 170.
16. Bathrellos, *Byzantine Christ*, 170.
17. Bathrellos, *Byzantine Christ*, 171.
18. Bathrellos, *Byzantine Christ*, 171. Perhaps even more clearly, he writes,

> If we were to say that it is the divinity or the divine will that moves the human will without at the same time stressing that the Logos as man allows

2d. Self-Determination and Being Moved

Constantinople III and the teachings of Maximus the Confessor cannot be understood properly if incompatibilism is presupposed. Ian A. McFarland demonstrates that Maximus rejected libertarianism. He writes, "In stark contrast to libertarian views, freedom of the will for Maximus is an expression *of* human nature rather than a power *over* it that puts us in conflict both with our natures and with the God who created them."[19] For Maximus, movement is simply a part of what it means to be a creature. "All creatures move, but the movement of human beings is free because humans are rational—and therefore willing-creatures."[20] Therefore, "Plants are distinguished by the property of a productive and growing motion, the sentient by the motion caused by impulse, but the rational by self-determination."[21] Self-determination *just is* having a rational will. Maximus writes:

> his human will to be moved by them in an act of obedience, not only the whole point of the obedience of the Son to the Father, but also the self-determination of the human will of the Son, both of which Maximus insists upon so strongly, would be nullified. On the contrary, by emphasizing that the Logos as God wills by his divine will and as man obeys the divine will by his human will, the self-determination of the human will is secured. (Bathrellos, *Byzantine Christ*, 174)

19. McFarland, "Theology of the Will," 1.

20. McFarland, "Theology of the Will," 5; cf. John Damascene:

> But that volition is implanted in man by nature is manifest from this. Excluding the divine life, there are three forms of life: the vegetative, the sentient, and the intellectual. The properties of the vegetative life are the functions of nourishment, and growth, and production: that of the sentient life is impulse: and that of the rational and intellectual life is freedom of will. If, then, nourishment belongs by nature to the vegetative life and impulse to the sentient, freedom of will by nature belongs to the rational and intellectual life. But freedom of will is nothing else than volition. The Word, therefore, having become flesh, endowed with life and mind and free-will, became also endowed with volition. (John Damascene, *De Fide Orthodoxa* 3:14)

21. Maximus, *Disputation with Pyrrhus*, 49. Likewise, Thomas Aquinas writes,

> It is proper to an instrument to be moved by the principal agent, yet diversely, according to the property of its nature. For an inanimate instrument, as an axe or a saw, is moved by the craftsman with only a corporeal movement; but an instrument animated by a sensitive soul is moved by the sensitive appetite, as a horse by its rider; and an instrument animated with a rational soul is moved by its will, as by the command of his lord the servant is moved to act, the servant being like an animate instrument, as the Philosopher says (Polit. i, 2,4; Ethic. viii, 11). And hence it was in

> If man be the image of the divine nature, and the divine nature be self-determining, then so is the image; since the image preserveth its likeness to the archetype, it too must be self-determining by nature. And if Christ is become both the archetype and the image by nature, then the same Person, subsisting in both His natures possesseth also the will proper to both natures. For it hath been demonstrated previously out of the Fathers that the will is the self-determination proper to [a rational] nature.[22]

Self-determination is not characterized by *choosing* but by *willing*. For Maximus, "freedom is fully and perfectly realized when rational beings will according to their natures, without the need for deliberation."[23] McFarland summarizes:

> Thus, where a monothelite like Pyrrhus could see no alternative between libertarian freedom on the one hand and the compulsion of nature on the other, Maximus insisted that "in a rational nature, nothing natural is involuntary." Even as God's infinite goodness is not any less an expression of divine freedom because God by nature cannot be otherwise than good, so the

---

> this manner that the human nature of Christ was the instrument of the Godhead, and was moved by its own will. (*ST* III, q. 18, a. 1, ad 2.)

22. Maximus, *Disputation with Pyrrhus*, 138.

23. McFarland, "Theology of the Will," 8. Harry Austryn Wolfson shows how Maximus understood Christ's freedom and necessity:

> Now, argues Maximus, necessity in the sense of acting under compulsion is the opposite of freedom, but necessity in the sense of acting in accordance with one's own nature and without any compulsion is the highest kind of freedom. This kind of freedom which follows from the necessity of one's own nature, he continues his argument, differs from the freedom of choice which is ordinarily attributed by philosophers to me, for freedom of choice implies a decision between two conflicting natures in the agent, whereas freedom which follows from the necessity of one's own nature implies no conflict of natures in the agent, and this is either of two sense, either because there is in the agent only one nature, as in the case of God, or because the two natures in the agent are always in harmony with each other, as was the case of Jesus. It is this highest kind of freedom in the first sense, he concludes, that God is said to possess when he is said to act in accordance with His own simple nature and similarly it is this highest kind of freedom in the second sense that Jesus is said to have possessed when he is said to have acted always in accordance with the will of the divine nature within him, with which the will of the human nature within him always harmonized. (Wolfson, *Philosophy of the Church Fathers*, 486)

> defining characteristics of human nature are rightly understood as expression of freedom rather than as a sign of limitations.[24]

Thomas Watts, likewise, understands Maximus to be a compatibilist with respect to Christ's human self-determination and God's moving. "Maximus insists that the natural will is free, not compelled. . . . He holds that true freedom is not the ability to choose anything at all, but the natural inclination towards what is good without ignorance or hesitation."[25] Watts sees Maximus' teaching on self-determination as consistent with God's moving. He explains that the human will

> is self-determining in the sense that there can be no direct action on a person's will by another person. All action on a person's will is mediated via the person. The will is actualized only in the person in which it subsists. . . . Rational creatures act normally *without* external impulse, whereas irrational creatures act only *with* external impulse. Self-determination in this sense is consistent with the idea of a will that is bound to act according to the nature in which it inheres.[26]

Self-determination does not nullify God's moving the will. "Jesus actively obeys as man, maintaining the self-determination of the human will, yet acting according to the natural inclination of the will towards God. The idea that Jesus' human will is superfluous because Jesus' flesh and will was moved by the Logos was rightly attacked by Maximus as Nestorian."[27]

Because Maximus taught that human self-determination is compatible with being moved by God, we ought to interpret Constantinople III in this light. The proper way to move rational creatures is not through compulsion

24. McFarland, "Theology of the Will," 13.

25. Watts, "Two Wills in Christ?," 469.

26. Watts, "Two Wills in Christ?," 476. In footnote 107, Watts claims that Maximus' view of the will is similar to Jonathan Edwards' view. He writes,

> Thus Maximus differs from Edwards only in terminology at this point. Against the Arminian position, Edwards argues that the will is not self-determining in order to make the point that it is not itself free to choose; rather, it is the vehicle by which the mind chooses that to which the soul is inclined (see, e.g., Edwards, *Freedom of the Will*, 2.2 [175–79]). Maximus makes the same point by arguing that the will is itself natural, and does not stand over nature; it is free to follow the inclinations of the nature in which it inheres. Yet he then uses the idea of self-determination in a different sense . . . to make the point that the will is only actualized in the person in which it naturally subsists. (Watts, "Two Wills in Christ?," 476n107)

27. Watts, "Two Wills in Christ?," 477.

but through their rational volition. To be moved is to will; and to will is to be self-determined. Pyrrhus, Maximus' disputant, rightly affirms "that the same [person, the Son] willed in a manner appropriate to each of His natures: on the one hand, determining as God, and on the other, obeying as man."[28] Thus, Christ's human self-determination is compatible with his being moved and subjected to the divine will.

3. Models of Volitional Non-Contrariety

God moves Christ's human will. It remains to be shown that the divine will causes or even determines the human will. Pawl argues, for instance, that the councils are underdetermined on the relationship between Christ's wills. He explains:

> The councils are not explicit on what amount of control the divine will employs over the human will. There are multiple interpretations one could give, and not all of them require complete docility of the human will. Perhaps the divine will subjects the human will by means of putting parameters on the sorts of activities the human will could will. Moreover, perhaps the human will does not resist or struggle against the parameters. Perhaps the moving of the human will that the divine will engages in is putting the human will in the position to have such parameters in place.[29]

In what follows, I evaluate several models of VNC according to their theological integrity and coherence. Four models that fit *prima facie* with VNC are the Parameter Model, the Beatific Vision Model, the Molinist Model, and the Causal Model.

3a. The Parameter Model of VNC

In his response to the objection that dyothelitism and VNC somehow threaten to diminish Christ's human mind, Pawl offers the following argument:

> Suppose the divine will just sets parameters around some activities of the human will. It is, say, similar to a parent teaching a

28. Maximus, *Disputation with Pyrrhus*, 56.

29. Pawl, *In Defense of Extended Conciliar Christology*, 129–30. It is important to note that Pawl does not reduce the divine will to mere moral commands. Whatever the relation between Christ's human and divine will, the language of Constantinople III, *prima facie*, "sounds like the wrong sort of situation to be in to be free." Pawl, *In Defense of Extended Conciliar Christology*, 126.

> child to walk. The child is doing the walking, but the parent is ready to swoop in and catch the child, were he to begin falling. In such a case, the child's power to walk (or legs) have observable consequences in the life of the child. The child could be, after a bit of training, an exemplar for teaching other little kids how to walk (were toddlers the sort of beasts who paid any attention to the exemplars their parents wish them to copy). The analogy is not important here, though. What is important is that whether or not the powers of the human desires are vanishingly small, whether the powers and mind threaten to disappear, whether the mind has observable consequences, and whether the exemplary role evaporates all depends upon the theory of subjection one embraces.[30]

Pawl's point is that one's model of dyothelitism and VNC need not diminish Christ's human mind. A model that preserves Christ's human intelligence, volition, and agency, and rejects compulsion and coercion does not undermine Christ's human mind. Pawl suggests that a parameter model would be consistent with Constantinople III and Christ having a true, undiminished human mind. I argue, however, that the parameter model is problematic.

Consider Pawl's analogy: the child is free to walk, but if the child begins to fall, the parent ensures that the child will not fall. It is not clear how this analogy ought to be applied to Christ. Consider any given choice in the human life of Christ: Christ has a limited number of good and bad alternatives from which to choose. The good alternatives are aligned with the divine will, and the bad alternatives are opposed to the divine will. Perhaps God's parameters are his restricting of the bad alternatives, so that Christ can only choose among the good alternatives. If Christ begins to choose a bad alternative (or shows some indication of being about to choose a bad alternative), God causes Christ to choose within the parameters, instead. Call this model the (proper) "Parameter Model." But there are other ways we might interpret the analogy and the notion of parameters. Perhaps God provides Christ's human mind with infallible knowledge of his divine will, so that he knows the good perfectly. In this case, because Christ has perfect knowledge and a desire to obey God, Christ would always choose a good alternative. The parameters in this model, then, are set by perfect knowledge of God's will and the desire to obey God's will. This interpretation is tantamount to the Beatific Vision Model below. Perhaps, instead, God knows what Christ would do in his human nature in any given circumstance, so he manipulates the circumstances in order that Christ always do what God wills. The parameters in this model, then, are simply the circumstances in

30. Pawl, *In Defense of Conciliar Christology*, 220.

which Christ finds himself. Christ is never put in a situation in which he would choose a bad alternative. We should view this model as tantamount to the Molinist Model below. Let us consider the *proper* Parameter Model in this section, and the other models in their own sections.

The *proper* Parameter Model, itself, is problematic because, first, it looks suspiciously like a Frankfurt-style counterexample (FSC) to the principle of alternative possibilities (PAP); and FSCs are notoriously complex and contentious.[31] FSCs are most often used in arguments for compatibilism or sourcehood libertarianism. The Parameter Model, however, tries to show that Christ has some leeway in his choices. Let us set aside Christ's leeway, for a moment, and address the boundaries. On this model, God, somehow, prevents the human will from choosing something contrary to the divine will. But the only mechanism by which God can prevent the human will from choosing a bad alternative must be divine causation (otherwise, it would belong to one of the following models, e.g., the Molinist Model). Divine causation is either compulsive or compatible with Christ's human freedom. If divine causation is compatible with human freedom, then compatibilism is true, and there would be no further need to defend an incompatibilist model. If divine causation is compulsive, then Christ is not free whenever the divine will prevents the human will from choosing a bad alternative. But can Christ ever choose (or be about to choose) a bad alternative, i.e., contrary to God's will? It seems that for Christ even to want to sin (or to act contrary to God's will) would itself be sin and a violation of his impeccability. At what point, then, would Christ be about to sin that would not itself be a state of sin? Indeed, it does not seem possible that Christ would ever be in a position that would require the divine will to intervene, i.e., to cause a *change* in his human will. Whatever keeps Christ's human will from willing badly must not, therefore, be something that *changes* his will from bad to good (or about-to-be-bad to about-to-be-good)—on pains of his impeccability. Unfortunately, this model does not explain *how* Christ is impeccable or *why* Christ's human will aligns with the divine will. Rather, it attempts to explain how God would prevent Christ from sinning if Christ were about to sin (which seems impossible on account of his impeccability).

31. FSCs are thought experiments in which an agent is prevented from doing otherwise than the agent in fact does. For example, the agent is given a choice between eating chocolate and vanilla ice cream. If the agent is about to choose chocolate, someone prevents the agent from choosing chocolate (by threat, by force, by electrodes in the brain, etc.), so the agent is unable to choose chocolate. But the agent actually chooses vanilla because the agent wants vanilla, not chocolate. FSCs purport to show that moral responsibility does not hinge on the agent's ability to do otherwise but in the agent's doing what the agent actually wants to do. The debate began with Frankfurt, "Alternative Possibilities and Moral Responsibility," 1–10. See chapters 1 and 4.

Perhaps the unintended consequence of this model is that it shows that Christ's human freedom and agency are located in his actual willing—not in an indifference of choice between good and bad alternatives. Christ must always choose the good, and yet, there is no reason to think that his inability to do other than the good diminishes his freedom or moral responsibility. This conclusion is precisely what FSCs seek to prove.

A second problem has to do with the leeway aspect of the Parameter Model. According to this model, Christ must choose within certain parameters set by the divine will. He must choose the good, but he has freedom to choose one good rather than an alternative good. This model implies that the divine will has a degree of openness or indeterminacy regarding Christ's human choices. But the divine will, in this discussion, cannot be reduced merely to God's moral commands. Rather, the Son has a mission; he is sent by God to fulfill a unique purpose. His life consisted repeatedly of fulfilling Old Testament prophecy, leading to his death and resurrection. But if there is some degree of openness or indeterminacy in Christ's human choices, then God's will is not meticulous over Christ's choices. And if God's will is not meticulous over Christ's human will, then God's will cannot be considered meticulous at all. Denying God's meticulous will is undesirable for many classical theists.

One might respond, however, by making the human will more fundamental than the divine will. In this case, God's will is meticulous as long as Christ's human choices are the grounds for the divine willing. In other words, God wills what Christ's humanity wills; Christ's human willing is logically prior to his divine willing. But this route hardly agrees with the language of Constantinople III. If Christ's human will is prior, it is hard to see how it is *moved by* and *subject to* the divine will. So, it seems either that God's will is open (i.e., not meticulous) or that Christ's human will is prior to his divine will—both of which options are untenable. A persistent objector might argue that the divine willing is logically simultaneous with the human willing—neither will is more fundamental. But, again, logically simultaneous willing does not seem consonant with the language of "moving" and "subjecting."

Third, this Parameter Model lacks a strong sense of unity between Christ's two wills. The divine and human wills are the wills of a single person: the divine Logos. Because there is an openness or indeterminacy regarding Christ's human choices, the unity of his person is threatened. The human will chooses independently from the divine will (within certain parameters), and, therefore, seems not to express the divine will. When Jesus chooses action A rather than action B, there is no divine reason for his choosing A rather than B. Richard Sturch expresses this concern when he argues that a proper model of the incarnation must satisfy the requirements of atonement and revelation.[32] In this case, the Logos being one person hypostatically uniting the divine and human natures satisfies the requirements of atonement. The man, Jesus, who died and was resurrected is the same person as the divine Logos. But the hypostatic union (in this case) provides "only half our 'two-way traffic' after all; we need some form of causal link whereby the Godhead affects the deeds of the Man."[33] Every act of the man, Jesus, must be a revelation of God, and, thus, be an expression of God's will. Without meticulous control over Christ's actions, the incarnation struggles to be a revelation of the divine Logos.

3b. The Beatific Vision Model of VNC

Thomas Joseph White thinks that the harmony and non-contrariety between Christ's wills depend on Christ's having the beatific vision. The beatific vision gives Jesus perfect knowledge of the divine will, so his choices are in perfect conformity with the divine will. He argues:

> If Jesus is truly the Son of God, and therefore a divine person, then his divine will is present in his person as the primary agent of his personal choices. This means that, necessarily, his human will, in its rational deliberation and choice making, must be continually subordinated to, informed by, and indefectibly expressive of his personal divine will. But of course movements of human choice follow upon knowledge (apprehension of the good as well as deliberative judgments) informing the human intellect.[34]

White contends that "it is only if Christ's human intellect is continuously and immediately aware of his own divine will (by the beatific vision . . .), that his human will can act in immediate subordination to his divine will as the 'assumed instrument' of his divine subject."[35] He concludes:

> Only due to the *immediate* knowledge of the vision can the human will of Christ be *directly* moved (or specified) by his divine will so as irremediably to correspond to its inclinations. Because of the beatific vision, the prophetic knowledge in Christ's consciousness is suffused by the evidence Christ has of the will he

32. Sturch, *Word and the Christ*, 121–41.

33. Sturch, *Word and the Christ*, 136.

34. White, *Incarnate Lord*, 256.

35. White, *Incarnate Lord*, 257.

> shares eternally with the Father. Thus, the human will of Christ acts "instrumentally," that is to say, through an immediate subordination to his divine will.[36]

Because Jesus has the beatific vision, he is "humanly conscious of his own divine will in all of his actions, so that his human actions are indicative of his personal, divine willing as God."[37] The Beatific Vision Model is superior to the Parameter Model because it provides a much stronger sense of unity between Christ's two wills.

White does not present his model of VNC as depending on divine causality.[38] It seems, nevertheless, that his model amounts to determinism.[39] White's argument depends on the notion that one's choices are determined by one's apprehension and deliberation.[40] The beatific vision removes all ignorance, doubt, and hesitation from Christ's mind. He always knows the will of God immediately and intuitively; he always acts in accord with right reason; and, thus, he always chooses to do the will of God. In this respect, White's model seems aligned with the general moral psychology of Reformed theologians John Calvin, Francis Turretin, and Jonathan Edwards;

36. White, *Incarnate Lord*, 259–60.

37. White, *Incarnate Lord*, 254.

38. It must be noted however, that White does affirm an analogical view of divine causality. He argues that

> only a doctrine of analogical causality allows us to understand that there can be no rivalry whatsoever between the existence of created freedom and divine freedom, and consequently no rivalry between the divine and human freedoms of Christ. . . . God in his sovereign will and freedom can be intimately present in the human nature of Christ (even through the medium of the hypostatic union) without changing the structure of Christ's created freedom. The presence of the divine will in Christ, on the contrary, liberates human freedom so that it can be fully itself. (White, *Incarnate Lord*, 200)

I agree that a doctrine of analogical causality allows for a non-competitive view of divine and human agency and freedom. Of course, I interpret this view as a version of compatibilism, whereas White interprets it as a version of incompatibilism.

39. Pawl addresses the matter of Christ's beatific vision, foreknowledge, and freedom in *In Defense of Extended Conciliar Christology*, 167–93. I, however, am putting forth an argument about determinism—not fatalism.

40. Aquinas:

> Choice presupposes counsel; yet it follows counsel only as determined by judgment. For what we judge to be done, we choose, after the inquiry of counsel, as is stated (Ethic. iii, 2,3). Hence if anything is judged necessary to be done, without any preceding doubt or inquiry, this suffices for choice. Therefore it is plain that doubt or inquiry belong to choice not essentially, but only when it is in an ignorant nature. (*ST* III, q. 18, a.4, ad 2.)

in each of Christ's human acts, his human will was determined by "the last dictate of the understanding"—his perfect apprehension of the good, i.e., God's will.[41] For each of these acts, his perfect apprehension of the good was both prior to and sufficient for Christ acting as he did.

One might object by appealing to the Thomistic teaching that Christ was determined to the good but not to any particular good. As Aquinas says, "The will of Christ, though determined to good, is not determined to this or that good. Hence it pertains to Christ, even as to the blessed, to choose with a free-will confirmed in good."[42] This objection could succeed only if God's will were not meticulous. If God's will were not meticulous, then the beatific vision would not determine that Christ do *this* good rather than *that* good. But there are compelling reasons to believe that God's will is, in fact, meticulous.[43] First, it is a staple of classical theism, scholasticism, and Thomism that God's will and providence are comprehensive. Second, the concept of the beatific vision presupposes a classical view of God. It

41. Calvin:

> Let it be enough for us that the understanding is, as it were, the leader and governor of the soul; and that the will is always mindful of the bidding of the understanding, and in its own desires awaits the judgment of the understanding. (Calvin, *Institutes* 1.15.7 [194]).

Turretin:

> For since the will is a rational appetite, such is its nature that it must follow the last judgment of the practical intellect; otherwise it could seek evil as evil and be turned away from good as good (which is absurd [*asystaton*]). For if the last judgment of the practical intellect is brought to the point of judging that this object, here and now (all circumstances weighed) is the best, and the will should be opposed to this judgment, then it would be turned away from good as good. Nor ought it to be objected that the will frequently seeks evil. It does not seek evil as evil, but as an apparent, useful or pleasant good. (Turretin, *Institutes* 1:663)

Edwards:

> The choice of the mind never departs from that which, at that time, and with respect to the direct and immediate objects of that decision of the mind, appears most agreeable and pleasing, all things considered. . . . It appears from these things, that in some sense, the will always follows the last dictate of the understanding. But then the understanding must be taken in a larger sense, as including the whole faculty of perception or apprehension, and not merely what is called reason or judgment. (Edwards, *Freedom of the Will*, 147–48)

42. *ST* III, q. 18, a. 4, ad 3.

43. Even if God's will were not meticulous *simpliciter*, it seems that God's will regarding Christ's human actions must be meticulous. Otherwise, we fall back into the Parameter Model.

presupposes that God has a knowledge of simple intelligence (i.e., natural knowledge) and a knowledge of vision (i.e., free knowledge).[44] And it presupposes that God knows and wills all things. Third, the manifestation of the unity of the Word depends on his human will being directed by his divine will. "The singularity and unity of the person of Christ can only be sufficiently manifest in his human actions if his divine and human wills cooperate concretely in all of his personal actions. . . . It is this cooperation of the two wills that permits the human willing of Christ to take on its filial mode of expression."[45]

Finally, one might object by appealing to the mode of God's will. Aquinas taught that God willed that Christ's acts be contingent—not necessary. "Now God wills some things to be done necessarily, some contingently, to the right ordering of things, for the building up of the universe. Therefore to some effects He has attached necessary causes, that cannot fail; but to others defectible and contingent causes, from which arise contingent effects."[46] Because Christ's acts were contingent, they were neither necessary nor determined.[47] But Aquinas was writing about the necessity or contingency of the *secondary* (i.e., the proximate) cause. With respect to God's will, Aquinas was careful to affirm the necessity of the consequence (not the necessity of the consequent): "For the conditional statement that if God wills a thing it must necessarily be, is necessarily true."[48] He explains, "Hence things effected by the divine will have that kind of necessity that God wills them to

44. Aquinas explains:

> Now a certain difference is to be noted in the consideration of those things that are not actual. For though some of them may not be in act now, still they were, or they will be; and God is said to know all these with the knowledge of vision. . . . But there are other things in God's power, or the creature's, which nevertheless are not, nor will be, nor were; and as regards these He is said to have knowledge, not of vision, but of simple intelligence. (ST I, q. 14, a. 9, co)

Compare Aquinas with Turretin, who writes:

> It is commonly distinguished by theologians into the knowledge of simple intelligence (or natural and indefinite) and the knowledge of vision (or free and definite). The former is the knowledge of things merely possible and is therefore called indefinite because nothing on either hand is determined concerning them by God. The latter is the knowledge of future things and is called definite because future things are determined by the sure will of God. (Turretin, *Institutes* 1:212-13).

45. White, *Incarnate Lord*, 154.

46. *ST* I, q. 19, a. 8, co.

47. See Solano and Aldama, *On the Incarnate Word*, 193–212.

48. *ST* I, q. 19, a. 8, ad 1.

have, either absolute or conditional. Not all things, therefore, are absolute necessities."[49] The point is that the Beatific Vision Model presupposes a Thomistic framework that posits a perfect knowledge, immutable will, and meticulous providence to God, which effectively make Christ's actions determined.[50] And the fact that Christ has the beatific vision only strengthens this determinism.

3c. *The Molinist Model of VNC*

Thomas P. Flint, following Luis de Molina, demonstrates how appealing to divine middle knowledge provides tools for reconciling Christ's impeccability and libertarian freedom.[51] We can easily adapt Flint's argument to the matter of VNC. Before we consider VNC, we must review the basic tenets of Molinism.[52] Molinism posits three moments of divine knowledge. God's *natural knowledge* includes those truths that are necessary and independent of God's will. God's *free knowledge* includes those truths that are contingent and dependent upon God's will. God's *middle knowledge* includes those truths that are contingent yet independent of God's will. Counterfactuals of creaturely freedom belong to God's middle knowledge. In other words, what free creatures would do in any given circumstance is both contingent and independent of God's will. God knows what free creatures would do in any given circumstance because of his middle knowledge. God knows, for example, that Tyre and Sidon would have repented in sackcloth and ashes had Christ's works been performed in them. Thus, God is able to preserve creaturely freedom while still accomplishing his sovereign will in providence by actualizing the world in which the created circumstances infallibly

49. *ST* I, q. 19, a. 8, ad 3.

50. Aquinas writes, "But since the very act of free will is traced to God as to a cause, it necessarily follows that everything happening from the exercise of free will must be subject to divine providence. For human providence is included under the providence of God, as a particular under a universal cause." *ST* I, q. 22, a. 2, ad. 4.

51. Flint, "Death He Freely Accepted," 3–20. This article sparked a series of articles and chapters on the incarnation from a Molinist perspective. See Flint, "Possibilities of Incarnation," 307–20; Craig, "Flint's Radical Molinist Christology Not Radical Enough," 55–64; Flint "Molinism and Incarnation," 187–207; Mullins, "Flint's 'Molinism and the Incarnation' Is too Radical," 1–15; Mullins, "Flint's 'Molinism and the Incarnation' Is Still Too Radical," 515–32; Flint, "Orthodoxy and Incarnation: A Reply to Mullins," 180–92; Rogers, "Christ's Freedom," 497–512. For a compatibilist version of Molinism, see Ware, *God's Greater Glory*, 97–130.

52. For more comprehensive accounts of Molinism, see Freddoso, *On Divine Foreknowledge*; Flint, *Divine Providence*.

lead creatures to choose freely what God wants them to choose according to his purpose.

Flint argues that Molinism is the answer to reconciling Christ's freedom with his impeccability. In order for Christ to have significant freedom, though, he cannot have the beatific vision in the sense that White advocates. Flint explains:

> According to Molina, then, God saw to it that CHN [Christ's human nature], though receiving a multitude of gifts from the Father, did not receive those gifts that would have rendered it incapable of sinning. Rather, in order that CHN's actions might prove truly meritorious, the Father saw to it that CHN was placed in what we might call *freedom-retaining circumstances*—circumstances in which the full natural effects of the beatific vision were blocked so as to retain CHN's freedom "not to do those things that he was obligated by precept to do."[53]

Christ maintains his status as impeccable because God could not possibly permit Christ to sin. Thus, there is no possible world in which CHN is assumed and Christ sins. Christ's freedom to sin is maintained because there are possible worlds in which CHN is not assumed by the divine Logos and CHN sins. "That is to say, CHN has the power so to act that CHN never would have been assumed had it so acted."[54] God chose to actualize a world in which Christ would certainly not sin.[55]

> But the only way God could have had certainty concerning CHN's remaining sinless would be if he had middle knowledge that CHN would freely remain sinless if placed in certain freedom-retaining circumstances. Given this middle knowledge, he could then decide both to assume CHN and to see to it that CHN is placed only in circumstances in which God knew it would in fact freely refrain from sinning.[56]

53. Flint, "Death He Freely Accepted," 8. Flint cites Luis de Molina, *Concordia Disputation* 53, Part 4, Section 23 (271).

54. Flint, "Death He Freely Accepted," 9.

55. Alvin Plantinga distinguished between *strong* and *weak* actualization. Strong actualization is tantamount to divine causation, but weak actualization is possible if "for each world *W* there is something he could have done—some series of actions he could have taken—such that if he had, *W* would have been actual." A. Plantinga, *Nature of Necessity*, 173. Molinists routinely appeal to weak actualization to explain how God can bring about certain states of affair without violating creatures' freedom.

56. Flint, "Death He Freely Accepted," 9.

In this way, Christ can be both impeccable and free in the libertarian sense. We can readily see how this Molinist schema can be used as a model for VNC: God chooses a world in which Christ's human will freely and infallibly aligns with the divine will.

This Molinist Model of VNC has several weaknesses. First, a minor weakness is that it undermines the Free Will Defense (FWD) against the logical problem of evil.[57] The logical problem of evil states that if God is all-powerful, all-knowing, and all-good, then evil could not possibly exist because God would be powerful, wise, and good enough to prevent it. Evil exists; therefore, God does not exist. For FWD to work, it must be possible that God cannot create a world with libertarianly free creatures but without evil. The FWD stipulates that it is possible for all libertarianly free creatures to suffer from transworld depravity: in every world in which these creatures exist, they sin. If it is possible that all free creatures suffer from transworld depravity, then it is possible that God cannot create a world with free creatures without evil. Presumably, adherents of Molinism view FWD favorably. But the Molinist Model of VNC must deny that all free creatures suffer from transworld depravity. Otherwise, there would be no human nature assumable by the divine Logos.

A second, more significant, weakness of the Molinist Model is that it seems to run contrary to an important element in classical Christology, namely, the twofold doctrine of the *anhypostasia* and the *enhypostasia*. This element maintains that Christ's human nature has no hypostasis apart from the Logos; considered apart from the Logos, it is without a hypostasis (i.e., it is *anhypostasis*). Furthermore, the Logos is the hypostasis that *personalizes* Christ's human nature (the *enhypostasis*). I interpret this doctrine to mean that Christ's human nature cannot be considered a person apart from the Logos. In other words, there is no possible world in which CHN is not assumed by the Logos.[58] If there is no possible world in which CHN is not assumed by the Logos, then there can be no world in which CHN sins, and,

57. For FWD, see A. Plantinga, *God, Freedom, and Evil*, 7–64. I have not seen the argument that this Molinist model undermines FWD in print, but Drew Sparks has made the argument in a personal conversation with me, though we discovered the argument independently.

58. That there is no possible world in which CHN is not assumed by the Logos is a matter of contention. For example, Crisp thinks otherwise: see *Divinity and Humanity*, 83n10. But in "Human Nature, Potency, and the Incarnation," Freddoso argues that CHN must necessarily be united to the Logos, and he believes Aquinas would agree. Gorman disagrees and thinks Aquinas would think it possible that CHN not be assumed by the Logos, in *Aquinas on the Metaphysics of the Hypostatic Union*, 73–100. See Fred Sanders' introduction to *Jesus in Trinitarian Perspective*, 30–36; Wellum, *God the Son Incarnate*, 316–24.

thus, Christ is never free to sin. This line of argument does not prove that the Molinist model of VNC is impossible; it merely shows that the Molinist Model is unsuccessful in reconciling Christ's impeccability with libertarian freedom.

Third, as Katherin A. Rogers has demonstrated, the Molinist Model is incoherent. The Logos assumed CHN in the actual world because God knew that it would not sin in the freedom-retaining circumstances in which it was placed. But he knew those things about CHN as unassumed by the Logos. Doubtless, then, CHN could be placed in the same circumstances without being assumed, and yet freely not sin. But if CHN were not assumed in those circumstances, it certainly *would* sin because it would make claims about its person that would be false and blasphemous. "Out of the mouth of CHN-B [the assumed human nature] come such claims as that He and the Father are one, that He existed before the creation of the world, and that salvation involves ingesting His body and blood. But if CHN-A [the unassumed human nature] says such things they are wildly, bizarrely false."[59] It is impossible for any human nature to be found in the same circumstances as Christ without sin unless it were assumed by the divine Logos.

Fourth, and perhaps most significantly, in whichever possible world CHN is not assumed by the Logos, that human nature is not the person of Christ.[60] And if it is not the person of Christ, its actions have no bearing on Christ's libertarian freedom. Thus, to argue that Christ could have done otherwise in a particular situation because some other person in some other world did otherwise in a similar situation is a *non sequitur*.

Perhaps we could salvage the Molinist Model by eliminating the notion that there are possible worlds in which CHN is not assumed by the Logos. In this way, there are no possible worlds in which CHN sins because in every world with CHN, CHN is assumed by the Logos. This version of the Molinist Model avoids at least the second, third, and fourth objections mentioned above. I argue, however, that all Molinist models fail to unify the person of Christ adequately. If the counterfactuals of Christ's human freedom are part of God's middle knowledge, then, by definition, what Christ would do freely in any given circumstance is contingent and independent of God's will, i.e., Christ's divine will. The famous "grounding objection" argues that Molinism is incoherent because there is nothing that grounds contingent and pre-volitional truths—*how can something be contingent if nothing causes it?* The problem of Christ's personal unity is related to the grounding objection. If Christ's human actions are expressive of the divine Logos, then they

59. Rogers, "Christ's Freedom," 508.

60. This problem was pointed out to me by an anonymous referee.

ought to be grounded in the Logos (recall Sturch's atonement and revelation requirements). But Christ's human actions are not grounded in the Logos. What Christ would do freely in any given circumstance is independent of the Logos. Therefore, Christ's human actions are not expressive of the divine Logos, and so the unity of Christ's person is jeopardized.[61]

3d. *The Causal Model of VNC*

In a discussion about divine concurrence with human wills, Turretin argues that there are only three ways by which "two free wills may be joined together and agree to elicit the same common action at the same time and immediately (and proximately and undivided) and that not casually and fortuitously but infallibly and so certainly as to imply a contradiction for one to elicit such an action without the other."[62] First, both wills are "conjoined by a very powerful superior cause to elicit the same action in the same point of time"; second, both wills "are by their own nature determined to that operation so that they cannot help producing it"; or third, "one determines the operation of the other and consequently determines the other cause to act."[63] The first option is impossible because there is no higher cause than God himself. The second option is also impossible "because God is not determined necessarily to operating, since in all external concourse he is perfectly free. Nor do many second causes act from necessity of nature, but freely (which therefore ought to be masters of their own acts, so however as to depend always upon the first cause both in being and in operation)."[64] Therefore, the third option is correct: "the infallibility of the event cannot arise from any other cause than the divine predetermination."[65]

Turretin's reasoning can be applied to Christ's divine and human wills. If Christ is free with respect to both his divine and human wills, then the only way for those two wills to agree infallibly is for the divine will to (pre)determine that the human will agree in all acts of volition. Both the Beatific Vision Model and the Molinist Model are consistent with Turretin's reasoning, here. The divine will ultimately decides what the human will actually chooses. But Turretin has a stronger mechanism for VNC than middle knowledge or the

61. Furthermore, Molinist models make Christ's human will ultimately prior to his divine will. What Christ would do freely in any situation is already set (logically) before God chooses to create.

62. Turretin, *Institutes* 1:508.

63. Turretin, *Institutes* 1:508.

64. Turretin, *Institutes* 1:508.

65. Turretin, *Institutes* 1:508.

beatific vision: divine causation.[66] By "divine causation," I mean what Turretin calls a "previous and predetermining concourse." Turretin explains, "antecedently to all operation of the creature or before the creature operates by nature and reason, he really and efficaciously moves it to act in single actions so that without this premotion the second cause could not operate, but (this premotion being posited) it would be impossible in the compound sense for the second cause not to do that same thing to which it was previously moved by the first cause."[67] The Causal Model, then, states that God, the first cause, determines the will and actions of Christ's human nature.[68]

The Causal Model is superior to the other models. Unlike the Parameter Model, the Causal Model explains *how* Christ's two wills always harmonize. The divine will causes the human will to choose what it does. Unlike the Molinist Model, the Causal Model is coherent, preserves the unity of Christ's person, and does not risk undermining an important element of conciliar and classical Christology. Like the Beatific Vision Model, the Causal Model can secure a strong sense of personal unity. There is no act of human will in Christ that is not caused by the divine will. Thus, Christ's human decisions and actions are expressive of his divine person and satisfy the requirement of

66. It is important to note that divine causation is just one aspect of the relation between the human and divine natures in the person of Christ. A full account of the incarnation is beyond the scope of this article. Certainly, much could be said, for example, about the divine decree, divine providence, eternal generation, the metaphysics of the hypostatic union, the *extra calvinisticum*, the mission of the Son, Christ's human knowledge, his impeccability and temptations, and his being empowered by the Spirit—all of which relate to the discussion at hand.

67. Turretin, *Institutes* 1:506. Moreover, this predetermining concourse is merely conceptually—not really—distinct from God's simultaneous concourse "because the simultaneous concourse is nothing else than continued previous concourse which not only flows into the causes themselves, that it may work in them, but into the effect itself, so as to act with them." Turretin, *Institutes* 1:506.

68. Unlike the weak actualization of Molinism, the Causal Model holds that the divine will strongly actualizes the operations of Christ's human will. But we should not understand "strong actualization" in this context to imply that divine and human causation are univocal concepts. The first cause is not in competition with second causes, nor is it merely the first in a series of causes. Karl Barth is right when he says, "When we think of the *concursus divinus* as the divine foreordination (*praedeterminatio*) of creaturely activity, this means that the divine activity has to be differentiated from all other forms of ordination or determination which may underlie creaturely activity, and that in its difference from such forms it has to be given precedence over them." Barth, *Church Dogmatics*, III/3:121. Herman Bavinck adds, "And precisely because the primary and secondary cause do not stand and function dualistically on separate tracks, but the primary works through the secondary, the effect that proceeds from the two is one and the product is one. There is no division of labor between God and his creature, but the same effect is totally the effect of the primary cause as well as totally the effect of the proximate cause." Bavinck, *Reformed Dogmatics*, 2:614.

a true revelation. Both the Causal Model and the Beatific Vision Model are consistent with Constantinople III and amenable to compatibilism. In fact, the Causal Model could affirm that Christ had the beatific vision and, thus, reap all the supposed benefits of the Beatific Vision Model.

Despite the similarities between the Causal and Beatific Vision Models, there are several reasons why we should affirm the Causal Model as the better explanation of VNC. The first three reasons place doubt on the claim that Christ had the beatific vision before his resurrection.[69] The last two reasons have to do with the superiority of the Causal Model in explaining the relationship between the divine and human wills.

First, the Thomist understanding of the beatific vision entails that Christ *qua* humanity knows all things actual: "Therefore the soul of Christ knows all things that God knows in Himself by the knowledge of vision, but not all that God knows in Himself by knowledge of simple intelligence."[70] In other words, Christ knows *qua* humanity everything included in God's free knowledge.[71] But the biblical data runs contrary to the notion that Christ had the beatific knowledge of vision prior to his resurrection. Reformed theologians unanimously denied that Christ knew all things in his humanity because the Bible teaches otherwise.[72] Jesus grew in wisdom and admitted that there were things he did not know.[73] If Christ did not know all things *qua* humanity, then the Beatific Vision Model is unviable. Second, the Beatific Vision Model makes Christ very much unlike us. Christ's having perfect knowledge of all things seems to transcend human ability, and, thus, it either undermines Christ's true humanity or results in a mix of human and divine—both of which are inconsistent with classical Christology. Jesus Christ is "perfect in humanity . . . like us in all respects except for sin . . . acknowledged in two natures which undergo no confusion, no change,

69. A full critique of Christ having the beatific vision before his state of glory is beyond the scope of this chapter. For further discussion, see Turretin, *Institutes* 2:347-56. See also Wellum, *God the Son Incarnate*, 210–17.

70. *ST* III, q. 2, a. 2, ad 2. Pawl cites this text as proof that "Aquinas thinks that Christ, by means of the knowledge had in his created soul in virtue of the beatific vision, knows all that there is to know about creation." Pawl, *In Defense of Extended Conciliar Christology*, 171.

71. The notion that Christ had the beatific vision (in the Thomist sense) since the moment of conception does not mean that Christ was omniscient. God is omniscient because he knows all things actual *and* all things possible. Aquinas explains, "[God] knows all things, not merely whatever are in act at any time, which things He is said to know by knowledge of vision, but also what ever He Himself can do which He is said to know by simple intelligence." *ST* III, q. 2. a. 2, ad 2.

72. See Bavinck, *Reformed Dogmatics*, 2:312; cf. Heppe, *Reformed Dogmatics*, 434–38.

73. See Matt 24:36; Luke 2:52.

no division, no separation."[74] Third, the Beatific Vision Model denies that Christ had faith. Christ's immediate apprehension of the divine will allowed him to identify with it as his own, intuitively and internally.[75] For Christ to have immediate awareness of his own identity as the Son of God, so the argument goes, he must have the beatific vision. To say that Christ had faith is to deny that he had immediate awareness of his divine will and to affirm that his apprehension of his divine identity was external and received by faith. Despite the appeal of this argument for the beatific vision, we ought rather to believe that Christ is the exemplar of faith. Jesus' faith was not in God's mercy (because he was sinless) but in God's goodness and provision.[76] Christ's having faith makes better sense of his prayer life and dependence on the Holy Spirit. Moreover, one need not appeal to the beatific vision to make sense of Christ's immediate divine self-awareness. The Causal Model can easily accommodate his immediate self-awareness; God causes Jesus (via the divine decree and providence) to have immediate awareness that Jesus is God and to know that what Jesus actually does is divinely appointed, so that

74. Tanner, *Decrees of the Ecumenical Councils*, 86. This objection is not about humanity sharing in the beatific vision *per se* (indeed, Protestants believe the saints in heaven will have the beatific vision) but the Thomist interpretation of the beatific vision and its implications on Christ's superhuman knowledge.

75. White thinks that Christ's lacking faith is a good thing:

> In the absence of the [beatific] vision, the infused science of Christ would lack such immediate evidence and would need to be accompanied by faith. In this case, the prophetic awareness Christ had of his own divinity and will would have to be continuously accompanied by an autonomous decision of faith in the human heart of Christ and a repeated choice to welcome in trust this revelation *from his own divine self*. This would create, in effect, a kind of psychological autonomy in the man Jesus distinct from the willing of his divine subject, resulting in a schism between the two operations of the incarnate Word. Jesus as man would have to will to believe in his divine activity as God. He would not perceive it directly. (White, *Incarnate Lord*, 259)

76. Turretin writes, "[Faith] is ascribed to Christ as to substance of knowledge and assent to a thing known (i.e., to the doctrine revealed of God) and as to trust, which rests in the goodness of God providing all things necessary for us." Turretin, *Institutes* 2:348. He explains:

> Although the soul of Christ even from the beginning rejoiced in happiness and enjoyed God himself in virtue of the hypostatical union, still he had not as yet its fulness (on account of the necessity of suffering). Rather he should at length obtain it after his resurrection and ascension when (being made an attainer) he was fully glorified both as to soul and body. Thus nothing hindered him from believing in God and hoping for the glory promised to him (Heb. 12:2). (Turretin, *Institutes* 2:348)

he always does the will of God. In this way, Jesus is moved both subjectively and objectively—as a matter of providence and obedience.

Fourth, the Causal Model gives the divine will a more active role by directly and effectively bringing about whatever Jesus does. Whatever perceived benefit the Beatific Vision Model may have on Jesus' human subjective experience, without a divine predetermining cause, it fails to make Christ's human operation a direct work of God. Fifth, the Causal Model is better at conveying the instrumentality of Christ's humanity—a matter that is especially dear to both Thomist and Reformed theologians.[77] Aquinas writes:

> Therefore in Christ the human nature has its proper form and power whereby it acts; and so has the Divine. Hence the human nature has its proper operation distinct from the Divine, and conversely. Nevertheless, the Divine Nature makes use of the operation of the human nature, as of the operation of its instrument; and in the same way the human nature shares in the operation of the Divine Nature, as an instrument shares in the operation of the principal agent.[78]

Paul G. Crowley explains, "The instrumental relation between the two operations is not merely a moral one; the principles of causality which bind the two operations are rather 'physical,' or real; they show how the two natures are realized, fulfilled, and perfected precisely in their operations in the person of Christ, each working in relation with the other."[79] Reformed theology agrees: "In producing the common ἀποτέλεσμα θεανδρικόν [God-man operations] the divine nature enters into such an alliance with the human, that as the soul acts in bare man as the principal and the body as the instrument, so in the action of Christ the θεάνθρωπος [God-man] the divine nature functions as the principal cause, the human as a less principal and assistant cause."[80]

77. Aquinas:

> It is proper to an instrument to be moved by the principal agent, yet diversely, according to the property of its nature. For an inanimate instrument, as an axe or a saw, is moved by the craftsman with only a corporeal movement; but an instrument animated by a sensitive soul is moved by the sensitive appetite, as a horse by its rider; and an instrument animated with a rational soul is moved by its will, as by the command of his lord the servant is moved to act, the servant being like an animate instrument, as the Philosopher says (Polit. i, 2,4; Ethic. viii, 11). And hence it was in this manner that the human nature of Christ was the instrument of the Godhead, and was moved by its own will. (*ST* III, q. 18, a. 1, ad 2)

78. *ST* III, q. 19, a. 1, co.

79. Crowley, "*Instrumentum Divinitatis* in Thomas Aquinas," 474.

80. *Leiden Synopsis* XXVI, 18–19, cited in Heppe, *Reformed Dogmatics*, 446.

One might object to the Causal Model because it seems to imply no distinction between the way God moves Christ's human will and the way God moves everyone else's will. The Causal Model implies that God's decree and providence are meticulous and efficacious (indeed, determinative), and moral creatures have a compatibilistic kind of freedom. But there is a real distinction between God's moving his own human will and his moving of our wills. The distinction is that the two natures of Christ are hypostatically united, but our human natures are not hypostatically united to God. When the Son *qua* divinity moves his human nature, he is moving his *own* human nature. For this reason, the language of instrumentality must be undergirded with language of identity or personal possession. For example, my hand may be said to be causally determined by my will because my will is the prior and sufficient condition for my hand's movement. And yet, my hand is still *my* hand—not an object distinct from me, unlike, say, a hammer which I may also cause to move. Likewise, Christ's human will may be said to be causally determined by his divine will because the divine will is the prior and sufficient condition for the human will's movement. And yet, Christ's human will is still the *Son's* will—not the will of another person.

4. Conclusion

I began this chapter by considering what Constantinople III means when it says that Christ had to be *moved*. I argued that rational creatures are moved by their wills, and to be moved is compatible with self-determination. Then I considered four models of VNC that were *prima facie* consistent with the language of Constantinople III and VNC: the Parameter Model, the Beatific Vision Model, the Molinist Model, and the Causal Model. The first three models intended to preserve an incompatibilist view of Christ's human freedom. I have shown that each of these models failed either to maintain classical Christology or a libertarian account of Christ's freedom. I have demonstrated further that the Causal Model of VNC is coherent, consistent with classical Christology, and the best way to understand the harmony of Christ's wills. This divine causation—or movement—is compatible with Christ's human self-determination. And if exhaustive divine causation is tantamount to determinism, then compatibilism is true. But not all believe that divine causation amounts to determinism. In the next chapter, I consider one proposal that affirms divine universal causation but denies theological determinism.

7

Christ and the Divine Decree

1. Introduction

In the last chapter, I began to consider the relationship between classical Christology and determinism. I argued that Christ's human will is *caused* by the divine will. But if divine causation is not tantamount to theological determinism, then, perhaps, there is room for a libertarian account of Christ's freedom after all. In this chapter, I consider an account of divine universal causation that purports to be non-determinative because it places the divine decree externally to God: the Extrinsic Model (EM). In response, I defend an intrinsic model of the divine decree, the Reformed Scholastic Intrinsic Model (RSIM), which is characteristic of the Reformed tradition. I offer biblical, theological, and christological support for affirming RSIM. Finally, I summarize the argument of this and the previous chapter: if classical Christology is true, then hard determinism is false.

2. Divine Universal Causality Without Determinism

W. Matthews Grant believes that divine universal causality (DUC) does not entail determinism. It may be true both that God causes all things and that creatures have libertarian freedom. Grant argues for a broadly Thomistic view of providence and free will that he calls "the Dual Sources Account." In what follows, I sketch the major elements of the Dual Sources Account and show how it is purported to preserve DUC without determinism.

According to Grant, DUC "holds that necessarily, for any entity distinct from God, God directly causes that entity to exist at any time it exists. It follows from DUC that creaturely acts are directly caused by God."[1] The Dual

1. Grant, *Free Will and God's Universal Causality*, 15.

Sources Account affirms both God's conservation of and concurrence with creaturely operations. God is the primary cause of all things; created entities are secondary causes. God *co-operates* with creatures and created entities. Grant distinguishes between "cooperation" and "co-operation." *Cooperation* occurs when "two (or more) causes work together to bring about an effect, each contributing only a portion of the effect."[2] *Co-operation* occurs when two (or more) causes bring about the whole of the effect. He explains, "Thus, whatever effects are brought about by creaturely substances are brought about by those substances in whole, not just in part. And since those effects are also brought about by God, they are brought about by him in whole, too."[3] This view of concurrence and co-operation allows for creaturely agency. Creaturely causes have real effects in the world. Moreover, Grant argues that the Dual Sources Account is consistent with agent-causation.[4]

Grant compares two models of divine and human agency: an intrinsic model that he calls "the popular model" (PM) and the extrinsic model (EM). According to PM, the following items exist whenever a statement like "God causes E" is true:

1. God
2. E
3. God's choice, decree, or intention to bring about E, which is intrinsic to God, is that in virtue of which God causes E and which would not exist were God not causing E.
4. The causal-dependence relation between God and E.[5]

Grant argues that PM entails determinism.

> For DUC implies that every creaturely act is directly caused by God. And PM implies that for every creaturely effect E that is caused by God, there is a factor—God's choice or decree (or etc.)—that is both prior to and logically sufficient for E. The factor is prior to E, since it either causes E or is that in virtue of which God causes E. This factor is logically sufficient for E, since it is not possible for the factor to occur or obtain without

2. Grant, *Free Will and God's Universal Causality*, 39.
3. Grant, *Free Will and God's Universal Causality*, 39.
4. Grant, *Free Will and God's Universal Causality*, 48–51. See chapter 1 for more on agent causation.
5. Grant, *Free Will and God's Universal Causality*, 56.

> E's occurring or obtaining. It follows that DUC and PM imply that every creaturely act is determined.[6]

Instead of PM, Grant insists we ought to affirm EM. EM depends on two scholastic doctrines: divine simplicity and the notion that God is not *really* but *rationally* related to creation. Divine simplicity is the notion that God has no parts "and that there are no entities intrinsic to, but distinct from, God. It follows from divine simplicity that whatever is intrinsic to God is simply identical to God."[7] According to scholastic theology, God is not *really* related to his creatures because "there is no real foundation in God for that relation."[8] Rather, he is *rationally* related to his creatures. "God's causing or bringing about some effect within creation will not involve any real or intrinsic state or property of God that would not be there were he not causing that effect."[9] With this view of God, according to EM, whenever a statement like "God causes E" is true, the following must exist:

1. God (with God's reasons)
2. E
3. The causal-dependence relation between God and E.[10]

On EM, God would be the same intrinsically whether or not he were to cause E. God's reasons for creating are intrinsic to him, but "these reasons leave God free to refrain from causing any creaturely effect."[11] In this way, God's reasons are consistent with his wisdom and goodness but also his purpose and intention. E and God's causing E, however, are completely extrinsic to God. Grant argues that EM does not entail determinism because none of the items involved in a causal act is a factor that is both prior and sufficient for that act. Grant demonstrates by considering all the items involved when God causes A:

1. God
2. A

6. Grant, *Free Will and God's Universal Causality*, 56.

7. Grant, *Free Will and God's Universal Causality*, 56.

8. Grant, *Free Will and God's Universal Causality*, 57.

9. Grant, *Free Will and God's Universal Causality*, 57.

10. Grant, *Free Will and God's Universal Causality*, 58. Grant explain that "On EM, God's reasons for causing what he does are not entities distinct from God. Rather, they are contained in God's knowledge of himself, much in the same way that Aquinas says the divine ideas are." Grant, *Free Will and God's Universal Causality*, 202n20.

11. Grant, *Free Will and God's Universal Causality*, 58.

3. God's reason for causing A
4. The causal-dependence relation between God and A
5. God's causal act, or causing of A, which consists in A plus the causal relation between God and A.
6. God's willing or choosing A, which is nothing else than God's causing A for a reason when God could have done otherwise.[12]

Then, Grant questions whether any of these items (listed 1–6) "constitute a factor both prior to and logically sufficient for A."[13] Here is his discussion of these items *in toto*:

> Well, as cause of A, God is causally prior to A. But God is not logically sufficient for A: It is possible for God to exist without A. A, by contrast, is logically sufficient for itself. But clearly A is not prior to itself. Thus, neither God nor A is a factor both prior to and logically sufficient for A.

God's reason for causing A is arguably prior to A. But on EM, at least if we assume DUC, God's reason is not logically sufficient for A. That's because, on EM, God's reasons for causing creaturely effects leave him free to refrain from causing those effects. But, given DUC, it is not possible for anything distinct from God to exist without God's causing it. So, given EM, DUC, and any creaturely effect E that God causes in the actual world, there is a possible world in which God has the same reason to cause E, but in which E does not exist. But then God's reason is not logically sufficient for E. And so neither is God's reason for causing A logically sufficient for A.

> What then of the causal relation between God and A? And what of God's act of causing A or God's willing and choosing A? We need not determine whether the causal relation between God and A is logically sufficient for A, for it is not prior to A; relations are not prior to their relata. God's act of causing A is certainly logically sufficient for A: There is no world in which God causes A, but A does not exist. Yet God's causal act is just as clearly not prior to A. For that act consists in A together with the causal relation between God and A, and, as we have just seen, neither of these is prior to A. And, since God's willing and choosing A is just God's act of bringing about or causing A for a reason, God's willing or choosing A is not prior to A, either.[14]

12. Grant, *Free Will and God's Universal Causality*, 60.
13. Grant, *Free Will and God's Universal Causality*, 60.
14. Grant, *Free Will and God's Universal Causality*, 60–61.

On EM, divine universal causality is not determinism because there is no prior and sufficient condition in God's causing an effect.

One objection to DUC and EM is that "God's causal acts are *explanatorily prior* to his effects," thus making God's causing the event to "constitute a factor both prior to and logically sufficient for" the event.[15] But Grant responds that God's causing E is not prior to E; rather, God's causing E is a basic act—his act consists in its effect. "We should say that God brings about his effects *in* his causal acts, not *by means of* his causal acts."[16] It is not God's *act* that causes E, but God *himself* causes E. E, then, is simultaneous with God's causing E.

Grant argues that this Dual Sources Account preserves both prongs of libertarianism: PAP and ultimate sourcehood. Agents have the ability to do otherwise because their actions are not determined by a prior and sufficient cause. When agent S performs A at *t*, God's eternal existence is an ontologically prior factor, but God being a prior factor is also consistent with S's performing not-A at *t*. God's causing S to perform A at *t* is sufficient for S to perform A at *t*, but God's act is simultaneous with—not prior to—S's performing A at *t*. S has the ability to perform A or not-A at *t* because God himself has the ability to bring about S's performing A or not-A at *t*.

The Dual Sources Account, likewise, claims to preserve the creature's ultimate sourcehood. Creaturely agents satisfy the conditions for ultimate responsibility.[17] "Since, given EM, God's causing a creaturely act does not remove that which suffices for its being within the creature's power and control whether or not the act occurs, neither should we think it removes the act's being ultimately up to its creaturely agent."[18]

15. Grant, *Free Will and God's Universal Causality*, 61.

16. Grant, *Free Will and God's Universal Causality*, 62.

17. Recall Kane's conditions for ultimate responsibility:

> (UR) An agent is *ultimately responsible* for some (event or state) E's occurring only if (R) the agent is personally responsible for E's occurring in a sense which entails that something the agent voluntarily (or willingly) did or omitted, and for which the agent could have voluntarily done otherwise, either was, or causally contributed to, E's occurrence and made a difference to whether or not E occurred; and (U) for every X and Y (where X and Y represent occurrences of events and/or states) if the agent is personally responsible for X, and if Y is an *arche* (or sufficient ground or cause or explanation) for X, then the agent must also be personally responsible for Y. (Kane, *Significance of Free Will*, 35)

See Grant, *Free Will and God's Universal Causality*, 68–70.

18. Grant, *Free Will and God's Universal Causality*, 69.

3. RSIM and the Decree in the Reformed Tradition

Whether Grant's external model (EM) succeeds in avoiding determinism is beyond the scope of this chapter. I argue, however, that we ought to affirm—for biblical and theological reasons—the intrinsic model espoused by the Reformed scholastics instead of EM. Call this model a "Reformed Scholastic Intrinsic Model" (RSIM) because it maintains that God's acts are intrinsic and essential—not accidental to God.[19] RSIM also fits with the scholastic notions of DUC, divine simplicity, and the *relatio mixta*.[20] Contrary to Grant's contention about scholastic intrinsic models, I and the Reformed tradition understand RSIM to be compatible with divine freedom.[21]

3a. The Decree in the Reformed Tradition

The Reformed Protestant scholastics considered the decree to be internal to God, i.e., as essential to God.[22] Louis Berkhof explains, "The decrees are an internal manifestation and exercise of the divine attributes, rendering the futurition of things certain but this exercise of the intelligent volition of

19. Grant, *Free Will and God's Universal Causality*, 77.

20. For example, Turretin writes:

> Although the essence of God (considered simply in itself) is absolute and implies no relation to creatures, yet this does not hinder it (when considered with relative opposition to creatures and as determining itself in the manner of vital principle to the production of this or that thing out of itself) from having a certain reference (*schesin*) and relation to creatures. Nor can that manifold relation make composition in God, more than the relation which his omniscience and omnipotence bear to things ad extra, constituted a real difference between God and his omnipotence and omniscience." (Turretin, *Institutes* 1:193)

21. Oliver Crisp argues that PAP libertarianism is compatible with Calvinism in *Deviant Calvinism*, 71–96. In *Freedom, Redemption, and Communion*, 3–23, Crisp argues, instead, for a sourcehood libertarian Calvinism. He writes, "To the extent that the libertarian Calvinist can avail herself of the resources of a two-source account of creaturely freedom such as that offered by the concurrence theorist [i.e., like Grant's Dual Sources account], they may also provide reasons for thinking that libertarian Calvinism is more deeply embedded in a kind of classical theological way of thinking about God's relation to creation and his action in meticulous providence, than some objectors might imagine." Crisp, *Freedom, Redemption, and Communion*, 21–22. Judging the merit of Crisp's arguments is beyond the scope of this book; but insofar as Calvinism holds to classical Christology, it must acknowledge that compatibilism is true: free will and moral responsibility are compatible with determinism—even if not all human activity is determined. See also Anderson and Manata, "Determined to Come Most Freely," 272–97.

22. These theologians also held to DUC and divine simplicity.

God should not be confounded with the realization of its objects in creation, providence, and redemption."[23] In other words, the decree is an internal act of God pertaining to God's plan for the world; and, although the decree entails the certainty of God's plan being fulfilled, the decree is not the same thing as the acts of creation, providence, and redemption. These Reformed theologians affirmed several conceptual distinctions in God's operations. One distinction is between immanent acts (*opera immanentia*) and external acts (*opera exeuntia*). Another distinction is between essential acts (*opera essentialia*) and personal acts (*opera personalia*). The essential acts of God are operations common to the whole Trinity. The personal acts of God are the operations proper to each person. Thus, the immanent *personal* acts are those operations which distinguish the divine persons within the Trinity, that is, the relations of opposition (*opera relationis*): the Father generates the Son, and the Spirit proceeds from the Father and the Son. These acts do not depend on God's deliberative will but are necessary to the divine nature. The immanent *essential* acts, however, do depend on God's deliberative will. These acts are sometimes called "*opera immanentia donec exeunt*" because, even though they take place within God, they have a respect to that which is outside God. The divine counsel and decree belong to God's immanent essential acts. Both the counsel and the decree, then, belong to the essence of God.[24] Heppe writes, "The expression therefore of God's counsel, the decree of it, is to be distinguished only conceptually from the counsel, as from the nature of God Himself; it is not different essentially."[25]

The Protestant Reformed held to the trinitarian axiom that all the operations of the Trinity outward are inseparable (*omnia opera trinitatis*

23. Berkhof, *Systematic Theology*, 103.

24. Richard Muller defines the Protestant scholastic understanding of the decree as follows:

> *decree*, specifically, the *decretum aeternum*, or eternal decree, according to which God wills and orders all things; in a restricted sense, the eternal *praedestinatio* (q.v.) of God. *The decretum aeternum* can be distinguished from the counsel of God (*consilium Dei*) only formally, not essentially, since the essential acts of God belong to the divine essence in its simplicity (*simplicitas*, q.v.) and are identical with the essence itself; nevertheless, in a formal sense, the *consilium* is the divine decision, and the *decretum* is the actual willing or expression of that decision. The *decretum*, like the *consilium* Dei (q.v.), is utterly free, absolute, and inalterable, logically antecedent to all things, predicated upon nothing but the nature of the divine essence, which is to say upon the *consilium* or, essentially speaking, on itself. (Muller, "Decretum," in *Dictionary of Latin and Greek Theological Terms*, 87)

25. Heppe, *Reformed Dogmatics*, 137.

ad extra indivisa sunt). "All the works ad extra: creation, providence, rule, incarnation, satisfaction (atonement), renewal, sanctification, and so on, are works of the Trinity as a whole."[26] In this respect, the *opera exeuntia* are *opera essentialia*. John Owen explains, "the several persons are undivided in their operations, acting all by the same will, the same wisdom, the same power. Every person, therefore, is the author of every work of God, because each person is God, and the divine nature is the same undivided principle of all divine operations."[27] But the Protestant Reformed also taught that there is a sense in which the *opera exeuntia* may be personal. Owen writes:

> But as to the manner of subsistence therein, there is distinction, relation, and order between and among them; and hence there is no divine work but is distinctly assigned unto each person, and eminently unto one. . . . Thus, the creation of the world is distinctly ascribed to the Father as his work, Acts iv. 24; and to the Son as his, John i. 3; and also to the Holy Spirit, Job xxxiii. 4; but by way of eminence to the Father, and absolutely to God, who is Father, Son, and Holy Spirit.[28]

Applying an outward work of God eminently to one person is known as appropriation (*opera appropriata*).

Thus, aside from the *opera appropriata*, the Reformed tradition distinguishes three aspects of divine acts. For example, Turretin writes:

> The divine acts admit of a threefold distinction. (1) There are immanent and intrinsic acts having no respect to anything outside of God (such are the personal acts—to beget, to spirate—of which there is an absolute necessity without power to be the opposite). (2) Others are extrinsic and transient acts which are not

26. Bavinck, *Reformed Dogmatics*, 2:320.

27. Owen, *ΠΝΕΥΜΑΤΟΛΟΓΙΑ*, 93.

28. Owen, *ΠΝΕΥΜΑΤΟΛΟΓΙΑ*, 93. Owen explains that a divine operation is eminently applied (i.e., appropriated) to one trinitarian person when either of the following two conditions is met:

> (1) When any especial impression is made of the essential property of any person on any work; then is that work assigned peculiarly to that person. So there is of the power and authority of the Father on the old creation, and of the grace and wisdom of the Son on the new. (2) Where there is a peculiar condescension of any person unto a work, wherein the others have no concurrence but by approbation and consent. Such was the susception of the human nature by the Son, and all that he did therein; and such was the condescension of the Holy Ghost also unto his office, which entitles him peculiarly and by way of eminence unto his own immediate works. (Owen, *ΠΝΕΥΜΑΤΟΛΟΓΙΑ*, 93–94)

> in God, but from him effectively and in creatures subjectively (as to create, to govern)—these are temporal acts and God is denominated extrinsic only from them. (3) There are acts immanent and intrinsic in God, but connoting a respect and relation (*schesin*) to something outside of God (such are the decrees, which are nothing else than the counsels of God concerning future things out of himself).[29]

The divine decree, therefore, is an immanent and intrinsic act in God connoting a relation to things outside God.[30] In other words, we might say that the decree is an immanent *ad extra* operation—a work that is internal but concerning the external.

3b. Divine Freedom and RSIM

Grant's chief objection to a view like RSIM is that it must deny that God has the freedom to do otherwise. He explains, "Thus, if God were identical to his acts of causing and choosing, then God could not exist without causing and choosing E, and so could not do otherwise than cause or choose E."[31] The Reformed tradition denies both that God is unfree and that absolute indifference renders one free.[32] The Reformed tradition contends that God's

29. Turretin, *Institutes* 1:311.

30. Concerning the decrees, Turretin writes:

> Since they cannot belong to God accidentally, we must necessarily say that they are in him essentially, as immanent acts of his will with a relation (*schesei*) and termination outside of him. Thus they do not differ really from his essence, since the will of God (with which they are identified) is nothing else than the essence itself willing (apprehended by an inadequate conception by us). In this sense, the decrees are rightly said to be identified with the essence, conceived after the manner of a vital act determining itself to the production of efficient and exemplar. Efficient because all future things are for this reason future—that God has decreed them (nor can any prior cause of his works be assigned). Exemplar because the decree of God is (as it were) the idea of all things out of himself, after which as the archetype (*archetypon*) they, as ectypes (*ektypa*), are expressed in time. (Turretin, *Institutes* 1:312)

31. Grant, *Free Will and God's Universal Causality*, 77.

32. Dolezal writes, "It should be readily confessed that the exact function of free will in God who is himself pure act is beyond the scope of human knowledge. . . . Though we discover strong reasons for confessing both simplicity and freedom in God, we cannot form an isomorphically adequate notion of *how* this is the case. In fact, this confession of ignorance is precisely what one finds in the Thomist and Reformed traditions." Dolezal, *God Without Parts*, 210–11.

decree is free in at least three senses.[33] First, the decree is not conditional but absolute. No aspect of the decree depends on what creatures might do.[34] Second, the decree is determined by God's good pleasure, not by anything external to God. Nothing but God himself determines the decree. Third, the decree is determined by God's wisdom, not by some irrational necessity in God. Although divine simplicity entails that God cannot exist apart from his knowing and willing, there is nothing about God apart from his wisdom that he decree *this* or *that*. Rather, God's wisdom determines what he decrees.

Berkhof explains, "The freedom of God is not pure indifference, but rational self-determination. God has reasons for willing as He does, which induce Him to choose one end rather than another, and one set of means to accomplish one end in preference to others."[35]

33. See Hodge, *Systematic Theology*, 1:539–40.

34. See Turretin, *Institutes* 1:316–19.

35. Berkhof, *Systematic Theology*, 78. Consider Bavinck's discussion of God's freedom:

> We can almost never tell why God willed one thing or another, and are therefore compelled to believe that he could just as well have willed one thing as another. But in God there is actually no such thing as choice inasmuch as it always presupposes uncertainty, doubt, and deliberation. He, however, knows what he wills—eternally, firmly, and immutably. Every hint of arbitrariness, contingency, or uncertainty is alien to his will, which is eternally determinate and unchanging. Contingency characterizes creatures and—let it be said in all reverence—not even God can deprive the creature of this characteristic. In God alone existence and essence are of one piece; by virtue of its very nature, a creature is such that it could also not have existed.
>
> But God, by his own eternal and unchanging will, willed all creatures to be contingent. For that reason it is not possible, nor even permissible, for us to look for some ground higher than the will of God. For all such efforts end up seeking a ground for a creature in the very nature of God, thus making it necessary, eternal, and divine, and divesting it of its creaturely, that is, contingent, character. In that sense it is true that the will of God, which has created things as its object, is free. But this freedom does not exclude other divine attributes such as wisdom, goodness, righteousness, and so on. After all, even among creatures true freedom of will is not the kind that needs a long period of doubt, deliberation, and decision; the greatest freedom, rather, is that which establishes all at once, by a single intuition, both the end and the means of an enterprise, and knows nothing of hesitation. Such freedom exists also in God. It is a freedom that must not be conceived as bound to the other perfections of God or, in nominalist fashion, made independent of them, but a freedom that is free in an absolute sense because it is the freedom of a wise, just, holy, merciful, and almighty God. (Bavinck, *Reformed Dogmatics*, 2:239–40)

With further precision, Turretin parses three elements to the decree:

> (1) the essence of God willing and decreeing after the manner of a principle; (2) its tendency outside himself, without however any internal addition or change because it indicates nothing but an external respect and habitude towards the creature, after the manner of a relation; (3) the object itself or the things decreed, which have a reason of the end.[36]

The decree is necessary in the first element but free in the latter ones.[37] The decree is necessary because it *just is* God willing. Turretin explains:

> The decrees of God are free, not absolutely and as to the principle, but relatively and objectively and as to the end. For there could be no external object necessarily terminating to the divine will, for God stands in need of nothing out of himself. Therefore they could be and not be. But this does not hinder them from being called necessary as to the principle and internal act because the act of intelligence and will could not be absent from God at all. He could not be God without intelligence and will. They are necessary, therefore, as to internal existence, but free as to external relation (*schesin*) and habit. Nor can the will of God be said to cease absolutely, but with respect to the external object on which it is terminated.[38]

Although God must will *something*, he is naturally indifferent to *this* or *that tendentia* (i.e., an external respect or relation). "This is because the *tendentia* of the act of decreeing is *merus respectus* and hence not identical with God's essence and so not characterized by the pure actuality and absolute necessity of God's essence."[39]

Because God is free with respect to the object of the decree, RSIM does not succumb to necessitarianism or modal collapse (i.e., the idea that all

36. Turretin, *Institutes* 1:313.
37. Turretin, *Institutes* 1:313.
38. Turretin, *Institutes* 1:193.
39. Duby: *Divine Simplicity*, 198. Turretin writes,

> The liberty of the divine decree does not hinder it from being God himself because it is free only terminatively and on the part of the thing, but not subjectively and on the part of God. It is free in the exercised act inasmuch as it resides in the liberty of God to decree this or that thing. It is not free in the signified act because to decree anything depends upon the internal constitution of God by which he understands and wills. It is free as to the respect and relation (*schesin*) outside himself, but not as to the absolute existence within. (Turretin, *Institutes* 1:313)

truths are necessary truths). Creation is contingent because God's decree is based on his wise reason, not from a necessity of nature. By nature, God has the power to create any number of worlds. To speak of possible worlds, then, is permissible insofar as their existence is possible due to God's power. In this sense, God *could* have created other worlds. But, since God has decreed *this* world, no other world is possible with respect to his will.[40]

4. In Support of RSIM

RSIM is preferable to EM because it enjoys support from Scripture and theological reflection. In what follows, I offer evidence in support of RSIM from the Bible and Christology.

4a. The Divine Decree in Scripture

Thinkers in the Reformed tradition held to an intrinsic model because they believed Scripture teaches that God's decree is a prior and sufficient condition for creation and providence. Moreover, they believed that Scripture situates the decree within God himself. The decree is intrinsic to God; it is his willing of his wisdom. Here, I argue that Scripture reveals the divine decree as (1) a prior condition for its effect in the world, (2) a sufficient condition for its effect in the world, and (3) an idea in the mind of God.

Scripture frequently refers to an act of God "before the ages" (πρὸ τῶν αἰώνων), "before the foundation of the world" (πρὸ καταβολῆς κόσμου), or "before all time" (πρὸ παντὸς τοῦ αἰῶνος), which is fulfilled or manifested in time. Phrases like "before the ages" should not be interpreted as a long time ago but as being logically prior to "the ages," i.e., prior to temporality.[41] This act is an eternal, timeless act of God; it is the divine decree. We

40. In *Eternal God*, Helm writes:

> If an alternative world is conceivable then an alternative world is possible. But there is a difference between saying that a state of affairs is internally consistent quite apart from the question of whether God would actualize it and saying that it is possible that God would actualize it. If the question, "Could God have instantiated a world different from the actual world?" is a question about God's power then the answer must be that if *A* is a consistent state of affairs then God's power could have actualized it. But that God is sufficiently powerful that he could is not to say that he would. In fact, we know from the actual world that he would not, because he has not. (Helm, *Eternal God*, 188)

41. English Bibles also use "beforehand" similarly in some cases, but in others, "beforehand" simply means temporally beforehand. For example, God spoke to us through

are right to view the decree as prior—not merely because it is "before the ages" but because the terms used to describe this act assume its priority. For example, the hope of eternal life is "*promised* [ἐπηγγείλατο] before the ages began and at the proper time manifested" (Titus 1:2, emphasis mine). God "chose us in [Christ] before the foundation of the world. . . . In love he *predestined* [προορίσας] us . . . according to the *purpose of his will* [τὴν εὐδοκίαν τοῦ θελήματος αὐτοῦ]" (Eph 1:4–5, emphasis mine). Likewise, God saved us "because of his own *purpose* [πρόσθεσιν] and grace, which he gave us in Christ Jesus before the ages began" (2 Tim 1:9, emphasis mine). God makes "known the riches of his glory for vessels of mercy, which he has *prepared* [προητοίμασεν] beforehand for glory" (Rom 9:23, emphasis mine). Again, "we are his workmanship, created in Christ Jesus for good works, which God *prepared* [προητοίμασεν] beforehand, that we should walk in them" (Eph 2:10, emphasis mine). The words used to describe this eternal decree (promise, predestination, purpose, preparation) indicate a logical priority to the event itself. A promise is prior to its keeping; a predestination is prior to its destination; a purpose is prior to its fulfillment; a preparation is prior to its performance; and a decree is prior to its manifestation. "Let them praise the name of the LORD! For he commanded and they were created. And he established them forever and ever; he gave a decree, and it shall not pass away" (Ps 148:5–6). The divine decree is a prior condition for its realization in time.

Scripture also portrays the divine decree as sufficient for its manifestation. Everything that God decrees does indeed happen. God keeps his promises, e.g., "the LORD did to Sarah as he had promised" (Gen 21:1). What God says he will do, he will do, e.g., "so I will stretch out my hand and strike Egypt with all the wonders that I will do in it" (Exod 3:20). "And I will put my Spirit within you, and cause you to walk in my statutes and be careful to obey my rules" (Ezek 36:27). And God never lies: "which God, who never lies, promised before the ages began" (Titus 1:2). God's decree is his plan for the world according to his wisdom and purpose. He "works all things according to the counsel of his will" (Eph 1:11). He has made "known to us the mystery of his will, according to his purpose, which he set forth in Christ as a *plan for the fullness of time* [οἰκονομίαν τοῦ πληρώματος τῶν καιρῶν]" (Eph 1:9–10, emphasis mine; cf. Eph 3:9). The decree is not an open-ended plan; for instance, Jesus was "delivered up according to the *definite plan and foreknowledge* [τῇ ὡρισμένῃ βοθλῇ καὶ προγνώσει] of God" (Acts 2:23, emphasis mine). The divine decree is a sufficient condition for its realization in time.

---

his prophets beforehand, i.e., before the coming of Christ (cf. Acts 1:16; Rom 1:2). "Beforehand" is usually the translation of a prefix attached to a verb, e.g., προητοίμασεν (he prepared beforehand), προεπηγγείλατο (he promised beforehand).

The divine decree is both prior and sufficient because it is the willing of a determinate plan *in the mind of God*. In a discussion of the revelation of the gospel of Christ, Paul writes, "But we impart a secret and hidden wisdom of God, which God decreed before the ages for our glory" (1 Cor 2:7).[42] Paul continues to show that this decree is in the mind of God: "These things God revealed to us through the Spirit. For the Spirit searches everything, even the depths of God. For who knows a person's thoughts except the spirit of that person, which is in him? So also no one comprehends the thoughts of God except the Spirit of God" (1 Cor 2:10–11). The decree, then, is the determination of God's wisdom existing as a thought in the mind of God. The Holy Spirit is able to reveal the thoughts of God because he is the very Spirit of God. Elsewhere, the Bible links together the priority, sufficiency, and internal character of the divine decree: "God is not man, that he should lie, or a son of man, that he should change his mind. Has he said, and will he not do it? Or has he spoken, and will he not fulfill it?" (Num 23:19). God has made up his mind—he has determined to act in a particular way. What his mind has determined, he will do.

4b. Christ, RSIM, and Ultimate Sourcehood

Grant's EM and Dual Sources account are inconsistent with classical Christology in at least two ways: The *pactum salutis* (i.e., the covenant of redemption) and the ultimate source of Christ's activity. First, the *pactum salutis*, like the divine decree according to RSIM, is intrinsic to God with a respect toward creation that implies theological determinism. Admittedly, the covenant of redemption is not one of the key features of classical Christology mentioned in chapter 2. It is, however, consistent with classical Christology, characteristic of Reformed theology, and supported by Scripture, the foundation of classical Christology. Second, Grant's account of ultimacy is contrary to classical Christology.

4b.i. The Pactum Salutis

The doctrine of Christ requires RSIM on account of the *pactum salutis*. The covenant of redemption is an eternal covenant among the persons of the Trinity with respect to salvation. Peter Gentry and Stephen Wellum explain:

42. ἀλλὰ λαλοῦμεν θεοῦ σοφίαν ἐν μυστηρίῳ τὴν ἀποκεκρυμμένην ἣν προώρισεν ὁ θεὸς πρὸ τῶν αἰώνων εἰς δόξαν ἡμῶν (1 Cor 2:7).

> The triune God has an eternal plan which is then executed in history (e.g., Eph. 1:4–14)—a plan conceived before the foundation of the world, made known on the stage of human history, and which involves the work of all three persons of the Godhead. Scripture speaks of this plan in terms of the Father giving a people to the Son (e.g., John 6:39; 10:29; 17:2, 6–10; Eph. 1:4–12), the Son accomplishing that plan by his life and death (John 6:37–40; 10:14–18; Heb. 10:5–18), and the Spirit's work to bring those same people to faith union in Christ (Rom. 8:29–30; Eph. 1:11–13; 1 Pet. 1:5).[43]

This covenant is part of the eternal and immutable decree which is intrinsic to God:

> We nevertheless treat this covenant as one of the intrinsic works of God, being repeatedly presented in such a manner throughout the Holy Scriptures. Concerning Christ it is stated that He "was foreordained before the foundation of the world" (1 Pet. 1:20). The elect are chosen in Him (Eph. 1:4), and grace has been given them "in Christ Jesus before the world began" (2 Tim. 1:9). Whatever Christ encountered in this world happened to Him according to the eternal decree, foreknowledge, and determinate counsel of God (cf. Psa. 2:7; Luke 22:22; Acts 2:23).[44]

The *pactum salutis* is an immanent act of God with a respect toward creation.

> This pact of salvation, however, further forms the link between the eternal work of God toward salvation and what he does to that end in time. The covenant of grace revealed in time does not hang in the air but rests on an eternal, unchanging foundation. It is firmly grounded in the counsel and covenant of the triune God and is the application and execution of it that infallibly follows.[45]

43. Gentry and Wellum, *Kingdom Through Covenant*, 60.
44. Brakel, *Christian's Reasonable Service*, 1:252.
45. Bavinck, *Reformed Dogmatics*, 3:214. Heppe writes:

> The *pactum* by which the Son, in order to become the mediator of the Father's testament, became its sponsor and the second Adam of the human race, is still not an event in the Trinity first produced temporally through the fall, different from the Father's eternal counsel. On the contrary it is essentially connected with the fallen human race and yet it is an element in the eternal and unalterable decree of God Himself. (Heppe, *Reformed Dogmatics*, 378)

The covenant of redemption is that part of the divine decree that pertains to the Triune God's definite work of salvation. With respect to Christ's human work, the covenant of redemption entails determinism because it is logically prior to and sufficient for Christ's incarnation, life, death, and resurrection. All that Christ did was planned in the mind of God before it was executed in time.

The notion that Christ's human work of salvation was preordained in the mind of God is not unique to Reformed theology. Aquinas, for example, taught that Christ was predestined. According to Aquinas, "predestination, in its proper sense, is a certain Divine preordination from eternity of those things which are to be done in time by the grace of God."[46] He continues:

> Now, that man is God, and that God is man, is something done by God through the grace of union. Nor can it be said that God has not from eternity pre-ordained to do this in time: since it would follow that something would come anew into the Divine Mind. And we must needs admit that the union itself of natures in the Person of Christ falls under the eternal predestination of God. For this reason do we say that Christ was predestined.[47]

For Aquinas, "predestination" implies an antecedence; and this predestination is in the mind of God: "Although the participle *predestined* [*praedestinatus*], just as the participle *made* [*factus*], implies antecedence, yet there is a difference. For *to be made* [*fieri*] belongs to the thing in itself: whereas *to be predestined* [*praedestinari*] belongs to someone as being in the apprehension of one who pre-ordains."[48] Thus, the plan for Christ's human activity was in the mind of God logically prior to its actuality in time.

EM cannot make proper sense of the covenant of redemption because it cannot posit a logically prior covenant, pact, plan, or decree within God. On EM, God's decreeing (planning, covenanting, predestinating, etc.) Christ and his work of salvation *just is* God's bringing about Christ and his work of salvation in the world. But Christ's work of salvation in the world does not correspond to a definite plan, counsel, or decision in God.

Grant argues that predestination does not have to be understood as prior or antecedent to the event:

> Just as one may plausibly hold that the essential feature of a commitment to divine foreknowledge is simply that God knows future events, and not that God or God's knowledge is prior to

46. *ST* III q. 24, a. 1, co.

47. *ST* III q. 24, a. 1, co.

48. *ST* III q. 24, a. 1, ad. 3.

> the future events God knows, so I maintain that the essential feature of predestination is that a person's attaining salvation is God's choice and within God's power, and not that God's choice is prior to the person's doing what is needed to attain salvation.[49]

But the concept of predestination in Scripture cannot be understood apart from a notion of antecedence or logical priority. Consider, for example, Romans 9:9–13:

> For this is what the promise said: "About this time next year I will return, and Sarah shall have a son." And not only so, but also when Rebekah had conceived children by one man, our forefather Isaac, though they were not yet born and had done nothing either good or bad—in order that God's purpose of election might continue, not because of works but because of him who calls—she was told, "The older will serve the younger." As it is written, "Jacob I loved, but Esau I hated."

As the text clearly shows, Jacob was chosen *before* he was born. He was chosen not on account of anything he had done or would do. This election of Jacob is not merely God's prediction of Jacob's success or faith; rather, it was a promise from God. God is the ultimate source of Jacob's election.

Now consider this passage from 1 Peter which shows that Christ's election was prior to his incarnation:

> As you come to him, a living stone rejected by men but in the sight of God chosen and precious, you yourselves like living stones are being built up as a spiritual house, to be a holy priesthood, to offer spiritual sacrifices acceptable to God through Jesus Christ. For it stands in Scripture:
>
> > "Behold, I am laying in Zion a stone,
> > a cornerstone chosen and precious,
> > and whoever believes in him will not be put to shame."
>
> So the honor is for you who believe, but for those who do not believe,
>
> > "The stone that the builders rejected
> > has become the cornerstone,"
>
> and

49. Grant, *Free Will and God's Universal Causality*, 175–76.

> "A stone of stumbling,
> and a rock of offense."
>
> They stumble because they disobey the word, as they were destined to do. (1 Pet 2:4–8)

Jesus is the stone that was chosen by God—a precious cornerstone to the house of God and a stumbling block to those who do not believe. That Christ's election is a prior condition to his incarnation can be seen from the fact it was promised and prophesied beforehand. And it is not merely Jesus' choices that are preordained but his incarnation—and there is no way that his birth was in any way *up to him* (i.e., up to his human will, choice, or power). It seems, then, that the *pactum salutis* and the language of Scripture require that Christ's work of salvation correspond to a plan in God logically prior to that work.

I end this section with a passage from Ephesians that brings together many of the ideas discussed in this chapter so far:

> Blessed be the God and Father of our Lord Jesus Christ, who has blessed us in Christ with every spiritual blessing in the heavenly places, even as he chose us in him before the foundation of the world, that we should be holy and blameless before him. In love he predestined us for adoption to himself as sons through Jesus Christ, according to the purpose of his will, to the praise of his glorious grace, with which he has blessed us in the Beloved. In him we have redemption through his blood, the forgiveness of our trespasses, according to the riches of his grace, which he lavished upon us, in all wisdom and insight making known to us the mystery of his will, according to his purpose, which he set forth in Christ as a plan for the fullness of time, to unite all things in him, things in heaven and things on earth. (Eph 1:3–10)

Notice the repeated mention of the *purpose* of God's will. The purpose can be no other than the divine wisdom (i.e., God's reason[s]). The "mystery of his will" is the gospel of Christ crucified, which is founded in divine wisdom and constitutes "a plan for the fullness of time."

4b.ii. The Ultimate Sourcehood of Christ's Activity

Christ's human activity must originate in his divinity. Dominic Legge, interpreting Aquinas, writes, "But the hypostatic union alone is not enough to account for how Christ's humanity acts as an instrument of his divinity. . . . [The human nature of Christ] must be actually moved by the divinity, with a motion that originates above and yet that is interior to it."[50] Classical Christology acknowledges that Jesus Christ does the work of God because he *is God* and is *from God* (John 1:1, 18). Jesus, himself, says, "For I have come down from heaven, not to do my own will but the will of him who sent me" (John 6:38).

Because Grant's Dual Sources account claims that humans have counterfactual power over God, it implies that the humanity of Christ has counterfactual power over his divinity. Grant writes:

> Given EM, I exercise counterfactual power over God's causing my act, since, all antecedent conditions remaining the same, I have the ability to do otherwise, and were I to do otherwise, God's act of causing my act would not occur. Since whether God's causing my act occurs is not outside my power, there is no reason on EM to think that whether or not my act occurs is ultimately up to God and not, at least also, ultimately up to me.[51]

Presumably, because Christ's humanity is like that of other human beings, he has the same counterfactual power over the divine will that other humans do. Thus, the origin of Christ's human activity is ultimately in his humanity *and* ultimately in his divinity. Whether this paradox is coherent is a matter beyond the scope of this chapter, but whether it is consistent with classical Christology *is* the matter of this chapter. I argue that the language of Constantinople III prohibits this implication of Grant's view. The council declares:

> And the two natural wills [of Christ] not in opposition, as the impious heretics said, far from it, but his human will following, and not resisting or struggling, rather in fact subject to his divine and all powerful will. For the will of the flesh had to be moved, and yet to be subjected to the divine will, according to the most wise Athanasius.[52]

The council teaches that Christ's human will was subordinate to his divine will; the wills are not co-ultimate. Constantinople III is built on the teachings of Scripture: "the Son can do nothing of his own accord, but only what he sees the Father doing. For whatever the Father does, that the Son does likewise" (John 5:19); "I can do nothing on my own. As I hear, I judge, and my judgment is just, because I seek not my own will but the will of him who sent me" (John 5:30). Because Grant's EM and Dual Sources account are

50. Legge, *Trinitarian Christology*, 194.

51. Grant, *Free Will and God's Universal Causality*, 70.

52. Tanner, *Decrees of the Ecumenical Councils*, 128.

inconsistent with classical Christology and cannot affirm the *pactum salutis*, RSIM is required in order to make sense of Christology.

5. Christ and Hard Determinism Summary

In this and the previous chapter, I have shown that if classical Christology is true, then hard determinism is false. Hard determinism is the thesis that (1) freedom and moral responsibility are incompatible with determinism, and (2) determinism is true. I have already shown that Jesus Christ is, indeed, a moral agent. So, whether or not determinism is true, hard determinism is ruled out. In chapter 6, I considered the relationship between Christ's divine and human will. I argued that the only way to account for the divine will moving the human will is by causation. In this chapter, I considered whether God's causation should be considered deterministically. I answered in the affirmative: because the decree is intrinsic to God, it is both prior to and sufficient for its manifestation in creation. Christ's human volitions and operations are included in the divine decree. Therefore, Christ's human volitions and operations were determined by God. Because Christ's human activity was determined, and yet he is a moral agent whose decisions are voluntary and uncoerced, hard determinism is false.

Part III:

The Positive Christological Case for Compatibilism

8

Christ's Teaching

1. Introduction

In the previous chapters, I demonstrated that classical Christology is inconsistent with PAP libertarianism, sourcehood libertarianism, and hard determinism. Therefore, the only viable alternative is compatibilism. In this part of the book, I present a positive case for compatibilism. I show that compatibilism is entailed by classical Christology using three modes of argument: (1) Jesus Christ's didactic ministry, including his revelation about his own mission and relation to the Father, and his teachings about humanity, (2) the biblical-historical unfolding of God's plan in Christ, and (3) the systematic theological features of classical Christology. These three modes of argument align roughly with the three forms of christological arguments for compatibilism: (1) appeals to Christ's own teachings, (2) appeals to the necessity of the incarnation and atonement, and (3) appeals to Christ's wills and impeccability.

I do not argue that compatibilism is the only possible way to understand every individual biblical or theological datum that follows (e.g., God's promises are fulfilled in Christ). Rather, I argue that (1) compatibilism is consistent with every datum that follows, (2) compatibilism is consistent with the whole counsel of Scripture, and (3) in light of the arguments made in part 2, compatibilism is entailed by classical Christology. Whereas the previous chapters tended toward philosophico-theological discourse, this chapter is decidedly a work of exegetico-biblical theology, and the next two are decidedly works of biblical and systematic theology.

By way of review, determinism is the thesis that every event is necessitated by a set of prior and sufficient conditions. Compatibilism is the thesis that determinism is compatible with freedom and moral responsibility. In this case, the determining condition is the divine will; and the freedom and responsibility in question is that of the humanity of Jesus Christ.

Classical Christology is the portrait of Jesus Christ given in Scripture and affirmed by Christian, historical orthodoxy. Classical Christology maintains that the man Jesus Christ is also the pre-existent Son of God, consubstantial with the Father and the Holy Spirit. Classical Christology affirms dyothelitism, non-contrariety of wills, and impeccability.

Christ's teaching about himself and his teaching about humanity are consistent with compatibilism and support the thesis that classical Christology entails compatibilism. Christ understood that he was sent by God to do the will of God. Everything he did was a fulfillment of prophecy set forth in Scripture. From his birth to his death and resurrection—his human life and activity were ordained by God for God's own purposes. Christ also taught both that (i) humans are free and moral creatures and yet (ii) they (at least sometimes) lack the ability to do otherwise. Moreover, Jesus taught divine judgment and meticulous providence over human activity.

2. Christ's Teaching About Himself

In chapter 5, I argued that Jesus saw his human life and actions as ultimately sourced in the Godhead. Here, first, I expand on the notion that Jesus is *from* the Father. Jesus' being *from* the Father is a theological concept drawn from the biblical language of sonship, dependence, and mission (i.e., being sent). Second, I show that Jesus taught that his life and activity were the fulfillment of God's purpose for the world. Third, I demonstrate that Jesus taught that he was free and morally praiseworthy. That Jesus is from the Father and the fulfillment of God's purpose for the world show that his life and activity are governed by God. And the notion that Jesus' life and activity are governed by God provides support for a compatibilist reading of his freedom.

2a. The Son Who Comes from God the Father

Jesus has come from heaven. He says, "For I have come down from heaven, not to do my own will but the will of him who sent me" (John 6:38). He calls himself "the bread of God . . . who comes down from heaven and gives life to the world" (John 6:33). John affirms that Jesus is from heaven: "He who comes from above is above all. He who is of the earth belongs to the earth and speaks in an earthly way. He who comes from heaven is above all" (John 3:31; cf. 1 Thess 1:10).

Jesus has come from the Father. He says, "You know me, and you know where I come from. But I have not come of my own accord. He who sent me is true, and him you do not know" (John 7:28). In the Garden of Gethsemane, Jesus implies that he comes from the Father when he prays, "Now is my soul troubled. And what shall I say? 'Father, save me from this hour'? But for this purpose I have come to this hour" (John 12:27). Perhaps most explicitly, Jesus says, "I came from the Father and have come into the world" (John 16:28). Jesus was sent by the Father; he says, "Whoever receives one such child in my name receives me, and whoever receives me, receives not me but him who sent me" (Mark 9:37). Jesus' parable of the tenants also teaches that Jesus was sent by the Father: "He had still one other, a beloved son. Finally he sent him to them" (Mark 12:6). John corroborates when he writes that Jesus was given and sent by the Father: "For God so loved the world, that he gave his only Son, that whoever believes in him should not perish but have eternal life. For God did not sent his Son into the world to condemn the world, but in order that the world might be saved through him" (John 3:16–17; cf. 13:3).

Jesus is the incarnate Son of God. Jesus often referred to himself as the Son of Man (e.g., Matt 8:20; 24:44; Mark 14:41; Luke 6:22). "The Son of Man" is not merely a designation of his humanity; rather, it signifies divine prerogative through humanity (see especially the "son of man" throughout Ezekiel and in Daniel 7). The Son of Man is the one who is to come to usher in God's kingdom (e.g., Matt 16:28; Mark 14:62). Although Jesus more frequently refers to himself as the Son of Man, he never rejects the title of Son of God (e.g., when Satan tempts Jesus in the wilderness: "If you are the Son of God . . ." [Matt 4]). Indeed, Jesus says that the church is built on Peter's confession: "You are the Christ, the Son of the living God" (Matt 16:16). And Jesus openly declared himself to be the Son of God (e.g., John 5:25; 10:36). The rest of Scripture corroborates Jesus' teaching that he is the incarnate Son of God: "And we know that the Son of God has come and has given us understanding, so that we may know him who is true; and we are in him who is true, in his Son Jesus Christ. He is the true God and eternal life" (1 John 5:20). Jesus' use of sonship language shows that he believed himself to be the Messiah—the one who was to come to fulfill the Law and the Prophets.[1]

1. I take Jesus' use of the messianic titles "Son of Man" and "Son of God" as a whole to indicate his divinity, not merely his Davidic kingship. For a high christological reading of these messianic titles in the Synoptic Gospels, see Gathercole, *Preexistent Son*, 253–83. See also Schreiner, *New Testament Theology*, 197–260; Bauckham, *Jesus and the God of Israel*, 46–50, 169–72. For extrabiblical Jewish sources on the title "Son of Man," see Bock and Herrick, *Jesus in Context*, 76–79, 177–81, 236.

Jesus taught that he is the Son of God incarnate who was sent by the Father from heaven. Jesus recognizes that this relationship to the Father orders his whole life. Jesus did not send himself; rather, he says, "I came not of my own accord, but he sent me" (John 8:42; cf. 7:28). He can do nothing apart from the Father: "Truly, truly, I say to you, the Son can do nothing of his own accord, but only what he sees the Father doing. For whatever the Father does, that the Son does likewise" (John 5:19). The Son always does the will of the Father: "I seek not my own will but the will of him who sent me" (John 5:30; cf. 6:38); "Nevertheless, not my will, but yours be done" (Luke 22:42). The Son always says what the Father would have him say: "For I have not spoken on my own authority, but the Father who sent me has himself given me a commandment—what to say and what to speak" (John 12:49). Everything Christ has, he received from his Father (e.g., Matt 28:18; John 8:38; 15:15), even the authority to lay down his life: "This charge I have received from my Father" (John 10:18). Christ's very body is God's possession to give on behalf of mankind: "This is my body, which is given for you" (Luke 22:19). Jesus does the work of the Father: "For the works that the Father has given to me to accomplish, the very works that I am doing, bear witness about me that the Father has sent me" (John 5:36).

2b. The Fulfillment of Divine Purpose

Jesus regularly taught that he was the fulfillment of divine purpose. Already, Jesus' use of sonship, mission, and dependence language supports the idea that God had a special purpose for Jesus' life. Likewise, Jesus' frequent remarks about the necessity of his work and the fulfillment of Scripture show that he taught that he was the fulfillment of divine purpose.

Jesus often said a particular act was necessary. For example, Jesus taught "that he must go to Jerusalem and suffer many things from the elders and chief priests and scribes, and be killed, and on the third day be raised" (Matt 16:21; cf. Mark 8:31; Luke 9:22; 13:33; 17:25). When he was a child, he said to his parents, "Did you not know that I must be in my Father's house?" (Luke 2:49). Jesus tells Zacchaeus that "I must stay at your house today" (Luke 19:5). Jesus says, "I must preach the good news of the kingdom of God to the other towns as well; for I was sent for this purpose" (Luke 4:43). After his resurrection, Jesus says to his disciples, "O foolish ones, and slow of heart to believe all that the prophets have spoken! Was it not necessary that the Christ should suffer these things and enter into his glory?" (Luke 24:25–26).

Jesus often grounded this necessity in the teachings of Scripture. Scripture must be fulfilled; and it is Christ who came to fulfill all Scripture: "Do not think that I have come to abolish the Law or the Prophets; I have not come to abolish them but to fulfill them" (Matt 5:17). Having read from the scroll of Isaiah in the synagogue, Jesus explains, "Today this Scripture has been fulfilled in your hearing" (Luke 4:21). He teaches that "everything written about me in the Law of Moses and the Prophets and the Psalms must be fulfilled" (Luke 24:44). This fulfillment of Scripture does not pertain merely to a few broad activities; rather, everything Jesus did was part of his fulfilling of divine purpose. Jesus' justification for his baptism was that "it is fitting for us to fulfill all righteousness" (Matt 3:15). His ministry began at the appointed time: "The time is fulfilled, and the kingdom of God is at hand; repent and believe in the gospel" (Mark 1:15). In his high priestly prayer, he says, "While I was with them, I kept them in your name, which you have given me. I have guarded them, and not one of them has been lost except the son of destruction, that the Scripture may be fulfilled" (John 17:12). Jesus' betrayal and capture were part of the fulfillment of Scripture; Jesus says, "For I tell you that this Scripture must be fulfilled in me: 'And he was numbered with the transgressors.' For what is written about me has its fulfillment" (Luke 22:37). He says to his captors, "Day after day I was with you in the temple teaching, and you did not seize me. But let the Scriptures be fulfilled" (Mark 14:49).

2c. Free and Morally Praiseworthy

Jesus' own words show that he is a rational agent who is free to act according to his will. Jesus claims to know things (e.g., Matt 11:27; John 3:11; 5:32) and to choose things (e.g., John 13:18; 15:16); thus, his claims imply that he has the faculties of a rational agent, namely, an intellect and will. Moreover, Christ's prayer in Gethsemane demonstrates that, even though his life and activity are directed by God, he wills freely—not by compulsion: "nevertheless, not as I will, but as you will" (Matt 26:39).

Jesus also claims to be good and righteous. He preaches the good news about the kingdom of God and teaches kingdom ethics. The Sermon on the Mount, for example, is concerned especially with righteousness. He judges between the righteous and unrighteous (e.g., Matt 7:21–23; 25:31–46). Jesus does good works. After healing the man with the withered hand, Jesus asks the scribes and Pharisees who sought to snare him, "I ask you, is it lawful on the Sabbath to do good or to do harm, to save life or to destroy it?" (Luke 6:9). Likewise, he says, "I have shown you many good works from the Father; for which of them are you going to stone me?" (John 10:32). Jesus is the self-avowed preacher, teacher, judge, and doer of righteousness. His obedience is pleasing to God (John 8:29).

2d. A Compatibilist Reading of Jesus' Teaching About Himself

Jesus' teaching about himself supports the central thesis of this book, namely, that classical Christology entails compatibilism. Jesus, himself, taught that he is completely dependent on God and that everything he does is part of God's purpose as prophesied in Scripture. He always does the Father's will; he speaks only what the Father gives him to speak; and he does the work of his Father alone. It was necessary that he carry out the Father's will and thus fulfill all of Scripture. As the Son of God, Jesus so identifies with the Father that he could say that the Father is in him (John 17:21) and, "I and the Father are one" (John 10:30; cf. 17:11). Because Jesus never did otherwise than the Father's will, the burden of proof is on the indeterminist to prove that Jesus *could* have done otherwise. Furthermore, because all that Jesus did was the fulfillment of God's word, purpose, and will, we ought to conclude that the ultimate source of Jesus' activity is found in the Godhead, not in the humanity of Christ. And because Jesus saw himself as a moral agent, compatibilism is a fitting reading of Jesus' teaching about himself.

3. Christ's Teaching About Humanity

Christ's teaching about humanity accords with compatibilism and seems to run contrary to both hard determinism and libertarianism. Christ taught that human persons are moral agents who are rightly judged according to their works. He taught that (1) a person's true and inner self (i.e., a person's heart) is known by the person's work, (2) God's grace is necessary for true repentance and faith, (3) God exercises meticulous providence over human activity, and (4) God judges human beings according to their work. These four points support a compatibilist reading of Jesus' teaching.

3a. Hearts Are Known by Works

Christ taught that people's actions are reflections of their true selves. Praiseworthy acts spring from righteous hearts. Blameworthy acts spill out of wicked hearts. Jesus frequently used fruit trees to illustrate this concept:

> Beware of false prophets, who come to you in sheep's clothing but inwardly are ravenous wolves. You will recognize them by

> their fruits. Are grapes gathered from thornbushes, or figs from thistles? So, every healthy tree bears good fruit, but the diseased tree bears bad fruit. A healthy tree cannot bear bad fruit, nor can a diseased tree bear good fruit. Every tree that does not bear good fruit is cut down and thrown into the fire. Thus you will recognize them by their fruits. (Matt 7:15–20; cf. Luke 6:43–45)

Good deeds come from hearts set on good; evil deeds come from hearts set on evil:

> Either make the tree good and its fruit good, or make the tree bad and its fruit bad, for the tree is known by its fruit. You brood of vipers! How can you speak good, when you are evil? For out of the abundance of the heart the mouth speaks. The good person out of his good treasure brings forth good, and the evil person out of his evil treasure brings forth evil. I tell you, on the day of judgment people will give account for every careless word they speak, for by your words you will be justified, and by your words you will be condemned. (Matt 12:33–37)

Jesus explains, "What comes out of the mouth proceeds from the heart, and this defiles a person. For out of the heart come evil thoughts, murder, adultery, sexual immorality, theft, false witness, slander" (Matt 15:18–19). The implication of this teaching is that one's inner self—including one's thoughts, reasons, beliefs, and desires—determine one's outer self—one's words and actions. Furthermore, this correspondence between one's inner self and outer self seems to preclude the principle of alternative possibilities (PAP).[2] And if PAP is false, then PAP libertarianism is false. If one's heart is set one way, then one's actions will follow that way. Libertarianism teaches that one's inner self cannot *determine* one's outer self: It is possible that a bad tree produce good fruit and a good tree produce bad fruit. Compatibilism, however, fits with Jesus' teaching about the inner and outer selves: One's words and deeds are determined by one's beliefs, desires, and reasons.

3b. Divine Grace Is Necessary

Jesus' teaching about the heart is fitting with his teaching about the need for divine grace for true repentance and faith. This idea is most pronounced in Jesus' conversation with Nicodemus:

2. That is, if this correspondence between the inner and outer self precludes the ability to do otherwise (which it seems to do), then the principle of alternative possibilities is false, and thus, PAP libertarianism is false.

> Now there was a man of the Pharisees named Nicodemus, a ruler of the Jews. This man came to Jesus by night and said to him, "Rabbi, we know that you are a teacher come from God, for no one can do these signs that you do unless God is with him." Jesus answered him, "Truly, truly, I say to you, unless one is born again he cannot see the kingdom of God." Nicodemus said to him, "How can a man be born when he is old? Can he enter a second time into his mother's womb and be born?" Jesus answered, "Truly, truly, I say to you, unless one is born of water and the Spirit, he cannot enter the kingdom of God. That which is born of the flesh is flesh, and that which is born of the Spirit is spirit. Do not marvel that I said to you, 'You must be born again.' The wind blows where it wishes, and you hear its sound, but you do not know where it comes from or where it goes. So it is with everyone who is born of the Spirit." (John 3:1–8)

In this passage, Jesus teaches that the Spirit's work of regeneration is a necessary precursor to seeing and entering the kingdom of God. Apart from regeneration, one cannot exercise true faith and repentance (cf. 1 Cor 2:6–16; 1 Pet 1:3–9; 1 John 3:9–10; 5:1–5).[3]

The absence and restoration of sight and hearing are major motifs in Jesus' ministry. Jesus' metaphors of blindness and deafness highlight the need for divine grace. Blessed are those who have eyes to see and ears to hear (Matt 11:15; 13:9–17; Mark 4:21–23; Luke 10:23–24). Jesus' healing of the blind and deaf is symbolic for the spiritual healing of regeneration to the spiritually blind and deaf (Matt 9:27–31; Mark 7:31–37; 8:22–26; John 9:1–41). But those who do not have eyes to see and ears to hear have hardened hearts and are stuck in darkness and sin (Matt 13:10–17; Luke 19:41–44). Only God can make the blind see and the deaf hear. After healing the "demon-oppressed man who was blind and mute," the Pharisees accused Jesus of doing so by the power of the prince of demons, but Jesus responds, "But if it is by the Spirit of God that I cast out demons, then the kingdom of God has come upon you" (Matt 12:22, 28). Jesus, moreover, is the light of the world; through him alone may anyone see God (John 8:12–20; 12:44–50). Likewise, those who hear Jesus' voice are blessed (John 10:27; Rev 3:20). The apostles were right to connect spiritual blindness and deafness with uncircumcision of the heart, that is, being unregenerate (Acts 7:51). Sight and hearing are also connected with faith and understanding.

3. A libertarian may invoke the notion of prevenient grace and claim that although prevenient grace is necessary, it is not sufficient for faith and repentance. But, as I show below, God himself brings about faith and repentance; thus, God's work is both necessary and sufficient for faith and repentance.

To see and hear is to have faith and to understand. To be blind and deaf is to lack understanding and to lack faith; and to lack understanding and faith is to be hard of heart (Mark 6:52; 8:17).

Jesus teaches that God takes the initiative in salvation. Jesus himself is the God-ordained means by which sinners are saved; he says, "I am the living bread that came down from heaven. If anyone eats of this bread, he will live forever. And the bread that I will give for the life of the world is my flesh" (John 6:51). But no one can come to God without God first drawing them; Jesus explains, "No one can come to me unless the Father who sent me draws him. And I will raise him up on the last day" (John 6:44). Jesus makes the same point with another metaphor; he says, "I am the vine; you are the branches. Whoever abides in me and I in him, he it is that bears much fruit, for apart from me you can do nothing" (John 15:5). Thus, Jesus is the God-ordained means of salvation. And he proceeds to say, "You did not choose me, but I chose you and appointed you that you should go and bear fruit and that your fruit should abide" (John 15:16). This language of drawing and choosing, along with the motifs of seeing/hearing and believing/understanding, link with the idea of effectual calling. Again, Jesus provides a metaphor: "I am the good shepherd. The good shepherd lays down his life for the sheep" (John 10:11).

> Jesus answered them, "I told you, and you do not believe. The works that I do in my Father's name bear witness about me, but you do not believe because you are not among my sheep. My sheep hear my voice, and I know them, and they follow me. I give them eternal life, and they will never perish, and no one will snatch them out of my hand. My Father, who has given them to me, is greater than all, and no one is able to snatch them out of the Father's hand. I and the Father are one." (John 10:25–30)

Those who are called by Jesus follow him (Mark 1:20; Luke 5:27). And this spiritual calling is symbolized by Jesus calling the dead girl to life: "But taking her by the hand he called, saying, "Child, arise" (Luke 8:54). Hence, Jesus teaches that God takes the initiative in salvation both in ordaining the objective means (the person and work of Jesus Christ) and the subjective means (bringing about faith in Jesus).

3c. *Providence Is Meticulous*

Jesus taught that everything happens according to God's will, and, by intension, all human willing and acting happens according to God's will. All that has been said already about Christ's fulfillment of God's word, will, and purpose supports the claim that Christ believed in meticulous providence. God must order all things surrounding Jesus' life, including his genealogy, his place of birth, his activity, the history and state of the nations, the reactions of the spiritual and political leaders, etc. That Jesus taught meticulous providence can also be deduced from a consideration of his teachings cumulatively.

Jesus reminds his disciples about God's exhaustive knowledge and care for humanity: "Are not five sparrows sold for two pennies? And not one of them is forgotten before God. Why, even the hairs of your head are all numbered. Fear not; you are of more value than many sparrows" (Luke 12:6–7; cf. 12:22–30). God sees the secret activities, hears the secret prayers, and knows the hearts of his creatures (Matt 6:1–6; Luke 16:15).

Jesus' own prayers and teaching about prayer demonstrate that God is provident over creation. For example, he prays, "I thank you, Father, Lord of heaven and earth, that you have hidden these things from the wise and understanding and revealed them to little children; yes, Father, for such was your gracious will" (Matt 11:25–26). In other words, God's will is sovereign over the understanding of human creatures. Because of God's sovereignty, Jesus teaches us to pray, "Give us this day our daily bread. . . . And lead us not into temptation, but deliver us from evil" (Matt 6:11, 13). Likewise, "If you then, who are evil, know how to give good gifts to your children, how much more will your Father who is in heaven give good things to those who ask him!" (Matt 7:11). We pray to God because he has the power to do what he wills. In fact, Jesus explains, "with God all things are possible" (Matt 19:26). And, in one respect, God's will determines what is possible; compare Matthew's account of Christ's Gethsemane prayer: "My Father, if it be possible [εἰ δυνατόν ἐστιν], let this cup pass from me; nevertheless, not as I will, but as you will" (26:39) with Luke's account: "Father, if you are willing [εἰ βούλει], remove this cup from me. Nevertheless, not my will, but yours be done" (Luke 22:42).[4]

Jesus recognizes that God has all authority: "Jesus answered him, 'You have no authority over me at all unless it had been given you from above. Therefore he who delivered me over to you has the greater sin'" (John 19:11).

4. I am not suggesting any sort of voluntarism wherein all notions of modality arise out of the divine will rather than divine self-knowledge (I affirm intellectualism in agreement with Thomism and the Reformed tradition). Rather, I suggest that we interpret the two verses as teaching that, given the divine will, only one series of events will be actual—and in that sense, no other series of events could be actual. In other words, together, these two passages teach a consequent necessity.

Likewise, "All authority in heaven and on earth has been given to me" (Matt 28:18).

Even sin, suffering, and evil fall under the providence of God. Jesus' disciples asked him, "'Rabbi, who sinned, this man or his parents, that he was born blind?' Jesus answered, 'It was not that this man sinned, or his parents, but that the works of God might be displayed in him'" (John 9:2–3). And, undoubtedly, Judas' betrayal was part of God's plan: "For the Son of Man goes as it is written of him, but woe to that man by whom the Son of Man is betrayed!" (Mark 14:21).

3d. God Will Judge

Even though Christ teaches that God's providence is exhaustive, he still teaches that God holds humans accountable for their deeds. In other words, Christ teaches divine judgment (Matt 12:36–37). Those who are wicked are condemned; those who are righteous are blessed and rewarded.

The righteous, Jesus says, will enter the kingdom of heaven, be comforted, inherit the earth, be satisfied, receive mercy, see God, be called "sons of God," and be rewarded in heaven (Matt 5:3–10). The reward is eternal life (Luke 18:29–30; John 5:24). Jesus also teaches that sinners are liable to judgment (Matt 5:21–22). Indeed, he teaches that hell is reserved for sinners; it is better to lose an eye or a limb "than that your whole body go into hell" (Matt 5:30).

Jesus himself will judge humanity on his throne. He will separate the sheep from the goats. The sheep, who represent the righteous, will be placed on his right, and he will say to them, "Come, you who are blessed by my Father, inherit the kingdom prepared for you from the foundation of the world" (Matt 25:34). The goats, who represent the unrighteous, will be placed on his left, and he will say to them, "Depart from me, you cursed, into the eternal fire prepared for the devil and his angels" (Matt 25:41). He concludes, "And these will go away into eternal punishment, but the righteous into eternal life" (Matt 25:46; cf. 13:36–43).

Divine judgment, moreover, is not arbitrary but just. Condemnation is for the guilty: "And if you had known what this means, 'I desire mercy, and not sacrifice' you would not have condemned the guiltless" (Matt 12:7). And no good deed goes unrewarded (Luke 14:14).

3e. A Compatibilist Reading of Jesus' Teaching About Humanity

Christ's teaching about humanity accords with compatibilism. God is sovereign, and his providence is meticulous; everything happens according to God's will. Humans are moral creatures who deserve blame or praise, condemnation or reward, depending on their works. Human works, moreover, correspond to human hearts; that is, one's actions are determined by one's inner life: one's thoughts, beliefs, and desires. Although humans are free to do what they want, they are unable *to want* to serve God (i.e., to have true faith, repentance, and obedience) apart from divine grace. Fallen creatures need God to open their eyes and ears, soften their hearts, and cause them to be born again. If either God's meticulous providence or the priority of human hearts over human acts (or both) entail determinism, then we should affirm that Christ's teaching about humanity implies compatibilism.

4. Conclusion

In this chapter, I reflected upon Jesus' teaching ministry. I showed that Jesus' teaching about himself is consistent with compatibilism. He was sent by God to do the will of God and to fulfill all Scripture. I also showed that Jesus teaching about humanity in general accords with compatibilism. Humans are under the meticulous sovereignty of God; they are held morally accountable for their deeds; and their outer lives properly express their inner lives. In the next chapters, I continue this positive case for compatibilism, reasoning from biblical and systematic theology.

9

The Necessity of Christ

1. Introduction

In this chapter, I review the metanarrative of Scripture in order to show the necessity of the advent and obedience of Jesus Christ. The storyline of Scripture has four major parts and six progressive covenants.[1] Stephen Wellum explains, "These parts and covenants work together to form the Bible's own theological framework that puts all of the intervening biblical data into place to display a clear and correct picture of Jesus. Apart from placing Jesus within this framework, we will fail to understand who he is, let alone what he has done."[2] After reviewing the metanarrative of Scripture, I consider several layers of necessity laid upon Christ. Then I argue that compatibilism is consistent with, and a helpful tool to understand, the necessity of Christ.

2. The Storyline of Scripture

The Bible's metanarrative has the following four major parts: creation, fall, redemption, and inauguration–consummation. In this section, I present the major parts of the storyline of Scripture in order to show how all of Scripture is directed toward and fulfilled by the person and work of Jesus Christ.

1. In this section, I follow the system of biblical theology called "progressive covenantalism" and Stephen Wellum's progressive covenantalist approach to Christology in his *God the Son Incarnate*; *Christ Alone*; and "New Covenant Work of Christ," 517–39. For more on progressive covenantalism, see Gentry and Wellum, *Kingdom Through Covenant*; see also Wellum and Parker, *Progressive Covenantalism*. Undoubtedly, a similar conclusion may be drawn from similar systems of biblical theology, but progressive covenantalism, in my view, is a more accurate framework for understanding Scripture.

2. Wellum, *God the Son Incarnate*, 112.

The Christ-centeredness of Scripture is one factor in a christological case for compatibilism based on biblical theology.

2a. Creation

According to Wellum, "Creation establishes a particular theistic-eschatological-typological framework that brings every reading of Scripture into a singular plan of God that carries certain expectations for humanity and all creation."[3] God is the "uncreated, independent, self-existent, self-sufficient, all-powerful Lord who created the universe and governs it by his word (Genesis 1–2; Ps. 50:12–14; Acts 17:24–25)."[4] The doctrine of creation implies the Creator–creature distinction. God is not part of creation, and creation is not part of God. Although creation is absolutely dependent upon God, God is absolutely independent. But God is not transcendent only; he is also immanent. He is present to creation as its Covenant Lord.

Creation is also eschatological. Creation begins a story which moves toward an end.

> Renewal of both creation and humanity . . . was part of God's eternal plan (1 Cor. 2:7; Eph. 1:5–11; 2 Tim. 1:9; Titus 1:2); the "new creation" represents the original eschatological goal of the old creation. The week of creation itself culminated in the rest of God on the seventh day (Gen. 2:1–3). And this one day of completion and rest became a pattern that grounds observance of the Sabbath day under the old covenant (see Ex. 20:8–11) but ultimately points to a final "sabbath rest for the people of God" (Heb. 3:7—4:13) under the new covenant that will never end (see Rev. 21:22–25), associated with great salvation rest inaugurated by Jesus himself.[5]

Furthermore, creation is typological. Mankind is created in God's image and is mandated to have dominion over creation as God's vice-regent. The *imago Dei* concept carries two further typological structures: sonship and federal headship. Adam is the son of God (Luke 3:38). "After Adam, both Israel (Ex. 4:22; cf. Hos 11:1) and the Davidic kings (2 Sam. 7:14ff; Psalm 2) bear this image-sonship precisely because each was made to represent the Covenant Lord and carry out his rule in the world in a special way,

3. Wellum, *God the Son Incarnate*, 118.
4. Wellum, *God the Son Incarnate*, 113.
5. Wellum, *God the Son Incarnate*, 116.

thus carrying on the Adamic role and function."[6] Adam is the representative of humanity as its federal head. "The first Adam had the dignity of representing what it means to be human—to be the vice-regent of God. But he also functioned as the first man to represent all humanity before God."[7]

Creation, then, sets up the identity of God, the goal of history, and significant typological trajectories:

> The Creator-Covenant Lord is bringing the goodness of his creation and the presence of his kingdom to its completion in a true and final image-Son-Adam. This coming *imago Dei* will precisely represent God; this coming Son will perfectly obey him; this coming Adam will provide faithful covenant headship—all for the sake of God's glory in a new humanity that will reign over a new creation according to the provisions of a new covenant.[8]

2b. Fall

In Genesis 3, Adam succumbs to temptation and disobeys God—thus bringing about the fall of humanity. Wellum writes, "The fall shows us that the entrance of human sin into God's creation was *internal* or *moral*, but not *intrinsic* or part of our original creation. The temptation to sin came externally, from Satan. The desire and will to act in disobedience to God, however, came from within Adam himself."[9] Adam failed in his role as federal head and son of God; and his failure led to the guilt and corruption of the entire human race. Thenceforth, all humans are born with original sin; all are depraved; all sin. Wellum explains the fallout of the fall:

> It is this basic *tension* between God's original creation and the subsequent fall of humanity that adds another dimension to the theistic-eschatological-typological framework of Scripture. We must soberly recognize that God cannot abide with a sinful humanity, and a sinful humanity cannot bring forth the plan of God to have a people for himself in a place of perfect provision. As the Creator-Covenant Lord, God is intrinsically holy, righteous, and just, such that his own perfect nature requires that he perfectly judge and punish his rebellious vice-regents.[10]

6. Wellum, *God the Son Incarnate*, 118.
7. Wellum, *God the Son Incarnate*, 118.
8. Wellum, *God the Son Incarnate*, 118–19.
9. Wellum, *God the Son Incarnate*, 119.
10. Wellum, *God the Son Incarnate*, 120.

A divine dilemma ensues: God must accomplish his end for mankind, but he also must punish mankind for sin.

2c. *Redemption*

The divine dilemma is solved by the redemption of humanity. Wellum explains that redemption—in the Bible's own terms—is shaped by two dimensions. The redemption and reign of humanity will come by God himself (e.g., Ps 3:8; Ezek 34:15) and by a man (e.g., Gen 3:15; Ps 2:6–8; Isa 53:5).[11] Redemption is accomplished in the person of Jesus Christ—who is both God and man:

> In him we have redemption through his blood, the forgiveness of our trespasses, according to the riches of his grace, which he lavished upon us, in all wisdom and insight making known to us the mystery of his will, according to his purpose, which he set forth in Christ, as a plan for the fullness of time, to unite all things in him, things in heaven and things on earth. (Eph 1:7–10)

2d. *Inauguration–consummation*

The Bible makes a division between "this present age" (e.g., Gal 1:4; Titus 2:12), which began at creation and extends to the present, and "the age to come" (e.g., Mark 10:30; Heb 6:5), which is the eschaton. The age to come is the consummation of all things: the new creation, but the age to come has already been inaugurated in the present age with the coming of Jesus Christ. This *already-not yet* notion of the *age to come* breaking into the *present age* is called "inaugurated eschatology." In one respect, the age to come is here: Christ reigns, the Spirit has been sent, sins are forgiven, Satan is defeated. In another respect the age to come is still to come: Christ will come again, the dead will rise, the world will be judged, the wicked will perish everlastingly, the righteous will put on immoral bodies and reign with Christ forever.

3. Progressive Covenants

The storyline of the Bible is set within the framework of six progressive covenants: the covenants with Adam, Noah, Abraham, Israel, David, and the new covenant. In this section, I describe each covenant in order to show that the

11. Wellum, *God the Son Incarnate*, 123.

advent of Jesus Christ was God's plan every step of the way. "Throughout this unfolding story, Scripture creates both the *expectation* and *necessity* that God would bring salvation in the person and work of Christ."[12] God's covenants throughout history necessitate the incarnation and atonement of Jesus. The necessity of Jesus Christ supports a compatibilistic reading of the Bible.

3a. The Creation Covenant

Gentry and Wellum describe the creation covenant as "an original and unique situation which involved, especially in light of the rest of Scripture, Adam in a representative role on behalf of the human race (cf. Rom. 5:12–21; 1 Cor. 15:20–21)."[13] Even though the word "covenant" does not appear in the context of Genesis 1–3, "all of the elements of Lord/vassal agreement are in the context, including conditions of obedience with sanctions for disobedience."[14] Associated with the creation covenant is the concept of "image" (cf. Gen 1:26–27) which "signifies our uniqueness, our dignity before God, and the representative role we play for the entire creation so that God deals with creation on the basis of how he deals with human beings."[15] The covenant of creation is also inseparable from the entrance of sin through Adam (Gen 3:1–13) and the promise of redemption (the protoevangelium, Gen 3:14–15).

3b. The Noahic Covenant

The Noahic covenant is a continuation of the creation covenant (Gen 8:20–22). Except now, God is covenanting with a fallen people. The Noahic covenant consists of God committing himself "to care for, preserve, provide for, and rule over all that he has made, and in light of sin, to not let the creation project fail."[16] This covenant is likewise universal, with Noah as its representative head (a second "Adam"), and the rainbow as the sign of God's faithfulness. As such, obedience is required from Noah and all humanity.

12. Wellum, *Christ Alone*, 34.
13. Gentry and Wellum, *Kingdom Through Covenant*, 613.
14. Gentry and Wellum, *Kingdom Through Covenant*, 613.
15. Gentry and Wellum, *Kingdom Through Covenant*, 614.
16. Gentry and Wellum, *Kingdom Through Covenant*, 628.

3c. *The Abrahamic Covenant*

The Abrahamic covenant is the "means by which God will fulfill his promises for humanity . . . through [Abraham's] family and offspring."[17] The Abrahamic covenant is a subset of the creation covenant with Abram/Abraham as its representative head (another "Adam"), and with a narrower scope: Abraham and his offspring (Gen 12, 15, 17, 22). God promises to give Abram a great name, to make a great nation from his seed, and to bless the nations through his offspring. This covenant follows the suzerain–vassal paradigm with unconditional elements (God's promises and commitments) and conditional elements (demands for obedience). The sign of the Abrahamic covenant is circumcision.

3d. *The Old Covenant*

The old covenant is the covenant with Israel. Gentry and Wellum explain, "God's calling and establishing his covenant with Israel is in fulfillment of the promises made to Abraham, which are then confirmed and passed to his sons Isaac and Jacob (Gen. 26:3–5; 28:13–15; 35:9–12)."[18] In other words, the old covenant is a subset of the Abrahamic covenant with a narrower focus: Israel. It is through Israel (another "Adam") that God will "bring about a resolution of the sin and death caused by the first Adam, ultimately in the dawning of a new creation."[19] The old covenant develops "many typological structures . . . which ultimately find their antitypical fulfillment in Christ and the new covenant."[20] For examples, the priesthood, the tabernacle and temple, and the sacrificial system all find their fulfillment in Christ. Whereas the bilateral/conditional elements are obvious (with the abundant laws and regulations), "one cannot understand the old covenant without also grounding it in God's ultimate purpose to bring about redemption—something which the covenant Lord must initiate and accomplish unilaterally."[21]

17. Gentry and Wellum, *Kingdom Through Covenant*, 631.
18. Gentry and Wellum, *Kingdom Through Covenant*, 636.
19. Gentry and Wellum, *Kingdom Through Covenant*, 636–37.
20. Gentry and Wellum, *Kingdom Through Covenant*, 637.
21. Gentry and Wellum, *Kingdom Through Covenant*, 638.

3e. *The Davidic Covenant*

The Davidic covenant is a subset of the old covenant, and the "sonship role of Israel is now supremely narrowed in the king as the corporate representative of the people." And so, the Davidic covenant is related organically to each previous covenant. God promises to establish David's house forever (2 Sam 7:12–16; 1 Chr 17:11–14) and he will relate to God as son (2 Sam 7:14; 1 Chr 7:13). Gentry and Wellum elaborate on the conditional/unconditional tension in this covenant:

> God demands perfect obedience from his image-bearers, which is evident for the covenant mediators as well. Yet none of these mediators, including David and his sons, were truly obedient and thus they did not fulfill their role and bring about God's promises. All of the previous mediators could only typify and anticipate another one to come, a Davidic son who would fulfill their role specifically through perfect obedience as the true Son. Yet it is also important to stress the strong unilateral emphasis of the biblical covenants, including the Davidic covenant, alongside the conditional.[22]

3f. *The New Covenant*

The new covenant supersedes all previous covenants because they are fulfilled by the new covenant in Christ. The previous covenants anticipated Christ (the last "Adam") who is God's perfect Son and Image. The new covenant differs from the old covenant in structure, nature, and forgiveness.[23] With regard to structure:

> The Old Testament pictures God working with his people as a tribal grouping whose knowledge of God and whose relations with God were uniquely dependent on specially endowed leaders—thus the strong emphasis on the Spirit of God being poured out, not on each believer, but distinctively on prophets, priests, kings, and a few designated special leaders (e.g., Bezalel).[24]

But the new covenant emphasizes that all believers will know God (Jer 31:31–34), not merely the special leaders. Moreover:

22. Gentry and Wellum, *Kingdom Through Covenant*, 642.
23. See Gentry and Wellum, *Kingdom Through Covenant*, 646–52.
24. Gentry and Wellum, *Kingdom Through Covenant*, 647.

> Under the previous covenants the genealogical principle, that is, the relationship between the covenant mediator and his seed, was *physical* (e.g., Adam, Noah, Abraham, Israel, David), but now, in Christ, under his mediation, the relationship between Christ and his people is *spiritual*. This is why all those within the covenant community know the Lord in contrast to the "mixed" nation of Israel.[25]

The new covenant consists of true believers only.[26]

Concerning its nature, unlike the members of the old covenant, all new covenant members are regenerate. Although both received the covenant sign of circumcision and both were considered covenant members, the spiritual seed and the merely physical seed of Abraham were distinct in the old covenant. "However, it was only the believers—the remnant—who were the spiritual seed of Abraham, the 'true Israel' in a salvific sense."[27]

Unlike old covenant reality, forgiveness in the new covenant is complete. In the old covenant, forgiveness was granted through the sacrificial system, but this forgiveness was incomplete and partial as evidenced by the repetitive nature of the sacrifices. All the previous covenants anticipated and longed for a mediator who would be perfectly obedient and bring about complete forgiveness. This mediator is found in Jesus Christ.

The person (God the Son incarnate; the prophet, priest, and king; the true David, the true Israel, the Seed of Abraham, the last Adam) and work (obedient life, death, resurrection, intercession, and reign) of Jesus Christ fulfill what all the previous covenants anticipated. God's promised salvation has come.

4. The Necessity of Christ

With the framework and storyline of Scripture in place, we can now consider the necessity of Christ. It was necessary that God become incarnate and that he make atonement for humanity. It was necessary according to (1) God's nature, (2) God's decree, (3) God's promises, and (4) the fulfillment of the Bible's own framework, including the covenantal and typological structures.

25. Gentry and Wellum, *Kingdom Through Covenant*, 648.

26. For more on the relationship between Israel, Christ, and the church, see Parker, "Israel-Christ-Church Relationship."

27. Gentry and Wellum, *Kingdom Through Covenant*, 649.

4a. God's Nature

With respect to God's nature, Christ's incarnation and atonement were made certain by a consequent absolute necessity. God's justice, love, and mercy demand that he make satisfaction for humanity—his image marred. God must punish sinful and corrupt humanity, but he also must accomplish his end in creation. God could not merely forgive without exacting payment. Thus, "God put forward [Christ Jesus] as a propitiation by his blood, to be received by faith. This was to show God's righteousness, because in his divine forbearance he had passed over former sins. It was to show his righteousness at the present time, so that he might be just and the justifier of the one who has faith in Jesus" (Rom 3:25–26). Francis Turretin expounds on the justice of God in the satisfaction of sins:

> For as sin is to be viewed in the threefold relation of debt, enmity and crime (and God in the relation of creditor, offended party and Judge), so Christ must put on a threefold relation: a surety who can pay the debt for us; a Mediator and peacemaker (*eirēnopoiou*), to take away enmity and reconcile us to God; and a Priest and victim, to substitute himself in our place for a penal satisfaction. Again the satisfaction exacted by the justice of God principally demanded two things: (1) that it should be paid by the same nature which had sinned; (2) that nevertheless it should be of an infinite value and worth to take away the infinite demerit of sin. Two natures were necessary in Christ for the making of a satisfaction—a human, to suffer; and a divine nature, to give an infinite price and value to his sufferings.[28]

It was necessary that the Mediator be both God and man. In sending his Son, not only is God's justice satisfied, but his love and mercy are, too: "God, being rich in mercy, because of the great love with which he loved us, even when we were dead in our trespasses, made us alive together with Christ" (Eph 2:4–5; cf. John 3:16; 1 John 4:9).[29]

Herman Bavinck provides six reasons for deeming Christ's incarnation and satisfaction as absolutely necessary—"not as a necessity that is imposed on God from without and from which he cannot escape, but as actions that are in agreement with his attributes and display them most splendidly."[30] First, "Scripture teaches that God does all things for his own

28. Turretin, *Institutes* 2:421.

29. See Turretin's discussion on the absolute necessity that Christ should make satisfaction for sins in *Institutes* 2:417–26.

30. Bavinck, *Reformed Dogmatics*, 3:371.

sake (Prov. 16:4; Rom. 11:36)."[31] Thus, the incarnation and atonement were not ultimately for the sake of humanity but for God's own sake. Second, "God as the absolutely righteous and holy one hates sin with divine hatred (Gen. 18:25; Exod. 20:5; 23:7; Ps. 5:6–7; Nah. 1:2; Rom. 1:18, 32)."[32] All that God is, being holy, is against sin. Third:

> God is not just a creator or injured party who can cancel the debt and forgive as well as forget the insult but is himself the giver, protector, and avenger of the law, righteousness in person, and as such he cannot forgive sin without atonement (Heb. 9:22). In that capacity he cannot nullify the just demands of the law, for we are not speaking here about personal rights or private rights, which one can relinquish, but about the righteousness, that is, the perfections and honor of God himself.[33]

"Fourth, the moral law as such is not an arbitrary positive law but law grounded in the nature of God himself."[34] Thus, the law is inviolable. Fifth, sin is a crime (in addition to being guilt, pollution, folly, etc.) worthy of judgment and death. "In this capacity it demands punishment, and there is no forgiveness without satisfaction (atonement); it can be completely overcome, as it concerns guilt and pollution as well as its power and control, only in the way of justice."[35] Sixth:

> Christ's incarnation and satisfaction occurred to the end that God would again be recognized and honored as God by his creatures. Sin was the rejection of God and all his perfections, a turning toward and adoration of creatures. But in Christ, God again revealed himself, restored his sovereignty, vindicated all his perfections, glorified his name, and maintained his deity.

4b. God's Decree

With respect to God's decree, Christ's incarnation and atonement were made certain by a hypothetical necessity. God, according to his wise counsel, willed that the Son would become incarnate and make atonement for the sins of humanity. Thus, it was necessary according to the divine will that the Son become incarnate and make atonement for sins. The Son was sent to

31. Bavinck, *Reformed Dogmatics*, 3:371.
32. Bavinck, *Reformed Dogmatics*, 3:371.
33. Bavinck, *Reformed Dogmatics*, 3:372.
34. Bavinck, *Reformed Dogmatics*, 3:373.
35. Bavinck, *Reformed Dogmatics*, 3:373.

be born as man "when the fullness of time had come" (Gal 4:4). Christ Jesus "gave himself for our sins to deliver us from the present evil age, according to the will of our God and Father" (Gal 1:4). He was "delivered up according to the definite plan and foreknowledge of God" (Acts 2:23), so that, "at the right time Christ died for the ungodly" (Rom 5:6). It was "for this purpose [that Jesus came] to this hour" (John 12:27). "This was according to the eternal purpose that he has realized in Christ Jesus our Lord" (Eph 3:11); it was God's "plan for the fullness of time" (Eph 1:10). This mystery of the gospel of Christ "God decreed before the ages for our glory" (1 Cor 2:7). Because God decreed the incarnation and atonement, they were made hypothetically necessary in addition to the absolute necessity mentioned above.

4c. *God's Promises*

God's promises in Scripture made the incarnation and atonement certain by another layer of hypothetical necessity. Whatever God promises surely comes to pass. God's first promise of the gospel is the protoevangelium: "I will put enmity between you [the serpent] and the woman, and between your offspring and her offspring; he shall bruise your head, and you shall bruise his heel" (Gen 3:15). God promised Abraham: "In your offspring shall all the nations of the earth be blessed" (Gen 22:18). God promised that he would raise up a new and better prophet than Moses: "And I will put my words in his mouth, and he shall speak to them all that I command him" (Deut 18:18). God promised that from the line of David would come a new and better king: "He shall build a house for my name, and I will establish the throne of his kingdom forever. I will be to him a father, and he shall be to me a son" (2 Sam 7:13–14). God even made a promise to Mary and Joseph: "She will bear a son, and you shall call his name Jesus, for he will save his people from their sins" (Matt 1:21).

Prophecies, likewise, are promises in the form of indirect discourse. Daniel saw a vision of a "son of man" before the Ancient of Days, and he was given "an everlasting dominion which shall not pass away, and his kingdom one that shall not be destroyed" (Dan 7:14). Isaiah spoke of the suffering servant who "was pierced for our transgressions; he was crushed for our iniquities; upon him was the chastisement that brought us peace, and with his wounds we are healed" (Isa 53:5). And the whole Psalter is rife with messianic prophecy: "The Lord said to me, 'You are my Son; today I have begotten you'" (Ps 2:7). "The Lord says to my Lord: 'sit at my right hand, until I make your enemies your footstool.' . . . 'You are a priest forever after the order of Melchizedek'" (Ps 110:1, 4).

Although both God's decree and his promises make the incarnation and atonement hypothetically necessary, there is an important difference between them. The divine decree is the willing of a determinate plan within God. God's act of creation and providence correspond perfectly with his decree. Divine promises, however, are created effects of the divine will in time that reveal certain aspects of the decree before they take place in time. For example, the protoevangelium is a created effect of the divine will that happens at a certain time, namely, a time soon after Adam sins. The protoevangelium, moreover, reveals a certain aspect of the decree before it takes place, namely, the Son defeating Satan. This distinction is significant because it shows that the incarnation and atonement are necessitated by God's decree—which is *logically* prior to its manifestation—and by God's promise—which is *temporally* prior to its fulfillment.

4d. The Bible's Framework

The framework of the Bible, with its various parts and covenantal structure, render Christ's incarnation and atonement certain by another hypothetical necessity. The structure of the Bible necessitates that God become man and make satisfaction for sins. The main parts of the Bible (creation, fall, redemption, inauguration-consummation) show the centrality of Christ. Christ is the true Image-Son of God and the head of a new humanity. He is the Lord of creation, the redeemer of humanity, and the one who brings all things together in the end. Christ is the foundation, center, and fulfillment of the whole storyline of Scripture:

> He is the image of the invisible God, the firstborn of all creation. For by him all things were created, in heaven and on earth, visible and invisible, whether thrones or dominions or rulers or authorities—all things were created through him and for him. And he is before all things, and in him all things hold together. And he is the head of the body, the church. He is the beginning, the firstborn from the dead, that in everything he might be preeminent. For in him all the fullness of God was pleased to dwell, and through him to reconcile to himself all things, whether on earth or in heaven, making peace by the blood of his cross. (Col 1:15–20)

Christ is the fulfillment of the covenantal structure of the Bible. He is the true and better Adam (Luke 3:23–38; Rom 5:12–21; 1 Cor 15:22, 45). Christ is the Son, who, though tempted by Satan, obeyed God perfectly (Matt 4:1–11). And whereas Noah was commanded not to drink or eat blood because the blood is a creature's life (Gen 9:4–5), Jesus offered his blood for the forgiveness of sins and the gift of eternal life (Matt 26:27–28; John 6:54–56). Christ is the offspring of Abraham through whom the whole world is blessed (Gen 17:1–8; Gal 3:16). The promise to Abraham of a place and a people is fulfilled in Christ. The place now is in spirit and truth (John 4:23) and in the age to come: a new heavens and a new earth (2 Pet 3:13). The people are the church (Eph 5:25–27). Christ is the true and better Israel. Israel, like the other covenant heads, is considered God's son (Hos 11:1). But unlike Israel, Jesus never failed to obey God or to love him with all his heart, soul, and might. Finally, Christ is the Davidic king whose reign is absolute in both scope and duration (Rom 1:1–4; Ps 145), as Isaiah declares:

> For to us a child is born,
>   to us a son is given;
> and the government shall be upon his shoulder,
>   and his name shall be called
> Wonderful Counselor, Mighty God,
>   Everlasting Father, Prince of Peace.
> Of the increase of his government and of peace
>   there will be no end,
> on the throne of David and over his kingdom,
>   to establish it and to uphold it
> with justice and with righteousness
>   from this time forth and forevermore. (Isa 9:6–7)

Through Jesus, God institutes the new covenant that was prophesied beforehand (Ezek 36:22–32).

Christ is the fulfillment of many typological structures in Scripture. We have already considered Christ's role as true Son and Image. Christ is also the biblical antitype of rest-peace-Sabbath (Matt 11:28; 12:8; Col 3:15), the tabernacle-temple (John 2:19; 1 Cor 3:16–17; Heb 8:1–7), and others. Perhaps most importantly, Christ is the antitype of prophet, priest, and king. Christ is the fulfillment of the role of prophet; he is the very Word and Wisdom of God (John 1:1–3; 1 Cor 1:24). Because he is God, he speaks on his own authority (Mark 1:27). In his priestly work, Christ offers himself up to God (Heb 7:27; 9:14). His atonement secures the salvation of his people (John 10:7–18). Because of his obedience, he was highly exalted and was seated at the right hand of the Father (Phil 2:9–11; Heb 12:2; Rev 3:21; 7:17). The entire Old Testament anticipates Christ's fulfillment of the covenants and these typological structures (Luke 24:27). Indeed, at Christ's transfiguration, both Moses and Elijah—personally representing the Torah (Moses) and the Prophets (Elijah)—appear to attest to Christ's superiority and deity (Matt

17:1–8). Thus, the framework and storyline of Scripture render the incarnation and atonement necessary. The Bible simply would not make sense if God did not become man—in the line of Adam, Noah, Abraham, Israel, and David—live obediently, and make atonement for sins.

5. Necessity and Compatibilism

In this section, I argue that compatibilism is both consistent with and a helpful tool to understand the necessity of Christ's incarnation and atonement. But, first, I consider the relationship between necessity and determinism in this context. Not every necessity amounts to determinism. Determinism claims that every event is caused (or brought about) by a set of sufficient prior conditions. It is impossible for those prior conditions to obtain without the event happening; if those prior conditions obtain, there is exactly one possible future. The absolute necessity of the incarnation and atonement that results from God's nature and the consequence of sin may not equate to determinism. For one might think that even with a necessary incarnation and atonement, the manner of incarnation and atonement might have been different.[36] Thus the prior condition (i.e., God's nature in light of the fall of the human race) would produce more than one possible future; in other words, God might have brought about an incarnation and atonement differently than he had.

But when we consider the layers of necessity—not only from God's nature—but from the framework of Scripture, God's promises, and, especially, God's decree, we are forced to affirm a meticulous providence. The layers of necessity with respect to the incarnation and atonement imply that God moved the events of history in precisely the right way to achieve his end. The fact that Jesus was in the line of Adam, Abraham, and David demonstrates that God had to preserve the line from Adam to Abraham to David to Jesus (Matt 1:1–17; Luke 3:23–38). Thus, God had to be provident over the free choices of dozens of generations of men and women, so that they produced children at the right times. Moreover, God had to preserve these people through wars, famines, plagues, natural disasters, captivities, evil schemes, and accidents—just to get to the birth of Jesus. To go from Jesus' birth to his death also requires meticulous providence. God had to direct the life of Jesus and the reactions of the crowds and the political and religious rulers, so that Jesus would be crucified at the right time and in the right way. The nature of the atonement, itself, is a rich interplay of biblical themes such as obedience, sacrifice, propitiation, redemption, reconciliation, conquest,

36. Recall my discussion of token and type acts in chapter 5.

justification, and moral example.[37] These themes could reach their fulfillment in Christ only if God orchestrated both the history of redemption leading up to Christ and the history of Christ's life leading up to his death and resurrection. The biblical theology of atonement is too rich to be coincidence.

Thus, the necessity of the incarnation and atonement lead to an affirmation of meticulous providence. But meticulous providence is not tantamount to theological determinism. Both Molinists and many Thomists, for example, affirm meticulous providence without affirming theological determinism.[38] Here, however, I argue merely that compatibilism is consistent with and a helpful tool to understand the necessity of the incarnation and the atonement. That compatibilism is consistent with the necessity of the incarnation and atonement is clearly true. Compatibilism claims that free will and moral responsibility are compatible with determinism. Thus, a creature's free act is consistent with God's *causing* that act. If God merely *brings it about* that a creature acts freely—certainly, the creature's act is still free. Compatibilism, then, is a helpful tool in understanding the necessity of the incarnation and atonement. God can direct all history—whether through causation or merely "bringing it about"—without undermining the freedom and moral responsibility of creatures. Indeed, God can direct the life of Christ without undermining *his* freedom.

6. Conclusion

In this chapter, I argued that the metanarrative of Scripture, including its major parts and typological and covenantal structures, shows that it was necessary that the Son of God become incarnate, live an obedient life, die an obedient death, and be raised again for our salvation. Indeed, there are several layers of necessity laid on the incarnation and atonement of Christ: the necessity derived from the divine nature, the hypothetical necessities of God's decree and promises, and the necessity derived from the biblical framework. Compatibilism is consistent with and a helpful tool for understanding these layers of necessity. In the next chapter, I argue that compatibilism is also consistent with and a helpful tool for understanding dyothelitism, volitional non-contrariety, and impeccability.

37. See Wellum, *Christ Alone*, 228–43.

38. In chapters 4–7, I have argued that incompatibilism is inconsistent with classical Christology. Because Molinists and most Thomists affirm incompatibilism, they are at odds with classical Christology.

10

The Case for Compatibilism

1. Introduction

In part 2, I demonstrated the inconsistency of classical Christology with incompatibilist accounts of freedom and moral responsibility. The most poignant christological features in the polemic against incompatibilism were dyothelitism, volitional non-contrariety (VNC), and impeccability. In this section, I show that these features of classical Christology fit with compatibilism.

2. Dyothelitism and VNC

Dyothelitism and VNC support a compatibilist reading of Christ's human nature. Dyothelitism is the doctrine that Jesus Christ has two wills—one according to each nature. He is the subject of the divine will which he has in common with the Father and the Holy Spirit. He is also the subject of his human will. This doctrine is derived from the Bible's attestation of Jesus' true humanity and true divinity, coupled with such texts that explicitly distinguish between the divine and human will; for example, "not as I will, but as you will" (Matt 26:39).

VNC claims that Christ's human will is never contrary but always in agreement with the divine will. VNC is derived both from the fact that Jesus always did the will of the Father, fulfilling the divine purpose, and from contemplation on the unity of his person. If Christ's divine and human natures willed contrary to each other, the unity of his person would be jeopardized, and we would seem to end up with a version of Nestorianism or adoptionism. Thus, the church universal has affirmed dyothelitism and VNC:

> And we proclaim equally two natural volitions or wills in him and two natural principles of action which undergo no division, no change, no partition, no confusion, in accordance with the teaching of the holy fathers. And the two natural wills not in opposition, as the impious heretics said, far from it, but his human will following, and not resisting or struggling, rather in fact subject to his divine and all powerful will. For the will of the flesh had to be moved, and yet to be subjected to the divine will, according to the most wise Athanasius.[1]

Here, it would be helpful to consider the divine will more carefully. The Reformed tradition distinguishes between two aspects of God's will: God's preceptive (revealed) will and God's decretive (hidden) will.[2] God's preceptive will includes his revealed commands. God's decretive will is his meticulous, creative-sustaining-provident will; all things come to pass according to God's decretive will—even those creaturely actions that are contrary to God's preceptive will.[3] One may not need to hold to a meticulous and universal decretive will in order to affirm classical Christology, but the preceptive–decretive distinction helps us think about the relation between Christ's divine and human wills. For Christ to have non-contrariety of wills, he must not only obey all God's commands, but he must also conform to God's will in the decretive sense. His human will—in all its exercises—must be subject to and moved by the divine will. In other words, God's decretive will is certainly meticulous over Christ's human will.

Denying VNC is detrimental to Christology. If Christ could will contrary to his divinity *qua* humanity, then, not only would the unity of his person be undermined, but so too would his impeccability and the divine purpose.

If Christ could act contrary to God's *preceptive* will, then he could disobey God's commands. And if Christ could disobey God's commands, then Christ is not impeccable. But impeccability is an essential feature of classical Christology. Therefore, Christ must obey God's commands. VNC and impeccability are thus shown to be intimately related.[4]

1. Tanner, *Decrees of the Ecumenical Councils*, 128.

2. See Turretin, *Institutes* 1:220–25; cf. Bavinck, *Reformed Dogmatics*, 2:242–45.

3. Most Calvinists, Thomists, and Molinists believe God's will to be meticulous, universal, and unthwartable. Acts 2:23 is an example of human agents fulfilling God's decretive will while disobeying his preceptive will: "This Jesus, delivered up according to the definite plan and foreknowledge of God, you crucified and killed by the hands of lawless men." See also Eph 1:7–12.

4. Timothy Pawl writes that Constantinople III may imply impeccability: "The human will is subjugated to the divine will, following it without resistance. But the divine

If Christ could act contrary to God's *decretive* will, then it seems possible that Christ could act contrary to God's purpose for him. But it is absurd that God's purpose for Christ might be thwarted, especially by Christ himself. For this reason, VNC cannot reduce to impeccability. God's preceptive will concerns fewer of Christ's actions than God's decretive will. For example, when Jesus heard that John the Baptist had been arrested, he left Nazareth and moved to Capernaum by the Sea of Galilee. This decision does not seem to be in response to a command or moral obligation. But Jesus' decision to move to Capernaum, whether intentionally or not, resulted in the fulfillment of Isaiah 9.[5] In other words, it was God's will that Jesus move from Nazareth to Capernaum, yet the decision itself seems to be a morally neutral one. Presumably, Jesus' impeccability would not be called into question if he had decided to stay in Nazareth. But if he had stayed, he would not have fulfilled God's purpose as revealed in Isaiah 9.[6]

VNC is essential to classical Christology, but some models of VNC are inadequate. In chapter 6, I argued that we ought to hold to the Causal Model of VNC. The Causal Model of VNC claims that Christ's human will is moved by the divine will in the manner of an efficient cause. The divine decretive will is decisive and sufficient for the movement of the human will in Christ. Christ, *qua* humanity, cannot do other than what he wills *qua* divinity. In this way, we ought to think of Christ's human nature as being the human instrument of the Word in creation. "Christ as man receives the form of an instrument of the Word—indeed, is ontologically constituted as such an instrument—by the hypostatic union, and is perfected as an instrument by the operative *habitus* he receives as gifts from the Spirit. But this instrument must also be moved."[7] Again, for this reason, there must be a causal connection between Christ's two wills: "If Christ's humanity were to act in perfect conformity with the divine will but without being moved by the divinity, his actions would not be truly instrumental or theandric. But in truth, Christ's own proper human operation is drawn into the very divine action itself, as its instrument."[8]

---

will could never will to sin. So, the human will of Christ could not will to sin. Thus, neither will could will sin. Therefore, Christ is incapable of willing sin, and hence is impeccable." Pawl, *In Defense of Extended Conciliar Christology*, 134.

5. See Matt 4:12–17 and Isa 9:1–2.

6. How one views the extent of Jesus' knowledge of the decretive will may complicate (or simplify) the matter. If Christ has the beatific vision, then he knows the decretive will perfectly. In that particular case, the distinction between decree and precept begins to blur. Jesus would seem to be morally obligated to fulfill God's purpose for him.

7. Legge, *Trinitarian Christology*, 199.

8. Legge, *Trinitarian Christology*, 199.

We should note, however, that when the divine will moves Christ's human will, there is both a similarity and a difference in the way that the divine will moves other humans.[9] All things happen according to God's will; God moves our created wills and Christ's created will to accomplish his ends in creation—that much is the same. But when God moves my will, for example, he is moving the will of an agent distinct from himself. But when God moves Christ's human will, it is not one agent moving another agent. Rather, the relation between the divine and human wills in Christ is even closer than the relation between my own will and my arms, for example, when I cause my arms to move. Legge explains:

> The movement of Christ's human will produces an action that is the human action of the Word, according to a union far more intimate than that between a master and his servant, or even between a soul and its body. This motion comes from above yet is *interior* to Christ's human nature, producing human actions that are at the same time moved by God and are voluntary.[10]

The Word that moves the human will is the *same person* whose will is moved.

This understanding of the movement of Christ's human will fits well with compatibilism. The divine will is prior to and sufficient for Christ's human activity; thus, divine willing amounts to theological determinism. Christ *qua* humanity cannot do otherwise than what his divinity determines; and the origin (the ultimate source) of all Christ's human actions is in the Godhead. Despite the fact that Christ's human will is determined by his divine will, his human acts are still voluntary and, thus, morally appraisable. If we assume incompatibilism, then we must do damage either to a proper understanding of VNC or to Christ's freedom and moral agency. Instead, classical Christology provides an example of an agent with compatibilistic freedom; thus, compatibilism is true.

3. Impeccability

Christ's impeccability supports the thesis that determinism is compatible with free will and moral responsibility. To say that Christ is impeccable means not only that Christ never sinned but also that he could not and cannot sin. In chapter 4, I provided three clarifications to Christ's impeccability.

9. Here, I assume a comprehensive, unthwartable decree and meticulous providence for the sake of comparing Christ's relation to the divine will to others' relation to the divine will—not for the sake of proving compatibilism because, in that case, I would be begging the question.

10. Legge, *Trinitarian Christology*, 200.

First, to say that Christ is impeccable is to say that Christ *qua* humanity cannot sin. Second, there is a difference between (1) someone wanting to sin and (2) someone wanting to do something *x* such that in doing *x*, one would be sinning. Christ never wanted to sin, even though, in some sense, he may have wanted to do something such that, if he were to do it, he would have sinned (e.g., shirking his mission in order to avoid pain and death). *Wanting to sin* is itself a sin. Third, impeccability means that, *necessarily*, Christ could not sin.

The matter of impeccability is almost always considered either in light of Christ's freedom or temptations, or both. Just as models of VNC abound, so, too, models of Christ's impeccability, freedom, and temptation (hereafter, IFT).[11] A full discussion of these models is beyond the scope of this book, but an adequate and satisfying model will include the following five items.[12]

First, the model of IFT must be committed to all the key features of classical Christology, including the Causal Model of VNC. Any model of classical Christology that accounts for Christ's impeccability and temptations must hold to classical Christology, obviously. Less obviously—but demonstrated from chapter 6—classical Christology requires a Causal Model of VNC.

Second, the model of IFT must include a plausible account of the structure of human moral psychology and theory of human action. I have argued that incompatibilism is inconsistent with classical Christology, but there are many plausible accounts of human willing and action that are compatible with classical Christology.[13]

Third, the model of IFT must include a reasonable account of Christ's knowledge. Classical Christology is a two-natured Christology, so the Son's knowledge must be considered both *qua* divinity and *qua* humanity. *Qua* divinity, the Son knows all things actual and possible because he is God. *Qua*

11. For an excellent survey of models of Christ's impeccability and temptation, see McKinley, *Tempted for Us*.

12. Note that I am not presenting a full doctrine of Christ; here, my argument requires only a minimalist account. Rather, I am listing the desiderata for a full account of Christ's impeccability, freedom, and temptation.

13. There are several accounts of the structure of human moral psychology and theory of action that are compatible with classical Christology, especially among the scholastics (preeminently, Thomas Aquinas) and the Reformed scholastics (e.g., Francis Turretin and John Owen). Eleonore Stump melds Aquinas' Christology with a Frankfurtian moral psychology which, apart from her incompatibilism (she espouses sourcehood libertarianism), is plausible. See Stump, *Atonement*, 190–93. Likewise, one could construct a guidance control model *à la* Michael Patrick Preciado's Reformed accommodation of the moral psychology of John Martin Fischer and Mark Ravizza. See Fischer and Ravizza, *Responsibility and Control*; Preciado, *Reformed View of Freedom*.

humanity, the Son's knowledge (during his humiliation) is more complex. Roman Catholics affirm a threefold distinction in Christ's human knowledge, but the Reformed hold to a twofold distinction.[14] Both affirm that Christ acquired knowledge by human nature, experience, and reason. Both affirm that Christ was infused with supernatural knowledge by the Holy Spirit akin to the way prophets attain supernatural knowledge. But Roman Catholics go beyond the Reformed by arguing that Christ also had beatific knowledge via the beatific vision.[15] In either case, Christ has certain knowledge about (at least some) of his own future; for example, Jesus predicts the future when he says, "For just as Jonah was three days and three nights in the belly of the great fish, so will the Son of Man be three days and three nights in the heart of the earth" (Matt 12:40). The notion that Christ knows (at least some) of his own future choices and actions is a problem for incompatibilists but not for compatibilists. A libertarian may say that Christ has alternative possibilities open to him—but not *actually*. In the actual world, there is only one path Christ takes. Moreover, Christ was not free *qua* humanity to choose which possible world was actualized—that decision was made in the mind of God.

Fourth, the model of IFT must include a biblically and theologically faithful account of the role of the Holy Spirit in the life of Jesus. In terms of the biblical presentation, the temptations of Jesus cannot be considered apart from the work of the Holy Spirit: "And Jesus, *full of the Holy Spirit*, returned from the Jordan and *was led by the Spirit* in the wilderness for forty days, being tempted by the devil" (Luke 4:1–2, italics mine). After his temptations (in which he quoted Spirit-inspired Scripture), "Jesus returned *in the power of the Spirit*" (Luke 4:14, italics mine).

In terms of theological precision, classical Christology is most fitting with classical theism and classical trinitarianism—which affirm that God is simple, and, thus, all his acts *ad extra* are inseparable. And yet, certain acts of God are rightly appropriated to certain persons of the Godhead in light of the Bible's own witness and contemplation on the trinitarian *taxis*: all things are from the Father, through the Son, by the Holy Spirit.[16] This contemplation on Scripture and the trinitarian *taxis* led John Owen to claim that "The Holy Ghost . . . is the *immediate, peculiar, efficient* cause of all external divine operations: for God worketh by his Spirit, or in him immediately applies the power and efficacy of the divine excellencies unto their operation; whence the same work is equally the work of each person."[17] Owen's understanding

14. See, for example, *ST* III q. 9–12; Turretin, *Institutes* 2:348–52.

15. In chapter 6, I argued against the Beatific Vision Model of VNC.

16. See my discussion of the Reformed Scholastic Intrinsic Model in chapter 7.

17. Owen, *ΠΝΕΥΜΑΤΟΛΟΓΙΑ*, 161–62.

of the Holy Spirit helps to flesh out the Causal Model of VNC; he writes, "[The Holy Ghost is] the immediate operator of all divine acts of the Son himself, even on his own human nature. Whatever the Son of God wrought in, by, or upon the human nature, he did it by the Holy Ghost, who is his Spirit, as he is the Spirit of the Father."[18] These things "wrought in, by, and upon the human nature" of Christ by the Spirit include the incarnation, sanctification, gifts, miracles, resurrection, etc. Indeed, Owen, expounding on Hebrews 9:14 ("Christ, who through the eternal Spirit offered himself without blemish to God"), argues that one of the principal graces of the Spirit on the human nature of Christ was "*His holy submission and obedience unto the will of God*."[19] He explains:

> It is true that the Lord Christ, in the whole course of his life, yielded obedience unto God, as he was "made of a woman, made under the law," Gal. iv. 4; but now he came to the great trial of it, with respect unto the especial command of the Father "to lay down his life," and to "make his soul an offering for sin," Isa. liii. 10. This was the highest act of obedience unto God that ever was, or ever shall be to all eternity; and therefore doth God so express his satisfaction therein and acceptance of it, Isa liii. 11, 12; Phil. ii. 9, 10. This was wrought in him, this he was wrought unto, by the Holy Spirit; and therefore by him he offered himself unto God.[20]

Fifth, the model of IFT must include a definition of "temptation" that is not question-begging; in other words, one that does not presuppose incompatibilism or indeterminism. Classical Christology, as I have argued throughout this book, is inconsistent with incompatibilism. Because Scripture and tradition teach that Christ was truly tempted, we must not presuppose that to be truly tempted is to be undetermined.

Christ's impeccability supports the thesis of compatibilism. Christ could not sin, yet he obeyed the will of the Father willingly and not by coercion or compulsion; and he was praised and rewarded for his obedience. Christ was determined not to sin, yet he was free to do what he desired most: to obey God. Compatibilism, likewise, makes good sense of Christ's temptations. Wellum summarizes,

> Assuming [compatibilism] to be the case, then our choices are viewed as true and genuine, even if causally determined, as long as we choose what we want and our choices are not constrained.

18. Owen, *ΠΝΕΥΜΑΤΟΛΟΓΙΑ*, 162.
19. Owen, *ΠΝΕΥΜΑΤΟΛΟΓΙΑ*, 178.
20. Owen, *ΠΝΕΥΜΑΤΟΛΟΓΙΑ*, 178–79.

> As applied to Christ, it is now possible to make sense of how he can resist temptation freely, not in the libertarian sense or even because he is constrained to do so, but because he freely chose to according to his wants and desires.[21]

Thus, the key features of classical Christology—dyothelitism, VNC, and impeccability—support (indeed, in light of the previous chapters, *entail*) compatibilism.

4. Conclusion

In this part of the book, I presented a positive case for compatibilism using three forms of christological arguments. First, I considered Jesus' didactic ministry. I demonstrated that Jesus' teaching about himself—that he was sent by God to do the will of God and to fulfill all Scripture—accords with compatibilism. And Jesus' teaching about humanity, likewise, fits well with compatibilism. Second, I considered the biblical-historical unfolding of God's plan in Christ. I argued that the storyline of Scripture, with its major parts and covenants, imply the necessity of the Christ-event—the incarnation and atonement. Third, I considered the systematic theological features of classical Christology. Dyothelitism, VNC, and impeccability fit well with compatibilism.[22] Because PAP libertarianism, sourcehood libertarianism, and hard determinism are inconsistent with classical Christology, and because compatibilism *is* consistent with classical Christology (and because there are no other options available), classical Christology entails compatibilism.

21. Wellum, *God the Son Incarnate*, 463.

22. And these key features of classical Christology make sense only in light of the broader features of the person of Christ, namely, that Christ is one person subsisting in and hypostatically uniting two natures—divine and human—and that Christ's activity was not limited to his humanity; rather, he continued to uphold the universe by his divine power in his act of decree, creation, and providence.

Conclusion

1. Introduction

The contemporary philosophical landscape offers four major views about the relationship between determinism and free will and moral responsibility. PAP libertarianism claims that free will and moral responsibility require the ability to do otherwise; thus, they are incompatible with determinism; but we do act freely and responsibility, at least sometimes; so determinism is false. Sourcehood libertarianism claims that free will and moral responsibility require that the agent be the ultimate source of his actions; determinism is incompatible with an agent's being the ultimate source of his actions; but we do act freely and responsibly, at least sometimes; so determinism is false. Hard determinism claims that free will and moral responsibility are incompatible with determinism, and determinism is true, so we never act freely. Compatibilism, however, claims that free will and moral responsibility are compatible with determinism; the truth or falsity of determinism cannot undermine human free will and moral responsibility. I have argued that classical Christology entails compatibilism. That freedom and moral responsibility are compatible with determinism is a necessary consequence of the teaching about Jesus Christ found in Scripture and affirmed in historical Christian orthodoxy.

A christological case for compatibilism is nothing new. I have shown that christological arguments for compatibilism date at least as far back as the Reformation. John Calvin, Francis Turretin, and Jonathan Edwards, for example, each employed christological arguments for the view of freedom and divine sovereignty that is today considered "compatibilism." Building on this tradition, I presented a complete christological case for compatibilism. I structured the case around a hypothetical syllogism between PAP libertarianism, sourcehood libertarianism, hard determinism, and compatibilism. By a process of elimination, I showed that classical Christology entails compatibilism. Both forms of libertarianism are ruled out by classical Christology because Jesus could not do otherwise than what the divine will intended, and the ultimate source of his actions is not found in his humanity but in God. Indeed, Christ's divine will is the ultimate cause of his human willing and acting. The divine will, moreover, corresponds to the divine decree which is intrinsic to God—which makes it logically prior to and sufficient for all of Christ's human operations. Hard determinism, likewise, is ruled out—not because determinism is proven false but because Scripture is abundantly clear that Jesus is morally praiseworthy for his obedience. Therefore, compatibilism is entailed by classical Christology—not only by a process of elimination but because Scripture and theological reflection support a compatibilistic understanding of the life of Christ.

2. Significance and Further Research

That classical Christology entails compatibilism is significant on several fronts. Recognition of this entailment should prompt further discussion and theological advancement in the following areas: classical Christian theology, christological anthropology, Reformed views of freedom, theological compatibilism, and models of divine providence.

2a. Classical Christian Theology

Classical Christian theology is the confluence of classical theism, classical trinitarianism, and classical Christology. Classical theism views God as *that than which nothing greater can be conceived*: a perfect being who is absolute, *a se*, simple, immutable, impassible, immense, atemporal, omnipotent, omnipresent, omniscient, and omnibenevolent. Classical theism bears a strong Creator–creature distinction and often affirms a mixed relation between God and creation. Classical trinitarianisms view the Trinity not as a *community* or *society* of persons, each instantiating a center of consciousness, knowledge, and will, but as one center of consciousness, knowledge, and will existing in three persons. According to classical theology, a person is an individual subsistence (or supposit) of a rational nature. With respect to the Trinity, Father, Son, and Spirit are subsisting relations in God who is a rational being. The Father is eternally unbegotten; the Son is eternally begotten of the Father; the Spirit eternally proceeds from the Father and the Son. And classical Christology has been discussed at length throughout this book. These three systems—classical theism, classical trinitarianism, and classical Christology—are often seen as inextricably linked. If they are inseparable, then the argument from classical Christology to compatibilism may be broadened to an argument from classical Christian theology to compatibilism.

2b. Christological Anthropology

Christological anthropology is the discipline that considers the doctrine of humanity in light of Jesus Christ. A proper understanding of human nature cannot be attained without considering the anthropological implications of the person of Christ. For example, the distinction between person and nature is influenced by our understanding of Christ's existing as one person in two natures. For another example, the telos of humanity is known via Christ's resurrection. The matter of Christ's freedom should inform (I say "inform" not "dictate") our understanding of our own freedom. If Jesus Christ's freedom must be understood in a compatibilistic sense, then, certainly, there are implications for the doctrine of humanity. Indeed, our understanding of Christ's freedom in relation to his temptations and impeccability may shed light on our understanding of our glorified selves in heaven.

2c. Reformed Views of Freedom

Scholars sharing Reformed views of freedom would do well to consider what the Reformed tradition has said about the relationship between free will and Christology. I have provided a brief overview of three key figures in the Reformed tradition. Current scholarship would benefit both from a deeper analysis of these figure's christological arguments for compatibilism and from a chronologically and geographically broader analysis of the Reformed tradition's Christology. Jesus may not be the paradigm for every theologian's view of human freedom, but what one says about Jesus' freedom will reveal whether one believes freedom and moral responsibility are compatible with determinism—even if Jesus' situation is viewed as dissimilar to ordinary persons.

2d. Theological Compatibilism

In this volume, I have developed a complete christological case for compatibilism. Although christological arguments for compatibilism have appeared throughout the Reformed tradition, there had yet to be a full-length treatment. Moreover, this book was the first to develop a taxonomy of christological arguments for compatibilism: (1) appeals to Christ's wills and impeccability, (2) appeals to the necessity of the incarnation and atonement, and (3) appeals to Christ's teaching. Christological arguments for compatibilism are valuable additions to the broader set of theological arguments for compatibilism. The dominant theological arguments usually concern the divine will and decree, providence, fallen human nature, and matters of salvation (e.g., regeneration, effectual calling, perseverance). Christology, however, is an especially poignant locus for the free will debate because it deals with a real, historical person (Jesus Christ) and with codified teachings (i.e., in Scripture and tradition) about his impeccability, temptations, willing obedience, and moral praiseworthiness.

Although I have not argued for a particular model of free will or theory of action for ordinary human activity, the fact that, in the case of Jesus, free will and moral responsibility are compatible with determinism, shows that determinism does not undermine free will and moral responsibility. Therefore, those who think free will consists in ultimate sourcehood or alternative possibilities cannot argue on the basis that incompatibilism is true—because incompatibilism has been shown to be false. Whether human beings ever are the ultimate source of their actions or ever have the categorical ability to do otherwise falls outside the scope of this volume—though the argument of chapter 7 that the divine decree is intrinsic to God certainly has implications on ordinary human freedom.

Although I have not addressed God's relation to sin and evil, one implication of this work is that compatibilism itself does not make God the author of sin in a sense that makes God blameworthy. Christ's free acts were determined; thus, he had a compatibilistic type of freedom. But, because he never sinned, the concept of compatibilism itself does not entail that God determines evil or sin. Only when compatibilism is applied to creatures freely sinning does the issue of God's relation to sin and evil arise—an issue that fell outside the scope of this text.

Further work is needed to investigate the relationship between compatibilism and other doctrines. For example, what is the relationship between the nature and extent of the atonement and free will? How does our understanding of the work of the Holy Spirit affect our understanding of moral responsibility? Is an evangelical view of Scripture possible apart from a compatibilistic view of human freedom? Similar questions may be posed about issues in prolegomena, ecclesiology, angelology, and eschatology. Likewise, similar questions may be posed about issues in theological philosophy: What does a Christian metaphysic tell us about human freedom? What is the relationship between a Christian epistemology and moral responsibility? What about biblical ethics? Does compatibilism have any bearing on how we understand a Christian philosophy of mind, philosophy of action, philosophy of science, or philosophy of language?

2e. Models of Divine Providence

I have shown that, if classical Christology is true, then compatibilism is true: free will and moral responsibility are compatible with determinism. I have not, however, argued for a particular model of providence. In chapters 7 and 8, I discussed several models of Christ's volitional non-contrariety and also two models of God's interaction with the world. I have shown that certain views of providence do not fit with classical Christology. I have also shown that theological determinism—at least localized to Christ's human nature—does not undermine human freedom and responsibility. Because theological determinism does not undermine freedom, we ought not to fear models of divine providence that imply theological determinism. Further work is needed to explore the relationship between classical Christology and divine providence.

Bibliography

Allison, Gregg R. *Historical Theology: An Introduction to Christian Doctrine*. Grand Rapids: Zondervan, 2011.

Anderson, James N., and Paul Manata. "Determined to Come Most Freely: Some Challenges for Libertarian Calvinism." *JRT* 11 (2017) 272–97.

Anselm. *Monologion and Proslogion with Replies of Gaunilo and Anselm*. Translated by Thomas Williams. Indianapolis: Hackett, 1995.

Aquinas, Thomas. *Scriptum super Sententis Magistri Petri Lombardi*. Edited by Maria Fabianus Moos. Vol. 3. Paris: Lethielleux, 1933.

———. *Summa Theologiae*. Translated by Laurence Shapcote. 8 vols. Green Bay, WI: Aquinas Institute, 2012.

Aristotle. *Categories* and *De Interpretatione*. Translated by J. Ackrill. Oxford: Clarendon, 1963.

Arndt, William, Frederick W. Danker, Walter Bauer, and F. Wilbur Gingrich. *A Greek-English Lexicon of the New Testament and Other Early Christian Literature*. 3rd ed. Chicago: University of Chicago Press, 2000.

Athanasius. *On the Incarnation*. Translated by a religious of C.S.M.V. Crestwood, NY: St. Vladimir's Seminary Press, 1996.

Augustine. *De Trinitate*. 2nd ed. Translated by Edmund Hill. New York: New City, 2015.

———. *On Free Choice of the Will, On Grace and Free Choice, and Other Writings*. Edited and translated by Peter King. New York: Cambridge University Press, 2010.

Barnes, Corey L. *Christ's Two Wills in Scholastic Thought: The Christology of Aquinas and Its Historical Contexts*. Toronto: Pontifical Institute of Mediaeval Studies, 2016.

Barrett, Matthew. *None Greater: The Undomesticated Attributes of God*. Grand Rapids: Baker, 2019.

Barth, Karl. *Church Dogmatics*. Edited by G. W. Bromiley and T. F. Torrance. Translated by G. W. Bromiley. 4 vols. London: T&T Clark, 2004.

Bathrellos, Demetrios. *The Byzantine Christ: Person, Nature, and Will in the Christology of Saint Maximus the Confessor*. Oxford: Oxford University Press, 2004.

Bauckham, Richard J. *Jesus and the God of Israel: God Crucified and Other Studies on the New Testament's Christology of Divine Identity*. Milton Keynes: Paternoster, 2008.

Bavinck, Herman. *Reformed Dogmatics*. Edited by John Bolt. Translated by John Vriend. 4 vols. Grand Rapids: Baker Academic, 2004.

Bayne, Tim. "The Inclusion Model of the Incarnation: Problems and Prospects." *Religious Studies* 37 (2001) 125–41.

Beebee, Helen. "The Non-Governing Conception of Laws of Nature." *Philosophy and Phenomenological Research* 16 (2000) 571–94.

Beeke, Joel R., and Randall J. Pederson, eds. "Jonathan Edwards." In *Meet the Puritans: With a Guide to Modern Reprints*, 193–233. Grand Rapids: Reformation Heritage, 2006.

Bergmann, Michael, and J. A. Cover. "Divine Responsibility Without Divine Freedom." *Faith and Philosophy* 23 (2006) 381–408.

Berkhof, Louis. *Systematic Theology*. Grand Rapids: Eerdmans, 1996.

Best, W. E. *Christ Could Not Be Tempted*. Houston: South Belt Grace Church, 1985.

Bignon, Guillaume. *Excusing Sinners and Blaming God: A Calvinist Assessment of Determinism, Moral Responsibility, and Divine Involvement in Evil*. Eugene, OR: Pickwick, 2018.

Blocher, Henri. "The Atonement in John Calvin's Theology." In *The Glory of the Atonement: Biblical, Historical & Practical Perspectives: Essays in Honor or Roger Nicole*, edited by Charles E. Hill and Frank A. James III, 279–303. Downers Grove, IL: IVP Academic, 2004.

Bock, Darrell L., and Gregory J. Herrick, eds. *Jesus in Context: Background Readings for Gospel Study*. Grand Rapids: Baker Academic, 2005.

Boethius. *Consolation of Philosophy*. Translated by Joel C. Relihan. Indianapolis: Hackett, 2001.

Brakel, Wilhelmus à. *The Christian's Reasonable Service*. 4 vols. Grand Rapids: Reformation Heritage, 1992.

Brower, Jeffrey E., and Michael C. Rea. "Material Constitution and the Trinity." *Faith and Philosophy* 22 (2005) 57–76.

Cain, James. "The Doctrine of the Trinity and the Logic of Relative Identity." *Religious Studies* 25 (1989) 141–52.

Calvin, John. *The Bondage and Liberation of the Will: A Defense of the Orthodox Doctrine of Human Choice Against Pighius*. Edited by A. N. S. Lane. Translated by G. I. Davies. Grand Rapids: Baker, 1996.

———. *John Calvin's Bible Commentaries on the Gospel of John, Vol. 1*. Translated by W. P. Auchterarder. Altenmünster, DE: Jazzybee Verlag, 2016.

———. *Institutes of the Christian Religion*. Edited by John T. McNeill. Translated by Ford Lewis Battles. 2 vols. Philadelphia: Westminster, 1960.

Caneday, Ardel. "Veiled Glory: God's Self-Revelation in Human Likeness—A Biblical Theology of God's Anthropomorphic Self-Disclosure." In *Beyond the Bounds: Open Theism and the Undermining of Biblical Christianity*, edited by John Piper et al., 149–99. Wheaton, IL: Crossway, 2003.

Carson, D. A. *Divine Sovereignty and Human Responsibility: Biblical Perspectives in Tension*. Reprint, Eugene, OR: Wipf & Stock, 1994.

Caruso, Greg. "Skepticism About Moral Responsibility." In *The Stanford Encyclopedia of Philosophy*, edited by Edward N. Zalta. Spring 2018. https://plato.stanford.edu/archives/spr2018/entries/skepticism-moral-responsibility/.

Claunch, Kyle David. "The Son and the Spirit: The Promise of Spirit Christology in Traditional Trinitarian and Christological Perspective." PhD diss., The Southern Baptist Theological Seminary, 2017.

Cobb, John B., Jr., and Clark H. Pinnock, eds. *Searching for an Adequate God: A Dialogue Between Process and Free Will Theists*. Grand Rapids: Eerdmans, 2000.

Cortez, Marc. *ReSourcing Theological Anthropology: A Constructive Account of Humanity in the Light of Christ*. Grand Rapids: Zondervan, 2017.

Cottrell, Jack. *What the Bible Says About God the Ruler*. Reprint, Eugene, OR: Wipf & Stock, 2000.

Craig, William Lane. "Flint's Radical Molinist Christology Not Radical Enough." *Faith and Philosophy* 23 (2006) 55–64.

———. "Response to Gregory A. Boyd." In *Four Views on Divine Providence*, edited by Dennis W. Jowers, 224–30. Grand Rapids: Zondervan, 2011.

Crisp, Oliver D. *Analyzing Doctrine: Toward a Systematic Theology*. Waco, TX: Baylor University Press, 2019.

———. *Deviant Calvinism: Broadening Reformed Theology*. Minneapolis: Fortress, 2014.

———. *Divinity and Humanity: The Incarnation Reconsidered*. New York: Cambridge University Press, 2007.

———. *Freedom, Redemption, and Communion: Studies in Christian Doctrine*. London: T&T Clark, 2021.

———. "John Owen on Spirit Christology." *JRT* 5 (2011) 5–25.

Crisp, Oliver D., and Michael C. Rea, eds. *Analytic Theology: New Essays in the Philosophy of Theology*. New York: Oxford University Press, 2009.

Crowley, Paul G. "*Instrumentum Divinitatis* in Thomas Aquinas: Recovering the Divinity of Christ." *Theological Studies* 52 (1991) 451–75.

Daeley, Justin. "Divine Freedom and Contingency: An Intelligibility Problem for (Some) Theistic Compatibilists." *Religious Studies* 51 (2015) 563–82.

Damascene, John. *An Exact Exposition of the Orthodox Faith*. Edited by Paul A. Böer Sr. Translated by S. D. F. Salmond. Dallas: Veritatis Splendor, 2019.

Davidson, Ivor J. "'Not My Will but Yours Be Done': The Ontological Dynamics of Incarnational Intention." *International Journal of Systematic Theology* 7 (2005) 178–204.

Davis, Leo Donald. *The First Seven Ecumenical Creeds (325–787): Their History and Theology*. Collegeville, MN: Liturgical, 1983.

De Molina, Luis. *On Divine Foreknowledge (Part IV of the Concordia)*. Translated by Alfred J. Freddoso. Ithaca, NY: Cornell University Press, 1988.

DeWeese, Garrett. "One Person, Two Natures: Two Metaphysical Models of the Incarnation." In *Jesus in Trinitarian Perspective: An Introductory Christology*, edited by Fred Sanders and Klaus Issler, 114–53. Nashville: B&H Academic, 2007.

Dolezal, James E. *All That Is in God: Evangelical Theology and the Challenge of Classical Theism*. Grand Rapids: Reformation Heritage, 2017.

———. *God Without Parts: Divine Simplicity and the Metaphysics of God's Absoluteness*. Eugene, OR: Pickwick, 2011.

Duby, Steven J. *Divine Simplicity: A Dogmatic Account*. London: T&T Clark, 2016.

———. *God in Himself: Scripture, Metaphysics, and the Task of Christian Theology*. Downers Grove, IL: IVP Academic, 2019.

———. *Jesus and the God of Classical Theism: Biblical Christology in Light of the Doctrine of God*. Grand Rapids: Baker Academic, 2023.

Dunn, James D. G. *Jesus and Spirit: A Study of the Religious and Charismatic Experience of Jesus and the First Christians as Reflected in the New Testament*. Philadelphia: Westminster, 1975.

Edwards, Jonathan. *Freedom of the Will*. Edited by Paul Ramsey. New Haven: Yale University Press, 1985.

Ekstrom, Laura W. "Event-Causal Libertarianism." In *The Routledge Companion to Free Will*, edited by Kevin Timpe, Meghan Griffith, and Neil Levy, 62–71. London: Routledge, 2017.

Erickson, Millard J. *Christian Theology*. 2nd ed. Grand Rapids: Baker Academic, 1998.

Evans, Stephen C., ed. *Exploring Kenotic Christology: The Self-Emptying of God*. New York: Oxford University Press, 2006.

Feinberg, John S. "The Incarnation of Jesus Christ." In *In Defense of Miracles: A Comprehensive Case for God's Action in History*, edited by R. Douglas Geivett and Gary R. Habermas, 226–46. Downers Grove, IL: InterVarsity, 1997.

———. *No One Like Him: The Doctrine of God*. Wheaton, IL: Crossway, 2001.

Finch, Alicia. "Logical Fatalism." In *The Routledge Companion to Free Will*, edited by Kevin Timpe et al., 191–202. London: Routledge, 2017.

Finch, Alicia, and Ted A. Warfield. "The Mind Argument and Libertarianism." *Mind* 107.427 (1998) 515–28.

Fischer, John Martin. *Our Fate: Essays on God and Free Will*. New York: Oxford University Press, 2016.

———. "Semicompatibilism." In *The Routledge Companion to Free Will*, edited by Kevin Timpe et al., 5–14. London: Routledge, 2017.

Fischer, John Martin, and Mark Ravizza. *Responsibility and Control: An Essay on Moral Responsibility*. Cambridge: Cambridge University Press, 1998.

Fischer, John Martin, and Patrick Todd, eds. *Freedom, Fatalism, and Foreknowledge*. New York: Oxford University Press, 2015.

Flint, Thomas P. "'A Death He Freely Accepted': Molinist Reflections on the Incarnation." *Faith and Philosophy* 18 (2001) 3–20.

———. *Divine Providence: The Molinist Account*. Ithaca, NY: Cornell University Press, 1998.

———. "Orthodoxy and Incarnation: A Reply to Mullins." *JAT* 4 (2016) 180–92.

———. "The Possibilities of Incarnation: Some Radical Molinist Suggestions." *Religious Studies* 37 (2001) 307–20.

———. "Molinism and Incarnation." In *Molinism: The Contemporary Debate*, edited by Ken Perszyk, 187–207. New York: Oxford University Press, 2011.

———. "Should Concretists Part with Mereological Models of the Incarnation?" In *The Metaphysics of the Incarnation*, edited by Anna Marmodoro and Jonathan Hill, 67–87. New York: Oxford University Press, 2011.

Forrest, Peter. "The Incarnation: A Philosophical Case for Kenosis." *Religious Studies* 36 (2000) 127–40.

Frame, John M. *The Doctrine of God*. Phillipsburg, NJ: P&R, 2002.

———. *Systematic Theology: An Introduction to Christian Belief*. Phillipsburg, NJ: P&R, 2013.

Frankfurt, Harry G. "Alternative Possibilities and Moral Responsibility." In *The Importance of What We Care About*, 1–10. New York: Cambridge University Press, 1998.

———. "Freedom of the Will and the Concept of a Person." In *The Importance of What We Care About*, 11–25. New York: Cambridge University Press, 1998.

———. *The Importance of What We Care About*. New York: Cambridge University Press, 1998.

Franklin, Christopher Evan. "The Luck and *Mind* Arguments." In *The Routledge Companion to Free Will*, edited by Kevin Timpe et al., 203–12. London: Routledge, 2017.

Freddoso, Alfred J. "Human Nature, Potency, and the Incarnation." *Faith and Philosophy* 3 (1986) 27–53.

———. *On Divine Foreknowledge: Part IV of the* Concordia. Ithaca, NY: Cornell University Press, 1988.

Garrigou-Lagrange, Reginald. *God, His Existence and His Nature: A Thomistic Solution of Certain Agnostic Antimonies*. Translated by Dom Bede Rose. 2 vols. St. Louis: Herder, 1936.

Gathercole, Simon. *The Preexistent Son: Recovering the Christologies of Matthew, Mark, and Luke*. Grand Rapids: Eerdmans, 2006.

Gentry, Peter J., and Stephen J. Wellum. *Kingdom Through Covenant: A Biblical-Theological Understanding of the Covenants*. Wheaton, IL: Crossway, 2012.

George, Timothy. *Theology of the Reformers*. Rev. ed. Nashville: B&H Academic, 2013.

Ginet, Carl. "Libertarianism." In *The Oxford Handbook of Metaphysics*, edited by Michael J. Loux and Dean W. Zimmerman, 587–612. New York: Oxford University Press, 2003.

Gorman, Michael. *Aquinas on the Metaphysics of the Hypostatic Union*. New York: Cambridge University Press, 2017.

Grant, W. Matthews. "Divine Universal Causality and Libertarian Freedom." In *Free Will & Theism: Connections, Contingencies, and Concerns*, edited by Kevin Timpe and Daniel Speak, 214–33. New York: Oxford University Press, 2016.

———. "Divine Universal Causality Without Occasionalism (and with Agent-Causation)." In *Free Will and Classical Theism: The Significance of Freedom in Perfect Being Theology*, edited by Hugh J. McCann, 175–200. New York: Oxford University Press, 2017.

———. *Free Will and God's Universal Causality: The Dual Sources Account*. New York: Bloomsbury Academic, 2019.

Griffith, Meghan. "Agent Causation." In *The Routledge Companion to Free Will*, edited by Kevin Timpe et al., 72–85. London: Routledge, 2017.

Grillmeier, Aloys. *Christ in Christian Tradition*. Vol. 1, *From the Apostolic Age to Chalcedon (451)*. 2nd ed. Translated by John Bowden. Atlanta: John Knox, 1975.

Grudem, Wayne. *Systematic Theology: An Introduction to Biblical Doctrine*. 2nd ed. Grand Rapids: Zondervan, 2020.

Haji, Ishtiyaque. "Obligation, Reason, and Frankfurt Examples." In *The Oxford Handbook of Free Will*, edited by Robert Kane, 288–305. 2nd ed. Oxford: Oxford University Press, 2011.

Harris, Sam. *Free Will*. New York: Free, 2012.

Hawthorne, Gerald F. *The Presence & the Power: The Significance of the Holy Spirit in the Life and Ministry of Jesus*. Reprint, Eugene, OR: Wipf and Stock, 2003.

Helm, Paul. *Calvin at the Center*. New York: Oxford University Press, 2010.

———. *Eternal God: A Study of God Without Time*. 2nd ed. New York: Oxford University Press, 2010.

———. *John Calvin's Ideas*. New York: Oxford University Press, 2004.

———. *The Providence of God*. Downers Grove, IL: InterVarsity, 1994.

———. *Reforming Free Will: A Conversation on the History of Reformed Views on Compatibilism (1500–1800)*. Fearn: Mentor, 2020.

Helseth, Paul Kjoss. "God Causes All Things." In *Four Views on Divine Providence*, edited by Dennis W. Jowers, 25–52. Grand Rapids: Zondervan, 2011.

Heppe, Heinrich. *Reformed Dogmatics*. Edited by Ernst Bizer. Translated by G. T. Thomson. Reprint, Eugene, OR: Wipf & Stock, 2008.

Hill, Jonathan. "Introduction." In *The Metaphysics of the Incarnation*, edited by Anna Marmodoro and Jonathan Hill, 1–19. New York: Oxford University Press, 2011.

Hodge, Charles. *Systematic Theology*. 3 vols. Reprint, Peabody, MA: Hendrickson, 2016.

Holmes, Michael, ed. *Greek New Testament: SBL Edition*. Atlanta: SBL, 2010.

Horrell, J. Scott. "Toward a Biblical Model of the Social Trinity: Avoiding Equivocation of Nature and Order." *JETS* 47 (2004) 399–421.

Horton, Michael. *The Christian Faith: A Systematic Theology for Pilgrims on the Way*. Grand Rapids: Zondervan, 2011.

———. "Hellenistic or Hebrew? Open Theism and Reformed Theological Method." *JETS* 45 (2002) 317–41.

Hunt, David P. "Moral Responsibility and Unavoidable Action." *Philosophical Studies* 97 (2000) 195–227.

Jaworska, Agnieszka. "Identificationist Views." In *The Routledge Companion to Free Will*, edited by Kevin Timpe et al., 15–26. London: Routledge, 2017.

Johnson, Randall K. "Christ and the Principle of Alternative Possibilities." *JAT* 9 (2021) 314–21.

———. "Christological Arguments for Compatibilism in Reformed Theology." *Themelios* 48 (2023) 125–39.

———. "On the Harmony of Christ's Wills. *JRT* 18 (2024) 76–98.

Kane, Robert. *The Significance of Free Will*. New York: Oxford University Press, 1998.

Kapitan, Tomis. "Doxastic Freedom: A Compatibilist Alternative." *American Philosophical Quarterly* 26 (1989) 31–41.

Kelly, J. N. D. *Early Christian Doctrines*. Rev. ed. New York: HarperSanFrancisco, 1978.

Leftow, Brian. "The Humanity of God," In *The Metaphysics of the Incarnation*, edited by Anna Marmodoro and Jonathan Hill, 20–44. New York: Oxford University Press, 2011.

———. "A Latin Trinity." In *Oxford Readings in Philosophical Theology*. Vol. 1, *Trinity, Incarnation, Atonement*, edited by Michael Rea, 76–106. New York: Oxford University Press, 2009.

Legge, Dominic. *The Trinitarian Christology of St. Thomas Aquinas*. New York: Oxford University Press, 2018.

Letham, Robert. "The Person of Christ." In *Reformation Theology: A Systematic Summary*, edited by Matthew Barrett, 313–46. Wheaton, IL: Crossway, 2017.

Levy, Neil. "Bad Luck Once Again." *Philosophy and Phenomenological Research* 77 (2008) 749–54.

———. *Hard Luck: How Luck Undermines Free Will and Moral Responsibility*. New York: Oxford University Press, 2011.

Lewis, David. "Are We Free to Break the Laws?" *Theoria* 47 (1981) 113–21.

Luther, Martin. *The Bondage of the Will*. Translated by J. I. Packer and O. R. Johnston. Grand Rapids: Revell, 1957.

Maximus the Confessor. *The Disputation with Pyrrhus of Our Father Among the Saints Maximus the Confessor*. Translated by Joseph P. Farrell. Waymart, PA: St. Tikhon's Monastery, 2014.

McCall, Thomas H. *An Invitation to Analytic Christian Theology*. Downers Grove, IL: InterVarsity, 2015.

———. *Which Trinity? Whose Monotheism? Philosophical and Systematic Theologians on the Metaphysics of Trinitarian Theology*. Grand Rapids: Eerdmans, 2010.

McCann, Hugh J. *Creation and the Sovereignty of God*. Indianapolis: Indiana University Press, 2012.

McFarland, Ian A. "The Theology of the Will." In *The Oxford Handbook of Maximus the Confessor*, edited by Pauline Allen and Bronwen Neil, 516–32. Oxford: Oxford University Press, 2015.

McKay, Thomas J., and David Johnson. "A Reconsideration of an Argument Against Compatibilism." *Philosophical Topics* 24 (1996) 113–22.

McKenna, Michael. "Incompatibilism, Ultimacy, and the Transfer of Non-Responsibility." *American Philosophical Quarterly* 38 (2001) 37–51.

———. "Reasons-Responsive Theories of Freedom." In *The Routledge Companion to Free Will*, edited by Kevin Timpe et al., 27–40. London: Routledge, 2017.

———. "Source Compatibilism and that Pesky Ability to Do Otherwise: Comments on Dana Nelkin's 'Making Sense of Freedom and Responsibility.'" *Philosophical Studies* 163 (2013) 105–16.

McKenna, Michael, and D. Justin Coates. "Compatibilism." In *The Stanford Encyclopedia of Philosophy*, edited by Edward N. Zalta. Spring 2021. https://plato.stanford.edu/archives/spr2021/entries/compatibilism/.

McKinley, John E. *Tempted for Us: Theological Models and the Practical Relevance of Christ's Impeccability and Temptation*. PTM. Reprint, Eugene, OR: Wipf & Stock, 2009.

Mickelson, Kristin. "The Manipulation Argument." In *The Routledge Companion to Free Will*, edited by Kevin Timpe et al., 166–78. London: Routledge, 2017.

Moreland, J. P., and William Lane Craig. "The Trinity." In *Oxford Readings in Philosophical Theology*. Vol. 1, *Trinity, Incarnation, Atonement*, edited by Michael Rea, 21–43. New York: Oxford University Press, 2009.

Morris, Thomas V. *Anselmian Explorations: Essays in Philosophical Theology*. Notre Dame: University of Notre Dame Press, 1987.

———. *The Logic of God Incarnate*. Reprint, Eugene, OR: Wipf and Stock, 2001.

———. *Our Idea of God: An Introduction to Philosophical Theology*. Vancouver: Regent College, 1991.

Muller, Richard A. *Dictionary of Latin and Greek Theological Terms: Drawn Principally from Protestant Scholastic Theology*. 2nd ed. Grand Rapids: Baker Academic, 2017.

———. *Divine Will and Human Choice: Freedom, Contingency, and Necessity in Early Modern Reformed Thought*. Grand Rapids: Baker Academic, 2017.

Mullins, R. T. "Flint's 'Molinism and the Incarnation' Is Still Too Radical—A Rejoinder to Flint." *JAT* 5 (2017) 515–32.

———. "Flint's 'Molinism and the Incarnation' Is Too Radical." *JAT* 3 (2015) 1–15.

Nelkin, Dana Kay. *Making Sense of Freedom and Moral Responsibility*. New York: Oxford University Press, 2011.

Nowell-Smith, P. "Freewill and Moral Responsibility." *Mind* (1948) 45–61.

O'Connor, Timothy. *Persons & Causes: The Metaphysics of Free Will*. New York: Oxford University Press, 2000.

O'Connor, Timothy, and Christopher Franklin. "Free Will." In *The Stanford Encyclopedia of Philosophy*, edited by Edward N. Zalta. Fall 2020. https://plato.stanford.edu/archives/fall2020/entries/freewill/.

Olson, Roger E. *Arminian Theology: Myths and Realities*. Downers Grove, IL: IVP Academic, 2006.

Owen, John. *ΠΝΕΥΜΑΤΟΛΟΓΙΑ*. Edited by William H. Gould. The Works of John Owen 3. Edinburgh: Banner of Truth, 2009.

Parker, Brent E. "The Israel-Christ-Church Relationship." In *Progressive Covenantalism: Charting a Course Between Dispensationalism and Covenant Theologies*, edited by Stephen J. Wellum and Brent E. Parker, 39–68. Nashville: B&H Academic, 2016.

Pawl, Timothy J. *The Incarnation*. New York: Cambridge University Press, 2020.

———. *In Defense of Conciliar Christology: A Philosophical Essay*. New York: Oxford University Press, 2016.

———. *In Defense of Extended Conciliar Christology: A Philosophical Essay*. New York: Oxford University Press, 2019.

Pereboom, Derk. *Free Will, Agency, and Meaning in Life*. Oxford: Oxford University Press, 2014.

———. *Living Without Free Will*. New York: Cambridge University Press, 2001.

———. "Responsibility, Regress, and Protest." In *Oxford Studies in Agency and Responsibility*, edited by David Shoemaker, 4:121–40. New York: Oxford University Press, 2017.

———. "Skeptical Views About Free Will." In *The Routledge Companion to Free Will*, edited by Kevin Timpe et al., 121–35. London: Routledge, 2017.

Pike, Nelson. "Omnipotence and God's Ability to Sin." *American Philosophical Quarterly* 6 (1969) 208–16.

Pinnock, Clark H. *Most Moved Mover: A Theology of God's Openness*. Grand Rapids: Baker Academic, 2001.

Pinnock, Clark H., et al. *The Openness of God: A Biblical Challenge to the Traditional Understanding of God*. Downers Grove, IL: InterVarsity, 1994.

Plantinga, Alvin. *God, Freedom, and Evil*. Reprint, Grand Rapids: Eerdmans, 2001.

———. *The Nature of Necessity*. New York: Oxford University Press, 1974.

———. "On Heresy, Mind, and Truth." *Faith and Philosophy* 16 (1999) 182–93.

Plantinga, Cornelius, Jr. "Social Trinity and Tritheism." In *Trinity, Incarnation, and Atonement*, edited by Ronald J. Feenstra and Cornelius Plantinga Jr., 21–47. Notre Dame: University of Notre Dame Press, 1989.

Preciado, Michael Patrick. *A Reformed View of Freedom: The Compatibility of Guidance Control and Reformed Theology*. Eugene, OR: Pickwick, 2019.

Rea, Michael C. "Relative Identity and the Doctrine of the Trinity." *Philosophia Christi* 5 (2003) 431–45.

Rogers, Katherine A. "Christ's Freedom: Anselm vs Molina." *Religious Studies* 52 (2016) 497–512.

———. *Perfect Being Theology*. Edinburgh: Edinburgh University Press, 2000.

Sanders, Fred. "Introduction to Christology: Chalcedonian Categories for the Gospel Narrative." In *Jesus in Trinitarian Perspective*, edited by Fred Sanders and Klaus Issler, 1–41. Nashville: B&H Academic, 2007.

———. *The Triune God*. Grand Rapids: Zondervan, 2016.

Sanders, John. *The God Who Risks: A Theology of Divine Providence*. 2nd ed. Downers Grove, IL: IVP Academic, 2007.

Schreiner, Thomas R. *New Testament Theology: Magnifying God in Christ*. Grand Rapids: Baker Academic, 2008.

Senor, Thomas. "Drawing on Many Traditions: An Ecumenical Kenotic Christology." In *The Metaphysics of the Incarnation*, edited by Anna Marmodoro and Jonathan Hill, 88–114. New York: Oxford University Press, 2011.

Shabo, Seth. "Uncompromising Source Incompatibilism." *Philosophy and Phenomenological Research* 80 (2010) 349–83.

Solano, Iesu, and J. A. Aldama. *Sacrae Theologiae Summa IIIA: On the Incarnate Word; On the Blessed Virgin Mary*. Translated by Kenneth Baker. Saddle River, NJ: Keep the Faith, 2014.

Spinoza, Baruch. *Ethics*. Translated by Samuel Shirley. Indianapolis: Hackett, 1992.

Stamps, R. Lucas. "Atonement in Gethsemane: The Necessity of Dyothelitism for the Atonement." In *Locating Atonement*, edited by Oliver D. Crisp and Fred Sanders, 118–38. Grand Rapids: Zondervan, 2015.

Strawson, P. F. "Freedom and Resentment." *Proceedings of the British Academy* 48 (1962) 1–25.

Stump, Eleonore. "Alternative Possibilities and Moral Responsibility: The Flicker of Freedom." *Journal of Ethics* 3 (1999) 299–324.

———. *Atonement*. New York: Oxford University Press, 2018.

———. *The God of the Bible and the God of the Philosophers*. Milwaukee: Marquette University Press, 2016.

Sturch, Richard. *The Word and the Christ: An Essay in Analytic Christology*. Oxford: Clarendon, 1991.

Swinburne, Richard. *The Christian God*. Oxford: Clarendon, 1994.

Tanner, Norman P., ed. *Decrees of the Ecumenical Councils*. 2 vols. Washington, DC: Georgetown University Press, 1990.

Timpe, Kevin. *Free Will: Sourcehood and Its Alternatives*. 2nd ed. London: Bloomsbury, 2013.

Turretin, Francis. *Institutes of Elenctic Theology*. 3 vols. Edited by James T. Dennison Jr. Translated by George Musgrave Giger. Phillipsburg, NJ: P&R, 1992.

Van Asselt, Willem J., et al., eds. *Reformed Thought on Freedom: The Concept of Free Choice in Early Modern Theology*. Grand Rapids: Baker Academic, 2010.

Van Inwagen, Peter. *An Essay on Free Will*. New York: Oxford University Press, 1983.

———. "Three Persons in One Being: On Attempts to Show That the Doctrine of the Trinity Is Self-Contradictory." In A *Reader in Contemporary Philosophical Theology*, edited by Oliver Crisp, 126–42. London: T&T Clark, 2009.

———. "When Is the Will Free?" *Philosophical Perspectives* 3 (1989) 399–422.

Velleman, David J. "Epistemic Freedom." In *The Possibility of Practical Reason*, 32–55. Oxford: Clarendon, 2000.

Vihvelin, Kadri. "Dispositional Compatibilism." In *The Routledge Companion to Free Will*, edited by Kevin Timpe et al., 52–61. London: Routledge, 2017.

———. "Free Will Demystified: A Dispositional Account." *Philosophical Topics* 32 (2004) 427–50.

Waller, Bruce N. *Against Moral Responsibility*. Cambridge: MIT Press, 2014.

———. *Freedom Without Responsibility*. New York: Temple University Press, 1990.

Ware, Bruce A. *God's Greater Glory: The Exalted God of Scripture and the Christian Faith*. Wheaton, IL: Crossway, 2004.

———. "The Gospel of Christ" In *Beyond the Bounds: Open Theism and the Undermining of Biblical Christianity*, edited by John Piper et al., 309–36. Wheaton, IL: Crossway, 2003.

———. *The Man Christ Jesus: Theological Reflections on the Humanity of Christ.* Wheaton, IL: Crossway, 2013.

Watts, Thomas A. "Two Wills in Christ? Contemporary Objections Considered in the Light of a Critical Examination of Maximus the Confessor's *Disputations with Pyrrhus.*" *WTJ* 71 (2009) 455–87.

Weinandy, Thomas G. *Does God Change? The Word's Becoming in the Incarnation.* Still River, MA: St. Bede's Publications, 1985.

———. *Does God Suffer?* Notre Dame: University of Notre Dame Press, 2000.

Wellum, Stephen J. *Christ Alone: The Uniqueness of Jesus as Savior.* Grand Rapids: Zondervan, 2017.

———. *God the Son Incarnate: The Doctrine of Christ.* Wheaton, IL: Crossway, 2016.

———. "The New Covenant Work of Christ." In *From Heaven He Came and Sought Her: Definite Atonement in Historical, Biblical, and Pastoral Perspective*, edited by David Gibson and Jonathan Gibson, 517–39. Wheaton, IL: Crossway, 2013.

Wellum, Stephen J., and Brent Parker, eds. *Progressive Covenantalism: Charting a Course Between Dispensational and Covenant Theologies.* Nashville: B&H Academic, 2016.

White, Thomas Joseph. *The Incarnate Lord: A Thomistic Study in Christology.* Washington, DC: The Catholic University of America Press, 2017.

Widerker, David. "Frankfurt-Friendly Libertarianism." In *The Oxford Handbook of Free Will*, edited by Robert Kane, 266–87. 2nd ed. Oxford: Oxford University Press, 2011.

Wolf, Susan. *Freedom Within Reason.* New York: Oxford University Press, 1990.

Wolfson, Harry Austryn. *The Philosophy of the Church Fathers.* Vol. 1, *Faith, Trinity, Incarnation.* Cambridge: Harvard University Press, 1956.

Zagzebski, Linda. "Does Libertarian Freedom Require Alternate Possibilities?" *Philosophical Perspectives* 14 (2000) 231–48.

Subject Index

www.ingramcontent.com/pod-product-compliance
Lightning Source LLC
LaVergne TN
LVHW090513110826
845146LV00003B/843

* 9 7 9 8 3 8 5 2 2 7 7 1 6 *